No Limits, Just Edges Jackson Pollock *Paintings on Paper*

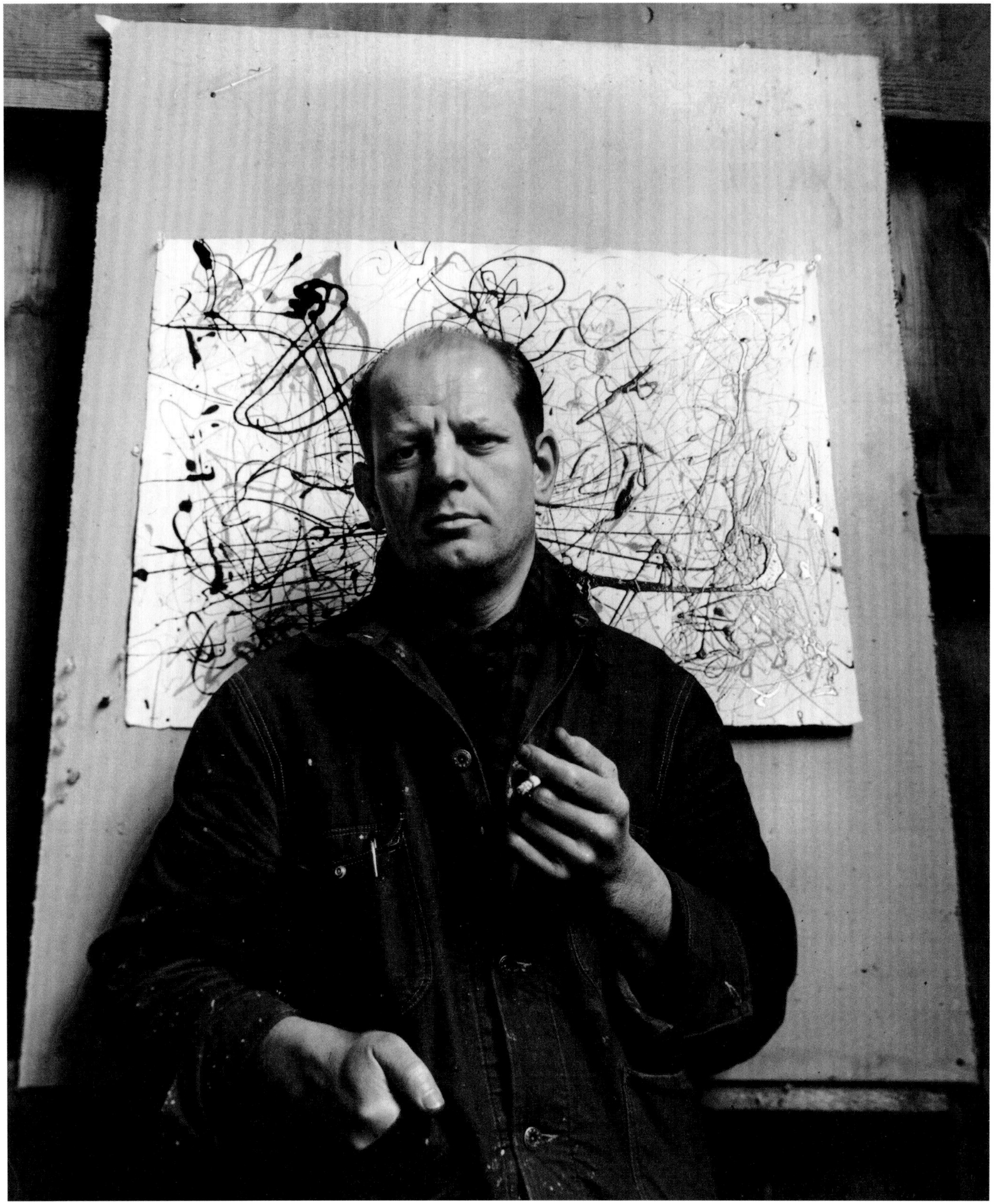

No Limits, Just Edges Jackson Pollock *Paintings on Paper*

Deutsche Guggenheim

Published on the occasion of the exhibition
No Limits, Just Edges: Jackson Pollock Paintings on Paper

Organized by Susan Davidson

DEUTSCHE GUGGENHEIM
January 29–April 10, 2005

PEGGY GUGGENHEIM COLLECTION
June 4–September 18, 2005

The exhibition at the Peggy Guggenheim Collection, Venice, has been made possible with the support of The Pollock-Krasner Foundation, Inc.

The artworks are numbered according to the archival system as indicated in Francis V. O'Connor and Eugene V. Thaw, *Jackson Pollock: A Catalogue Raisonné of Paintings, Drawings, and Other Works*, 4 vols. New Haven: Yale University Press, 1978, and Francis V. O'Connor, *Supplement One*, 1995.

ISBN: 0-89207-326-8

Deutsche Bank & Solomon R. Guggenheim Foundation

Guggenheim Museum Publications
1071 Fifth Avenue, New York, New York 10128

Deutsche Guggenheim
Unter den Linden 13/15, 10117 Berlin

English edition available through:
D.A.P./Distributed Art Publishers
155 Sixth Avenue, 2nd floor, New York, New York 10013
Tel.: (212) 627–1999; Fax: (212) 627–9484

Distributed outside the United States and Canada,
excluding German-speaking countries,
by Thames & Hudson, Ltd., 181A High Holborn Road
London WC1V 7QX, United Kingdom

Design: Don Quaintance, Public Address Design
Production assistant: Elizabeth Frizzell
Production: Melissa Secondino
Editorial: Elizabeth Franzen, Stephen Hoban

Printed in Italy by Conti Tipocolor

Cover: Jackson Pollock, *Number 4, 1948: Gray and Red* (detail), 1948. Enamel on paper, 22 5/8 x 30 7/8 inches (57.5 x 78.4 cm). Frederick R. Weisman Foundation, Los Angeles JPCR 2:202

Frontispiece: Jackson Pollock with an untitled drawing (JPCR 3:784) in his studio, The Springs, Long Island, New York, January 3, 1949. Photograph by Arnold Newman

CONTENTS

Deutsche Guggenheim

DEUTSCHE GUGGENHEIM is a unique joint venture between a corporation—Deutsche Bank—and a nonprofit arts foundation—The Solomon R. Guggenheim Foundation. Designed by American architect Richard Gluckman, the 510-square-meter gallery is located on the ground floor of the Deutsche Bank headquarters in Berlin. Since opening in fall 1997, Deutsche Guggenheim has presented four important exhibitions each year, many of which showcase a specially commissioned work by an artist. The exhibition program and day-to-day management of the museum is the responsibility of the two partners.

Deutsche Guggenheim joins the Solomon R. Guggenheim Foundation's other existing locations: the Solomon R. Guggenheim Museum in New York; the Peggy Guggenheim Collection in Venice; the Guggenheim Museum Bilbao; and the Guggenheim Hermitage Museum in Las Vegas. Deutsche Bank regularly supports exhibitions in renowned museums and since 1979 has been building its own collection of contemporary art under the motto "art at the workplace." The Deutsche Guggenheim initiative further represents a milestone in Deutsche Bank's advancement of the arts.

EXHIBITIONS AT DEUTSCHE GUGGENHEIM
since its founding in 1997

1997
Visions of Paris: Robert Delaunay's Series

1998
James Rosenquist: *The Swimmer in the Econo-Mist*•
From Dürer to Rauschenberg: A Quintessence of Drawing. Masterworks from the Albertina and the Guggenheim
Katharina Sieverding: Works on Pigment
After *Mountains and Sea*: Frankenthaler 1956–1959

1999
Andreas Slominski•
Georg Baselitz: Nostalgia in Istanbul
Amazons of the Avant-Garde: Alexandra Exter, Natalia Goncharova, Liubov Popova, Olga Rozanova, Varvara Stepanova, and Nadezhda Udaltsova
Dan Flavin: The Architecture of Light

2000
Sugimoto: Portraits•
Förg—Deutsche Bank Collection
Lawrence Weiner: Nach Alles/After All•
Jeff Koons: Easyfun-Ethereal•

2001
The Sultan's Signature: Ottoman Calligraphy from the Sakip Sabanci Museum, Sabanci University, Istanbul
Neo Rauch—Deutsche Bank Collection
On the Sublime: Mark Rothko, Yves Klein, and James Turrell
Rachel Whiteread: Transient Spaces•

2002
Bill Viola: Going Forth By Day•
Kara Walker—Deutsche Bank Collection
Chillida/Tàpies
Gerhard Richter: Eight Gray•

2003
Kazimir Malevich: Suprematism
Richard Artschwager: Up and Down/Back and Forth
Tom Sachs: Nutsy's
Bruce Nauman: Theaters of Experience

2004
Miwa Yanagi—Deutsche Bank Collection
Nam June Paik: Global Groove 2004
Robert Mapplethorpe and the Classical Tradition: Photographs and Mannerist Prints
John Baldessari: Somewhere Between Almost Right and Not Quite (With Orange)•

2005
No Limits, Just Edges: Jackson Pollock Paintings on Paper

•Commissioned work by Deutsche Guggenheim

FOREWORD

No Limits, Just Edges—this is a concise description of Jackson Pollock's work. In his famous action paintings, the artist fully ignores what is conventionally regarded to be the real pictorial space; color and movement virtually break through the prescribed surface of the canvas.

Just as fascinating as the large-format paintings, with which Pollock was a founding member of Abstract Expressionism, are his drawings—his artworks on paper. Much less well-known and only seldom displayed, these drawings form a self-contained, independent body of work, but there are recognizable parallels to the development of Pollock's painting: from object-focused beginnings with a strong European influence, to a coalescing liberation in form, up to the abstract compositions in later years. These were works in which Pollock arrived at his own personal language of images that facilitated the creation of something entirely new. Something that the entire group of artists known as the New York School had been striving to achieve after the end of World War II: genuine North American art fully unrelated to all of the predecessors from old Europe.

Today, Pollock's paintings can be found all over the world in museums and private collections, but so are his drawings. We are therefore very pleased to have been successful in bringing together these rare pieces of art from international collections for the exhibition *No Limits, Just Edges: Jackson Pollock Paintings on Paper* in the Deutsche Guggenheim. This is the first time that Pollock's illustrative works can be seen together in this scope in a retrospective exhibition in Berlin. But the exhibition also highlights an important aspect of the Deutsche Bank Collection, for which works on paper have always played the central role.

The exhibition comprises sheets from the artist's early sketchbooks as well as studies of paintings by old masters and murals by Mexican artists. Other pieces show the influence painters such as Joan Miró and Pablo Picasso had on the artist. The exhibition focuses on drawings and paintings on paper from the years 1940 to 1950, when Pollock showed the way with his unmistakable style of allover abstraction for an entire generation of artists.

With this exhibition, we are very pleased to have contributed to casting a new light on Jackson Pollock's overall work and hope the exhibition, which will be exhibited in Venice after Berlin, will be seen as an outstanding success.

—Dr. Tessen von Heydebreck
Member of the Board of Managing Directors of Deutsche Bank AG

PREFACE and ACKNOWLEDGMENTS

THE GUGGENHEIM MUSEUM has long been associated with the work of Jackson Pollock. In 1943, Peggy Guggenheim offered the then relatively unknown artist his first solo exhibition at her influential museum/gallery Art of This Century. For the next five years Guggenheim subsidized Pollock with a monthly stipend, which in turn allowed her to amass significant holdings of the artist's work. After Art of This Century closed, Guggenheim's patronage continued. In 1950 she organized his first European solo show at Venice's Museo Correr, and then began to disseminate his work through gifts to museums from Omaha, Nebraska to Amsterdam. Her support throughout his brief, yet brilliant career was unwavering and she fondly called Pollock her greatest discovery. Today, Pollock's iconic, large-scale canvases are recognized by museumgoers the world over. Yet his smaller, more intimate scaled works on paper often come as a revelation to even the most seasoned art audiences.

No Limits, Just Edges: Jackson Pollock Paintings on Paper—the first retrospective devoted exclusively to Pollock's works on paper in twenty-five years—specifically considers Pollock's draftsmanship as an essential component in his transformation of the traditional figurative line into nonfigurative graphic expression. We are particularly pleased to have this opportunity to build upon the museum's relationship with one of the most important artists of the twentieth century. The present exhibition is inspired in part by the donation to the museum of Untitled (*Green Silver*) (pl. 62). A classic painting dating from around 1949 when Pollock mastered the use of his innovative pouring technique, Untitled (*Green Silver*) greatly enriches the museum's collection of Pollock works. On behalf of the Solomon R. Guggenheim Foundation, I would like to extend our sincere gratitude to the donor, Barbara Slifka. Her generosity joins that of numerous individuals and institutions in America and Europe who have allowed us to share their treasured artworks. No exhibition can succeed without the kind support of its lenders and we are especially grateful to all of them for their philanthropy.

Throughout the organization of this exhibition, we have enjoyed the unparalleled support from those people charged today with furthering Pollock's name. In particular, Charles Bergman, Chairman of the Board of The Pollock-Krasner Foundation; Samuel Sachs II, President; and Helen A. Harrison, Director of the Pollock-Krasner House and Study Center, have offered guidance and commitment, while Joan Washburn, whose gallery represents the Pollock estate, and who wholeheartedly championed the project.

Numerous individuals graciously provided assistance in obtaining loans. At the Metropolitan Museum of Art, Nan Rosenthal, Ida Baboul, and Megan Heuer allowed viewing of Pollock's early sketchbooks. Similarly, at the Museum of Modern Art, Gary Garrels and Kathy Curry kindly provided access to that museum's considerable holdings of Pollock's work. Jennifer Vorbach of C&M Arts was unwavering in providing access to numerous private collections. Carol Mancusi-Ungaro, Director of Conservation, Whitney Museum of American Art and founding director of the Center for the Technical Study of Modern Art at the Harvard University Museums, offered insights into the composition of Pollock's paintings on paper. Additional help in locating works of art, preparing them for travel, and the faithful exchange of scholarship with curator Susan Davidson was provided by Amelia Abdullahsani; Emily Braun; Stephen M. Cadwalader; James Elliot; André Emmerich; Angela Gratzl; Paul Gray; Alison de Lima Greene; Laurie Haley; Marla H. Hand; Loretta Howard; Jennifer Benz Joy; Mary Kadish; Judy

Kwon; Josette Lamoureux; Ellen Landau; Jason McCoy; Jennifer McDaniel; Edward Nahem; David Mirvish; Bob Monk; Laura Paulson; Mary-Ellen Powell; Dennis Reid; Patricia Relay; Barbara Schwan; Gail Stavitsky; Lucille Stiger; Bonnie K. Verado; and Barry Walker.

I would like to gratefully acknowledge Dr. Tessen von Heydebreck, Member of the Board of Managing Directors of Deutsche Bank, for his continued cooperation. In addition, I thank the Curators of Deutsche Bank, Dr. Ariane Grigoteit and Friedhelm Hütte for their continued support. Svenja Gräfin von Reichenbach, Deutsche Guggenheim Gallery Manager and Sara Bernshausen, Associate Gallery Manager, as well as Silvie Buschmann and Lutz Driever, have enthusiastically embraced the exhibition and carefully overseen all aspects of its presentation in Berlin. Jörg Klambt, MuseumsShop Manager, offered inventive solutions in realizing the Deutsche Guggenheim's Limited-Edition Number 30. Thanks are also due to Uwe Rommel and his team for managing the construction and installation. Nikoline Kästner, Conservator; Fabienne Lindner, Graphic Designer; Kathrin Conrad; Sabine Ebner; Ulrike Heine; and Daniela Mewes have each contributed to the realization of the exhibition.

Appropriately, *No Limits, Just Edges* will be seen at the Peggy Guggenheim Museum in Venice, 57 years after Peggy's first debut of Pollock's work at the 24th Venice Biennale when she showed her collection of abstract and Surrealist art in the Greek Pavilion. It was the work of the young American artists who would become known as the New York School that enjoyed the greatest response on that occasion. In particular, we would like to thank our colleagues in Venice, Philip Rylands, Director, and his staff including Chiara Barbieri, Liesbeth Bollen, Siro De Boni, Sandra Divari, Paul Schwartzbaum, and Jasper Sharp for their unwavering support.

At the Guggenheim in New York, numerous individuals have contributed to the success of the exhibition. Particular acknowledgment is due to Susan Davidson, Curator, who selected and organized this exhibition, and whose catalogue essay deftly weaves a stylistic overview of Pollock's technique with a detailed accounting of the reception his works on paper received during his lifetime. She has ably clarified the approach to Pollock's work and brought together an international roster of important loans. Robin Kaye Goodman, Curatorial Assistant, managed critical aspects of this project, while Tatiana Cuevas-Guevara, the Hilla Rebay International Fellow, assisted with the initial research for the checklist. Curatorial Interns, Megan Fontanella and Courtney Strimple, tackled a variety of tasks with efficiency and good humor.

This catalogue was made possible by the Guggenheim's outstanding Publications department, in particular Elizabeth Levy, Director of Publications; Elizabeth Franzen, Managing Editor; Stephen Hoban, Assistant Editor; Jennifer Knox-White, Editor; Melissa Secondino, Production Manager; Cindy Williamson, Associate Production Manager; and Lara Fieldbinder, Production Assistant. In addition to contributions too numerous to list here, I am most grateful to Don Quaintance of Public Address Design, who created the elegant book design.

I would also like to recognize with gratitude the invaluable efforts of Lisa Dennison, Deputy Director and Chief Curator; Marion Kahan, former Exhibition Program Manager; Meryl Cohen, Head Registrar; Janet Hawkins, Project Registrar; Ana Luisa Leite, Manager of Exhibition Design; and Alison Weaver, Director of Program Management, Affiliates. Conservation for Untitled (*Green Silver*) was thoughtfully undertaken by Gillian McMillan.

The book has benefited from the written contributions made by David Anfam, the noted Abstract Expressionist scholar, whose insights illuminate Pollock's motives and milieu, and Margaret Holben Ellis, Professor of Conservation at the Institute of Fine Arts, New York University, and Director of the Thaw Conservation Center at the Morgan Library, New York, whose knowledge of the artist's materials and working techniques reveal an area of study too often over looked in exhibition catalogues.

—Thomas Krens
Director,
Solomon R. Guggenheim Foundation

The Gesture of Intimate Scale: Jackson Pollock Paintings on Paper

Susan Davidson

At last I see what you see. Jackson has learned to draw—
like an *angel.* —Clement Greenberg[1]

WHEN JACKSON POLLOCK had his first one-person exhibition, in the Daylight Gallery of Peggy Guggenheim's Art of This Century in November 1943, the artist chose to exhibit both paintings and drawings. This may have been due, in part, to practical considerations, as smaller works tended to attract ready sales. In fact, Howard Putzel, Guggenheim's gallery director, had pragmatically reminded Pollock in a postcard the month before: "Hope you're producing some small pictures for poor people."[2] Another factor may have been the lack of a sufficient body of newly finished paintings—Pollock had had only three and a half months in which to prepare for his exhibition debut. However, the primary motivation was Pollock's conviction that his paintings on canvas and his works on paper deserved equal attention as expressions of his artistic aims. From this exhibition on, at least half of his solo shows during his lifetime included approximately equal numbers of paintings and works on paper.

Pollock's defining innovation has been characterized as the transition from "drawing into painting."[3] Though apt, this phrase implies that the mechanics of drawing occurred first and moved in a linear progression toward painting, when in fact distinctions between the two mediums are quite elusive in Pollock's work. Line would remain the governing principle in all his work, regardless of whether he applied pencil to paper or paint to canvas. Pollock's preoccupation with drawing is well documented, yet the artistic endeavors of his youth marked him as a less than facile draftsman. By the time he arrived at his first major gallery exhibition, at the age of thirty-one, his confidence in his ability as a draftsman had gone through a long and somewhat painful progression. Even late in his career, some critics—unwilling to embrace Pollock's revolutionary new techniques—erroneously suggested that his allover poured surfaces were an attempt to mask his inability to deftly control line. Pollock's brother Sande (the one closest to him in age) recalls that, as a teenager enrolled at the Manual Arts High School in Los Angeles, "[Jack] couldn't make images out of other images."[4] Pollock expressed a similar appraisal of his ability in a letter to his brother Charles in 1930: "My drawing I will tell you frankly is rotten it seems to lack freedom and rhythm it is cold and lifeless. It isn't worth the postage to sent [sic] it."[5] Pollock's perceived deficiency as a draftsman resulted in part from the expectation that he draw realistically. He worked at this exercise avidly, drawing and sketching both from available art reproductions and from nature. During high school, Pollock and his friend Manuel Tolegian spent their afternoons in Tolegian's backyard "studio" (a converted chicken coop), scrutinizing library books about Renaissance art and making sketches. Berthe Pacifico, a high-school sweetheart, recalled the hundreds of sketches Pollock made of her in the afternoon while she practiced piano or when he accompanied her to recitals, carrying a small sketchpad in his shirt pocket, eager to document his surroundings.[6]

Later, between 1930 and 1935, on cross-country road trips between New York and California during summer breaks from the Art Students League, stops for refueling sometimes turned into long sketching sessions (fig. 1). The future *New Yorker* cartoonist Whitney Darrow, along for some of these trips, recalled the Chinese ink sticks that Pollock used to capture the color of the landscape by "putting it down on paper with great physical energy."[7] At the Art Students League, Pollock studied with Thomas Hart Benton, whose doctrinal teachings were founded on realism. Benton felt that Pollock lacked an understanding of the fundamentals of art, anatomy, and perspective and ultimately admitted that Pollock "was incapable of drafting logical sequences."[8] Pollock's fellow students at the League, on the other hand, were stunned by his drawings. "They were so individual," one recalled. "They had tremendous energy. Everyone talked about them."[9] Years later, after Pollock's fame as a radical abstractionist had been cemented, the art historian Selden Rodman agreed. Visiting Pollock in his studio a few months before the artist's fatal car crash on August 11, 1956, Rodman noted "stacks of drawings going back into the 1930s, [that] indicated beyond contention that Pollock can draw fluently from nature, or in the realm of nature-derived fantasy if he wants to."[10]

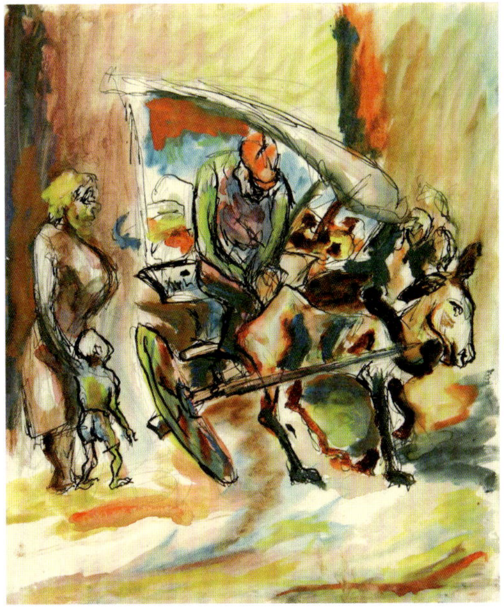

FIG. 1
JACKSON POLLOCK
The Peddler, 1934–38
Watercolor on paper
10 x 9 inches (25.4 x 22.9 cm)
Smithsonian American Art Museum, Washington, D.C. Gift of Thomas Hart Benton
JPCR 4:930

Pollock's high-school drawings, the landscape sketches, and the Western-style scenes depicting daily life made under the tutelage of Benton comprise the earliest stylistic grouping of Pollock's drawn oeuvre. After these initial youthful expressions —most of which were destroyed or lost—Pollock went on to produce approximately 700 works on paper in a variety of traditional drawing mediums—pencil, ink, watercolor, gouache, and collage—as well as, later in his career, poured enamel. Generally, the stylistic development of Pollock's drawings mirrors that of his paintings, and four loosely grouped categories can be defined.

The first, from around 1935 to about 1941, is characterized by figuration of both human and imaginary beings. It includes three accomplished sketchbooks that surfaced after his death and a group of unbound drawings that are most often connected to the psychoanalytical treatment the artist underwent in an attempt to deal with his alcoholism. The second stylistic grouping, a body of fully mature works dating between around 1942 through 1947 and corresponding approximately to Pollock's association with Peggy Guggenheim's Art of This Century museum/gallery, is distinguished by an idiosyncratic iconography he developed in part as a response to Surrealist influences. Employing mythical subject matter, calligraphic markings, and a vibrant and distinctive color palette, Pollock produced emotionally charged paintings and works on paper that retain figurative subject matter yet emphasize abstract qualities.

Arising from this confluence of abstraction and figuration, the third set comprises Pollock's breakthrough works, commonly perceived as pure abstraction and made over the course of a very explosive and intense period from mid-1947 to 1950. Here, not only did Pollock move away from a reliance on traditional figuration and subject matter, but he also broke free from the standard use of drawing and painting implements, usually abandoning their direct contact with the surface. Instead, he worked from distances above the picture plane, using dripping, pouring, and splattering techniques—methods that were not necessarily Pollock's invention alone but that he pushed to new extremes. The traditions of Renaissance perspective (the use of the rectangular plane as a kind of picture window into the depicted world) were dissolved with the transformation of the pictorial space into a site for the allover patterning of the receptor surface, whether paper or canvas. This was accompanied by a new emphasis on the materiality of the painted surface.

The fourth and final group represents a further refinement of Pollock's pouring techniques. Here the drawings are still stylistically related to his works on canvas of the time, but whereas earlier drawings had a clear connection to larger canvases, these later drawings are distinct explorations that specifically exploit the qualities of working with fluid mediums on porous paper. Like the canvas paintings completed between 1950 and 1952, these drawings exhibit a more open, light ground scattered with lyrical compositions of calligraphic forms. The last four years of Pollock's life are almost devoid of drawings; correspondingly, his output of paintings also diminished.

Pollock's seriousness about enhancing his graphic abilities is fully expressed in the three sketchbooks that represent the first period of his stylistic development, now in the collection of the Metropolitan Museum of Art, New York (see pls. 3 and 5–7). This unified body of work—initially intended as private studies—undercuts earlier negative criticism of Pollock's drawing ability. They reveal an artist keen to understand the traditions of line drawing in the manner of Renaissance and Baroque painters such as Michelangelo, Peter Paul Rubens, and El Greco. The first two sketchbooks suggest a fascination with anatomy and the depiction of volume and were probably done from life models, works in museums, or art reproductions. The third sketchbook displays Pollock's deep reverence for the Mexican muralists Diego Rivera, José Clemente Orozco, and David Alfaro Siqueiros. Pollock first encountered the work of these artists as a teenager, in California, and came in direct proximity with it after joining the mural division of the Works Progress Administration's

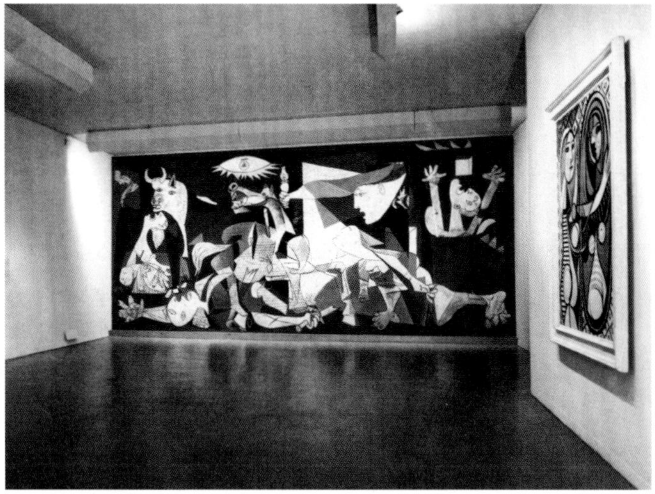

FIG. 2
Installation view, Pablo Picasso, *Guernica* (1937), The Museum of Modern Art Galleries, New York, 1947. Other work shown is *Girl before a Mirror* (1932).

Federal Art Project in the mid-1930s. The artist's confident expression of emotion graphically dominates the 77 sheets of recto/verso drawings. The fully figurative drawings of the three sketchbooks foreshadow principal aspects of Pollock's style in the remaining two decades of his artistic life. The Cubistic angularity, the tortured and fantastic imagery that appears to explode past the edge of the page, and the overwrought intensity would be subsumed in various guises into the later paintings on paper. Nan Rosenthal correctly suggests that the first two sketchbooks may have been executed while Pollock underwent treatment for acute alcoholism between June and September 1938.[11] Indeed, the sketchbooks reveal internal conflicts, which would become increasingly prominent as Pollock confronted personal turmoils through professional psychoanalysis. Early in 1939, he entered Jungian analysis with Dr. Joseph L. Henderson, a process that continued for a period of eighteen months. These sessions were Pollock's second, but not last, psychoanalytical effort to confront his alcohol dependency.[12] As an extension of his therapy, Pollock produced 83 drawings on 70 sheets, some double-sided, that delve into Jungian archetypes and suggest dramatic confrontations with his subjective being. When Pollock brought the drawings to Dr. Henderson's sessions, they became vehicles for facilitating the analysis of the extremely reticent artist. More than the sketchbooks that immediately preceded them, these drawings demonstrate a frenzied assuredness and an imaginative use of bold, earthen color—browns, yellows, and reds in particular. Pollock gave this body of work to Dr. Henderson, who released them to the Maxwell Galleries in San Francisco in 1969, when they were sold to museums and private collections.

Coincidentally, and somewhat providentially, at the time that Pollock began sessions with Dr. Henderson, Pablo Picasso's *Guernica* (1937) was on view at the Valentine Dudensing Gallery in New York to raise funds for refugees of the Spanish Civil War (fig. 2). Commissioned for the Spanish Pavilion of the 1937 Paris World's Fair, Picasso's mural-sized grisaille painting visualized the atrocities General Franco had levied on the small Basque town. Seeing Picasso's wrenching work had a galvanizing effect on numerous young American artists, including Pollock, who went often to see the painting, standing alone in the gallery, making sketches. Enthralled, Pollock adapted the violent representation of its subject matter to his more subjective renderings. Other Picasso works were much in evidence in New York at that moment, in the retrospective exhibition *Picasso: Forty Years of His Art* at the Museum of Modern Art. Pollock's growing friendship with John Graham, a Russian born avant-garde artist and critic of highly sophisticated tastes, further fueled his awareness of the Spanish master. Graham's erudite interest in tribal cultures and their effect on Modern art appealed to Pollock's Western sensibility and stirred memories of his youthful exposure, in the 1920s, to Native American sand paintings in California and Arizona. Pollock also visited the exhibition *Indian Art of the United States* (1941) at the Museum of Modern Art, which opened the door for the artist to explore the primitive, primordial, and mythical aspects of non-European cultures and their influence on the art of Picasso.[13] Pollock's drawings of this early period are heavily influenced by the Spaniard's bold fractured imagery, but they are also highly personal expressions of Pollock's own sensibilities.

This body of work, much discussed in the Pollock literature,[14] served as a laboratory that provided the seed for the mythic psychological figuration inhabiting the works on canvas of the early 1940s. One such breakthrough canvas was *Birth* (ca. 1941, JPCR 1:77), included in *American and French Paintings* at the McMillen Inc. gallery in New York from January 20 to February 6, 1942. This exhibition, organized by Graham, was one of the few shows in the United States since the 1913 Armory Show to pair European and American modernist artists. The exhibition itself was not significant and received little critical attention, but Pollock's painting impressed Lee Krasner, who, along with Stuart Davis, Willem de Kooning, and Walter Kuhn, made up the rest of the American contingent.[15]

The McMillen exhibition was one of a confluence of circumstances that brought Pollock to Peggy Guggenheim's attention. Another was Guggenheim's friendship with Howard Putzel, the West Coast art impresario who, in Paris in 1940, had been among an elite circle of advisors to Guggenheim as she formed her art collection and who would assume the role of gallery director at Art of This Century after it opened in October 1942.[16] Putzel was highly influential in initially recognizing the artists who came to be known as the New York School. He likely saw Pollock's submission to the McMillen exhibition and sought out the maker of such an energized and fresh picture.

Putzel, who had met many of the Surrealists while he was living in Paris and during his earlier art gallery days in California, facilitated the interaction of Pollock and other young Americans with artists such as Roberto Matta, the Surrealist who, like many of his European colleagues, sought refuge in New York during the course of World War II. The forced exile of many of Europe's premier artists during this time unleashed a series of artistic exchanges with the emerging American artists drawn into the Surrealist milieu surrounding Guggenheim and the gatherings at her Beekman Place townhouse.[17] A ready dialogue developed between artists such as William Baziotes, Peter Busa, Robert Motherwell, Richard Pousette-Dart, Mark Rothko, and Charles Seliger—all of whom showed at Art of This Century—and the Europeans André Masson, Matta, and Joan Miró. Masson's and Miró's works were frequently on view in New York galleries. (Miró's *Constellations*, shown at Pierre Matisse Gallery in January 1945, most likely served as a source for Pollock's works of 1945 and 1946 in which bold, pictographic lines and shapes appear against flat planes of bold color [see pls. 45–47].) Matta, in true European fashion, hosted salon-style evenings in his apartment on Tenth Street, where he introduced the Americans to the concept of automatic drawing and other methods of European Modernism. Many observers have connected these explorations of accessing the subconscious to the free-flowing spontaneity of Pollock's mature style of poured allover composition. But over the next several years, Pollock absorbed and mined another fundamental component of Surrealism, which dovetailed with his own interest in psychological states: the attempt to depict the truth of reality by seeking insights into the unconscious mind from imagery outside the bounds of logic.

Pollock's first four solo exhibitions, all at Guggenheim's Art of This Century, were drawn from the paintings and drawings of this period. When Art of This Century opened in 1942, Guggenheim's museum/gallery offered intimate access to masterworks of abstract and Surrealist art and also to the exiled European artists themselves, who frequented Frederick Kiesler's visionary interiors.[18] The first public exposure of Pollock's work at Art of This Century was in *Exhibition of Collage* (April 16–May 15, 1943). Matta had encouraged Pollock, Motherwell, and Baziotes to submit works for the exhibition, even instructing them in aspects of collage as none of the Americans had previously practiced the technique. The exact work submitted by Pollock is unknown, but plates 19 and 21 are likely candidates.[19] Baziotes's *The Drugged Balloonist* and Motherwell's *The Joy of Living* (both 1943) were sold to the Baltimore collector Saidie A. May just days after the exhibition opened, but Pollock's collage went unsold. While Pollock virtually abandoned collage after this brief foray (in contrast to Motherwell, who adopted the technique as an integral part of his practice), this first appearance at Art of This Century and the inclusion of his painting *Stenographic Figure* (1942, JPCR 1:88) in the 1943 Spring Salon, which immediately followed the collage exhibition, cemented Pollock's fruitful relationship with Guggenheim, whose museum/gallery provided the springboard for the artist's blossoming career.

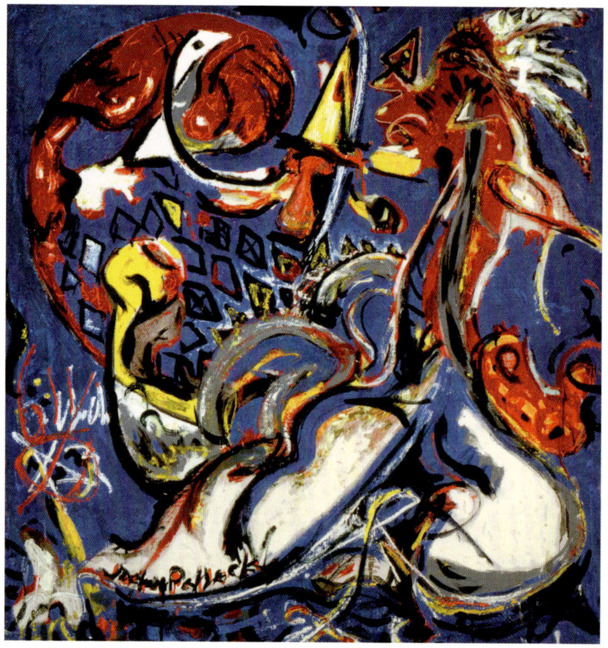

FIG. 3
JACKSON POLLOCK
The Moon-Woman Cuts the Circle, ca. 1943
Oil on canvas
42 x 40 inches (106.6 x 101.6 cm)
Musee national d'art moderne,
Centre Georges Pompidou, Paris
JPCR 1:90

The fact that Pollock's "Surrealist" drawings (see pls. 23–49) are often viewed simply as the precursors to his more renowned poured paintings has resulted in these purely imaginative compositions sometimes being underrated. The Surrealist-period drawings are populated with intensely realized personages who seem to emerge from mythic landscapes or are veiled or nearly buried in fields of color and expressive brushwork. C. L. Wysuph, referring to the drawings of 1939 to 1942, felt that Pollock "sought by camouflaging his imagery to disguise even inadvertent self-revelation."[20] Pollock commented: "I'm very representational some of the time, and a little all of the time. But when you're painting out of your unconscious, figures are bound to emerge."[21] Many of these works, such as *The Moon-Woman Cuts the Circle* (ca. 1943; fig. 3) and *Male and Female* (ca. 1942, JPCR 1:87), have highly activated backgrounds with free-floating calligraphic symbols and pictograms. In some, such as plate 24, the frenzied background itself becomes the subject of the drawing, highlighting the materiality of the painted surface and the prominence of purely abstract line. This particular work also represents a short interlude in Pollock's paintings on paper in which the painted ground is primarily black (see also pl. 25).

This dark coloration recalls Pollock's early fascination with the brooding palette of the Mexican muralists. In plate 42, the puzzling interplay between the allover abstract qualities of the form and line complicates recognizing the figures.

The works of this period fluctuate between dense, almost muddy planes of color (as in pl. 42), and light grounds infused with intersecting colored lines, swirls, and geometric shapes (as in pl. 38). Clement Greenberg wrote: "[Pollock] is the first painter I know of to have got something positive from the muddiness of color that so profoundly characterizes a great deal of American painting."[22] In plate 38 and related works, bolder, more spontaneous lines are built up with and surrounded by short repetitive patterning strokes. Volcanic shapes arising from agitated lines mark a number of drawings from this period, such as plates 33 and 36. In these works—in contrast to the allover fields he was developing concurrently, in which the picture plane is seemingly viewed from above, in the same manner as their making—Pollock centered the forms on a grounded horizon at the bottom of the sheet. Oriented more like traditional landscapes, these works seem to depict a more defined and confined space than the patterned abstractions; the line does not push past the edges of the paper. Pollock's concerns about the proper subject matter for modern painting, the transition from a traditional upright picture plane to a less strictly oriented expanse, and from the figurative to the abstract were shared by a coterie of emerging Americans whose paintings were characterized by a type of biomorphic representation laden with built-up paint, cellular compositions, and pictographic forms that would later evolve into Abstract Expressionism.

The precise number of works on paper Pollock exhibited at Art of This Century is unknown, but an examination of the accountant reports for three of the four solo shows he had there allows the identification of artworks sold and thereby offers an understanding of the public reception Pollock's work enjoyed at that moment.[23] Greenberg was the first to suggest in print that the works on paper provided a pathway to understanding Pollock's work in general: "Those who find his oils overpowering are advised to approach him through his gouaches, which in trying less to wring every possible ounce of intensity from every square inch of surface achieve greater clarity and are less suffocatingly packed than the oils."[24] This endorsement, written on the occasion of Pollock's second exhibition at Art of This Century, set in motion a consistent pattern of sales—chiefly among private collectors—for Pollock's small-scale paintings on paper. Indeed, Pollock came to rely on the income from these sales, which supplemented the monthly stipend he received as part of his annual contract with Guggenheim.[25]

Six drawings from Pollock's first exhibition sold—although not all during the run of the exhibition—at prices ranging from $50 to $225.[26] Barbara Reis, the artist daughter of Guggenheim's accountant, purchased JPCR 3:697; Davidson Taylor paid $75 for the Surrealist gouache on black ground described earlier (pl. 24); and the English avant-garde filmmaker and bon vivant Kenneth Macpherson purchased his second Pollock work, *Animals and Figures* (1942, JPCR 4:961), having earlier acquired *Horizontal on Black* (date unknown).[27] (*Animals and Figures* is one of two works known to have been in the exhibition that correspond to Pollock's earlier, more imagistic style.) The following year, a Mr. Elliot and Paul Osborne each bought drawings (an unidentified work and pl. 23, respectively) and Macpherson purchased the most expensive work on paper from the show, a gouache priced at $225 (probably JPCR 4:974).[28] Perhaps as a token of appreciation for her support and as a measure of their growing trust and friendship, Pollock gave Guggenheim an untitled drawing (pl. 30) as a gift. This work may be considered a bridge between Pollock's earlier style and the Surrealist works that dominated the first exhibition.

Sales were slightly better at Pollock's 1945 show, his second at Art of This Century. Seven works on paper were sold, at prices ranging from $75 to $200. The Dial Press, who would publish Guggenheim's memoir *Out of This Century* the following year, purchased an unidentified work on paper. Bill Davis was so impressed by the two works on paper he purchased (an unidentified gouache and drawing) that he encouraged Guggenheim to double Pollock's monthly stipend from $150 to $300 when Pollock's contract came up for renewal that year. Davis would go on to purchase three paintings from Pollock's third exhibition, in April 1946.[29] Princess Evangeline Zalstem-Zalesky, art patron and heiress of the Johnson and Johnson pharmaceutical company, purchased a black-ground gouache (JPCR 4:978), and the artist, botanist, and collector Dwight Ripley acquired three drawings (JPCR 4:1012, 4:1013, and 4:1014 [pl. 37]) for a total of $375. Ripley, like Davis, would become a significant collector of Pollock's work in all mediums. From the same show, he purchased two paintings: *Composition with Pouring II* (1943, JPCR 1:94) for $100 and an unknown (though evidently larger, given its price) work for $200.

Pollock's third show was a complete sellout. The demand for his works on paper required the artist to bring in additional works, since only eight were on exhibit and there were nine first-time buyers. San Francisco banker W. W. Crocker purchased a gouache; Monroe Wheeler, the director of exhibitions and head of the Museum of Modern Art's design department, acquired another gouache (JPCR 4:976); Selden Rodman paid $100 for a work (possibly JPCR 3:766); and a Lt. Lyndon paid $175 for plate 41. The English collector and later gallery owner Arthur Jeffress purchased an unidentified drawing; poet Charles Olsen purchased an unidentified gouache; and Allen Wolfe snapped up two gouaches. One institutional sale was made, of an unidentified drawing to the Society of the Four Arts, a cultural center in Palm Beach, Florida, that presented avant-garde exhibitions throughout the 1940s. It is possible that more works on paper sold after the close of the exhibition; however, this information cannot be confirmed due to the absence of accountant reports for the year ending 1947.

Pollock's last exhibition with Art of This Century, like all three exhibitions he would have in the 1950s at the Sidney Janis Gallery, were devoted exclusively to large-scale paintings. It should be noted that Pollock's production of drawings had dramatically slowed by the time of his first show at Janis, in 1952, and therefore their omission was a practical matter rather than signaling a split in the close relation between small- and large-scale works.

Contrary to how many artists work, Pollock did not produce preparatory sketches for his paintings, nor did he work out overall compositions on paper first. Once he chose the surface, whether canvas or paper, he worked instinctively. When asked about his working method by William Wright in a 1950 interview, Pollock responded: "I approach painting in the same sense as one approaches drawing; that is, it's direct. I don't work from drawings, I don't make sketches and drawings and color sketches into a final painting."[30] In other words, the two mediums were interchangeable for the artist.

Pollock's fourth exhibition at Guggenheim's Art of This Century occurred just months before she permanently closed the museum/gallery in May 1947 and returned to Europe. After much cajoling, Guggenheim convinced dealer Betty Parsons to assume the remainder of Pollock's contract. At his first show with Parsons, in January 1948, Pollock presented a new body of work: seventeen large-scale paintings representing the poured, allover abstractions that are now commonly thought to be Pollock's major innovation. By late 1946, Pollock often laid his surfaces flat, on a horizontal plane, as he worked on them. From above this level surface, he dripped and poured enamel paints on the canvas or paper below, a method that he felt enabled him to more precisely control the application of line. Fluid paint spilling from a can or drizzling from the tips of sticks or trowels replaced traditional means of drawing in his work. The nature of the surface's support medium—whether paper or canvas—was of less consequence initially (though later Pollock would more fully exploit the effects of enamel, ink, and watercolor on the physical properties of both unprimed canvas and porous papers). Pollock described the effects of the process: "I need the resistance of a hard surface. On the floor I am more at ease. I feel nearer, more a part of the painting, since this way I can walk around it, work from the four sides and can literally be *in* the painting."[31]

In the paintings and drawings of Pollock's mature period, figuration was, for the most part, nearly subsumed into the swirling, gyrating patterns of his painted surfaces. However, as Pepe Karmel has shown, Pollock often began his canvases with loose figurative forms.[32] Some of the pictures of this allover period, such as *Number 4, 1948: Gray and Red* (1948; pl. 50) and *Number 22A, 1948* (1948; pl. 52), are characterized by lyrical lariats of

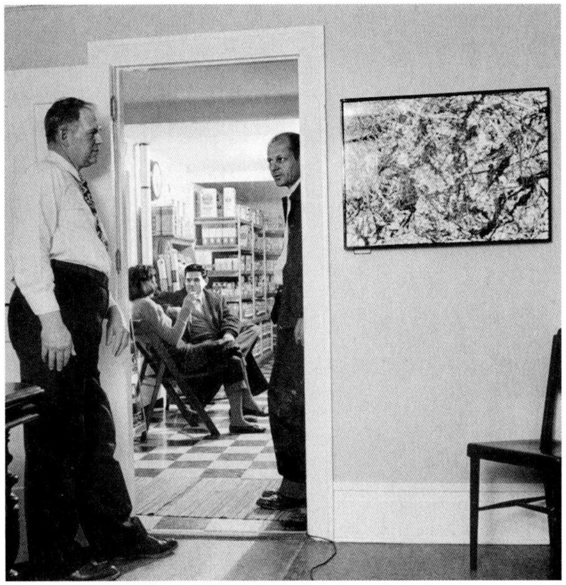

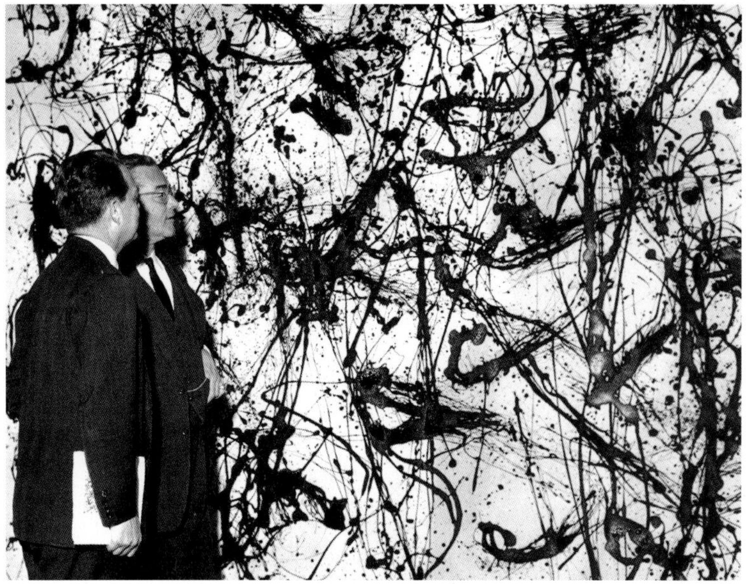

paint floating in essentially open, light backgrounds, while in others, such as *Composition (White, Black, Blue, and Red on White)* (1948; pl. 53) and *Number 33, 1949* (1949; pl. 56), the repetition of looping lines produces a thick, impenetrable thicket almost entirely obscuring the ground. Slashes of shimmering aluminum paint or splashing drips and splatters of brightly colored enamel in works such as *Number 20, 1949* (1949; pl. 57) and *Number 34, 1949* (1949; pl. 59) convey the residue of their violent execution. If the viewer follows these lines, they regularly extend past the edges of the support, suggesting that it is a pictorial frame binding a larger expanse of patterning. The insistent push of the pictorial elements past the outer dimensions of the support illustrates Pollock's working method, once described by the artist, succinctly, as having "no limits, just edges."[33]

During the height of Pollock's mature phase of poured paintings, his further eradication of the delineation between painting and drawing based on the receptor surface—canvas or paper—continued. Approximately 25 small-scale paintings on paper were probably executed flat during 1948 and 1949 (most lack the tacking holes that are left in paper when attached vertically to a studio wall). As many as fourteen of these paintings on paper were mounted onto canvas or composition board sometime after their execution, giving them a prominence not afforded any of his previous drawings (see fig. 4). Despite the radical shift in scale, Pollock's smaller works convey the same commanding sense of space, control of line, and complex organization evident in mural-sized canvases such as *Number 1A, 1948* (1948, JPCR 2:186) and *Number 32A, 1950* (1950; see fig. 5). Though the larger works seem to invite the viewer to walk into the activated space, as the artist did during its execution, the smaller ones remarkably retain a similar effect.

Pollock's unconventional working method and the physical nature of his creative process assumed an epic stature even before his untimely death. The protean myth of the artist as action painter is in part due to the extensive documentation of the artist as he worked on allover poured works in the early 1950s, recorded in photographs and films by Hans Namuth, Martha Holmes, and others. These visual records capture the elaborate choreography and gestural movements that Pollock used to create many of the large canvases of this period, pouring and splattering paint as they lay on the floor of his twenty-foot-square studio in

FIG. 4
Grocer Dan Miller and Jackson Pollock standing near *[Silver over Black, White, Yellow, and Red]*, (1948, pl. 58), The Springs General Store, The Springs, Long Island, New York, April 1, 1949. Photograph by Martha Holmes

FIG. 5
U.S. Ambassador to Great Britain John Hay Whitney, and Museum of Modern Art Director of Circulating Exhibits Porter McCray looking at Pollock's *Number 32A, 1950* (1950), *Jackson Pollock: 1912–1956*, Whitechapel Art Gallery, London, November 1958

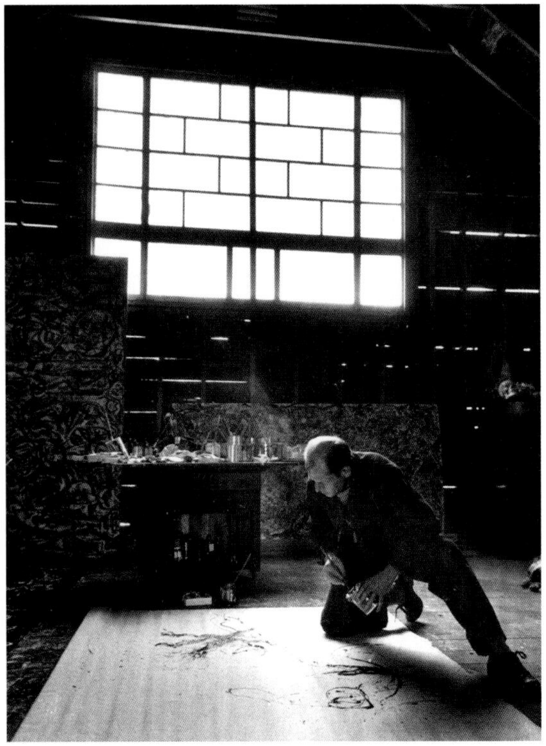

FIG. 6
Pollock working on a painting in his studio, The Springs, Long Island, New York, April 1, 1949. Photograph by Martha Holmes.

The Springs (fig. 6). At the same time, in the much smaller confines of his drawings, he was able to focus the same effects on sheets of paper whose area, in general, was roughly eight times smaller than that of most canvases of the period. There seems to be no record of whether Pollock worked on smaller works atop tables or on the floor, although the former seems more likely; in some photographs, drawings can be seen piled on low tables or atop a large flat file in The Springs studio (see figs. 7 and 23). Pollock once commented on the difficulty of transitioning from a large to a small scale: "I'm just more at ease in a large area than I am on something 2 x 2; I feel more at home in a big area."[34] This ability to scale the sweep of his gestures to widely variable dimensions demonstrates Pollock's extreme coordination of eye and hand as controlled by the movement of his wrist, then his arm, and finally his entire torso. Matta later described the physical mechanics involved in Pollock's movement from a small paper size to the full sweep of a mural-size canvas: "This freedom of Pollock . . . was like going from hand-painting to arm-painting."[35]

Pollock's first solo exhibition at Betty Parsons Gallery was followed by two more in 1949: one in January, of works executed in 1948, and one in November, of works made exclusively in 1949. Both exhibitions consisted of approximately thirty-five large-scale and small-scale paintings on canvas and paper. Together, these shows offered viewers a continuous exploration of Pollock's breakthrough abstract poured technique, which dominated his production during the two years he was "on the wagon." Both exhibitions were a critical success, and consequently sales (the benchmark for public acceptance) were respectable. Priced at $250 each, six paintings on paper from the first show sold to private collectors (Fred Hauck, Mrs. Daniel Longwell, Sue Mitchell, Kay Ordway, Edward Root, and Lynne Thompson), and one, the only institutional sale, was purchased by the Museum of Modern Art.[36] A handwritten note on a Parsons Gallery ledger indicates that the work identified as number 12 on the exhibition checklist also sold, although in fact it joined Parsons's personal collection. This painting, along with number 6, which collector Sue Mitchell acquired, were singled out for their "'accidental' development and spatial depth" in Emily Genauer's review, substantiating just how "good a painter Pollock could really be."[37] The excitement generated by Pollock's classic poured paintings was dramatically charged by the time of his second 1949 show, and just over half of the works in the exhibition were sold; all but two of these sales were for small-scale paintings on paper, whose prices had risen by $50 since the beginning of the year. Some of the buyers were repeat customers, like Dwight Ripley, who now added *Number 18, 1949* (1949, JPCR 2:226) to the body of Surrealist works on paper he had acquired from Art of This Century, and Edward Root, who purchased *Number 34, 1949* (1949; pl. 59), perhaps as a companion to *Number 20, 1948* (1948, JPCR 2:191), the work he had purchased from the first 1949 show. Alfonso Ossario, one of Pollock's main patrons, also purchased two small paintings on paper, *Number 19, 1949* (1949, JPCR 2:229) and *Number 33, 1949* (1949; pl. 56). Other purchasers included Edgar Kaufmann, Jr., critic and director of the industrial design department at the Museum of Modern Art from 1946 to 1948, who would donate the work to the museum's collection in 1952, and the collectors Dorothy Noyes, Priscella Peck, Abbott Kimbell, and Theodore Dragon.[38] It is interesting to note that women accounted for a number of the early collectors actively acquiring Pollock, whose work is generally characterized as masculine.[39]

Pollock's fourth show at Parsons, in late November 1950, was again devoted to a single year's production, although the artist chose not to include any of the drawings that he was then working on.[40] Following this exhibition, Pollock's works on paper began to diverge from the paintings of the same period as he became increasingly sensitive to the specific effects of specialized papers. He used Japanese papers with a translucent quality and porous fiber structure, into which his inks and watercolors bled

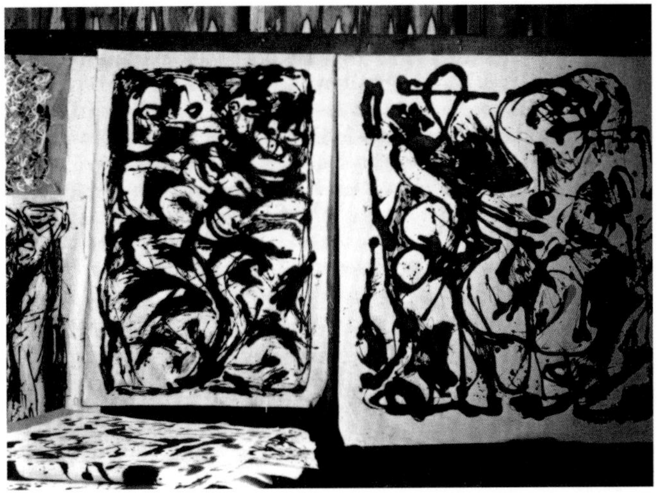

due to the capillary action of the fibers. His markings changed from bold, gestural continuous lines to sensitive, calligraphic half-swirls, squiggles, dots, and splotches resulting from the pooling effects of the wet mediums. Many of the dots on these sheets were formed by a new method, in which Pollock stacked sheets of paper while working, allowing the mediums to bleed through and thus transferring similar patterns to sheets underneath. Working on the lower sheets separately, he then further transformed this accidental staining. This process, a new variation of the automatist technique, can be seen in pairs of works, such as plates 68 and 69, in which the marks on one sheet correspond to the marks on the other. In JPCR 3:819 and 3:820 (pl. 72), Pollock turned over the bottom sheet before working further into the existing design, so that it is in part an inverted mirror image of the original top sheet. While Pollock's use of this transfer technique is confined to his works on paper of this period, his contemporaneous paintings demonstrate the same limited color range and more open composition as the drawings, as well as a related exploration of staining effects—in this case, the reaction of paint to unprimed and unsized canvas. The larger-scale canvases, such as *Easter and the Totem* and *Portrait and a Dream* (both 1953, JPCR 2:374 and 2:368), re-emphasize figuration, albeit in a very loose and abstract manner.

A corollary avenue of experimentation in the early 1950s involved Pollock's use of specialty handmade papers. Pollock and Krasner first saw the special art papers created by Douglass Morse Howell in an exhibition of collages by Anne Ryan at Parsons Gallery in 1951, held concurrently with a showing of works by Krasner. Howell's handmade papers had crevice-like textures and distinct colorations that absorbed fluid mediums and introduced irregular edges to drawn lines. In works incorporating these papers, such as plates 74 and 78, Pollock's allover lines, rather than exploding past the edges of the sheet, seem to organize themselves into more centralized shapes, as if responding to centripetal forces. A number of drawings and watercolors that revealed Pollock's experiments on specially made papers were included in his last exhibition with Parsons, devoted to works executed in 1951.

Today, the literature on Pollock routinely accepts the reciprocal interrelationship between the artist's canvases and smaller works on paper. Strikingly, however, the works on paper generally escaped significant contemporaneous critical comment, despite the fact that the drawings sold well and frequently. Likewise, Pollock's interviews and written statements almost never touch on the drawings per se, except where he rejects the idea that they served a preparatory role in relation to his paintings. This omission, which minimizes any differentiation between the two mediums, is a tacit recognition of Pollock's high evaluation of his many works on paper. The doubt and rejection associated with drawing in his early years as an artist, dating as far back as his childhood pocket sketchbooks, were supplanted by the silence of self-assuredness. Pollock had certainly tamed the line, in the process helping to reinvent pictorial space, not only at mural size but also at an intimate scale.

FIG. 7
Enamel on canvas paintings tacked on the wall of Pollock's studio and paintings on paper laid on a worktable (foreground), The Springs, Long Island, New York, ca. 1951. Photograph by Hans Namuth

NOTES

1. Clement Greenberg to Lee Krasner, ca. 1951, quoted in Steven Naifeh and Gregory White Smith, *Jackson Pollock: An American Saga* (New York: Clarkson N. Potter, 1989), p. 678.

2. Howard Putzel to Jackson Pollock, October 2, 1943, quoted in Francis V. O'Connor and Eugene V. Thaw, eds., *Jackson Pollock: A Catalogue Raisonné of Paintings, Drawings, and Other Works*, vol. 4 (New Haven, Conn.: Yale University Press, 1978), p. 229.

3. William S. Rubin was the first to use the phrase "drawing into painting" in relation to Pollock's work, in his "Jackson Pollock and the Modern Tradition, Part I," *Artforum* 5, no. 6 (February 1967), p. 21. Bernice Rose later adopted the phrase in the title of a traveling exhibition she organized for the International Council of the Museum of Modern Art, New York, in 1969, which was reconstituted as a European touring exhibition in 1980.

4. Sande Pollock, quoted in Naifeh and White Smith, op. cit., p. 124.

5. Jackson Pollock to Charles Pollock, January 31, 1930, quoted in Helen Harrison, ed., *Such Desperate Joy: Imagining Jackson Pollock* (New York: Thunder's Mouth Press, 2000), p. 9.

6. Naifeh and White Smith, op. cit., p. 148.

7. Ibid., p. 221.

8. Ibid., p. 164.

9. Quoted in Dorothy Seiberling, "A Shy and Turbulent Man Who Became a Myth," in Harrison, op. cit., p. 59.

10. Selden Rodman, "Jackson Pollock" (interview), 1956, in Harrison, op. cit., p. 57.

11. Nan Rosenthal, "The Pollock Sketchbooks: An Introduction," in *The Jackson Pollock Sketchbooks in the Metropolitan Museum of Art* (New York: Metropolitan Museum of Art, 1997), p. 25. This publication is a limited-edition facsimile of the three sketchbooks. Pollock's sources are convincingly presented in essays by Katharine Baetjer and Lisa Mintz Messinger, and Rosenthal's text offers sound evidence for dating the first two sketchbooks to 1938–39 as opposed to O'Connor and Thaw's dating of 1933–39 (see O'Connor and Thaw, op. cit., vol. 3, pp. 13–15).

12. Pollock left Dr. Henderson for sessions with Dr. Violet Staub de Laszlo, whom he saw from 1940 until 1943. He went into therapy again, although not psychoanalysis, with Dr. Elizabeth Wright Hubbard, who had a holistic approach to treatment, in the fall of 1944. Pollock's most successful treatment occurred under Dr. Edwin Heller in The Springs, when Pollock stopped drinking for two years, between 1948 and 1950, one of his most prolific periods of artistic production.

13. *Picasso: Forty Years of His Art*, organized by Alfred H. Barr, Jr., was held from November 15, 1939 to January 7, 1940, at the Museum of Modern Art. See also John Graham, "Primitive Art and Picasso," *Magazine of Art* 30, no. 4 (April 1937), pp. 236–39, 260; and Kirk Varnedoe, "Comet: Jackson Pollock's Life and Work," in *Jackson Pollock*, exh. cat. (New York: Museum of Modern Art, 1999), pp. 32–34.

14. C. L. Wysuph, *Jackson Pollock: Psychoanalytic Drawings* (New York: Horizon Press, 1970); Judith Wolfe, "Jungian Aspects of Jackson Pollock's Imagery," *Artforum* 11, no. 3 (November 1972), pp. 65–73; David Freke, "Jackson Pollock: A Symbolic Self-Portrait," *Studio International* 184, no. 950 (December 1972), pp. 217–21; Betsy Carter, "Jackson Pollock's Drawings Under Analysis," *Artnews* 76, no. 2 (February 1977), pp. 58–60; Elizabeth L. Langhorne, *A Jungian Interpretation of Jackson Pollock's Art through 1946* (Ann Arbor, Mich.: University Microfilms, 1979); Charles F. Stuckey, "Another Side of Jackson Pollock," *Art in America* 65, no. 6 (November–December 1977), pp. 80–91; Langhorne, "Jackson Pollock's 'The Moon Woman Cuts the Circle,'" *Arts Magazine* 53, no. 7 (March 1979), pp. 128–37; Hélène Lassalle, "Jackson Pollock: 'La Femme-lune coupe le cercle,' ou Pollock et Jung," *Cahiers du Musée national d'art moderne*, no. 4 (April–June 1980), pp. 288–98; Langhorne, "Pollock, Picasso and the Primitive," *Art History* 12, no. 1 (March 1989), pp. 66–92; William S. Rubin, "Pollock as Jungian Illustrator: The Limits of Psychological Criticism" (parts I and II), *Art in America* 67, nos. 7 and 8 (November and December 1979), pp. 104–23 and 72–91, respectively; and Claude Cernuschi, *Jackson Pollock: "Psychoanalytic" Drawings*, exh. cat. (Durham, N. C.: Duke University Museum of Art, 1992).

15. The French artists represented included Georges Braque, André Derain, Henri Matisse, and Pablo Picasso.

16. For more on Putzel and Guggenheim's relationship, see Susan Davidson, "Focusing an Instinct: The Collecting of Peggy Guggenheim," in *Peggy Guggenheim and Frederick Kiesler: The Story of Art of This Century* (Venice: Peggy Guggenheim Collection, 2004), pp. 50–89. For biographical information on Putzel, see Melvin P. Lader, "Howard Putzel: Proponent of Surrealism and Early Abstract Expressionism in America," *Arts Magazine* 56, no. 7 (March 1982), pp. 85–96.

17. For more on Surrealist artists in America, see Martica Sawin, *Surrealism in Exile and the Beginning of the New York School* (Cambridge, Mass.: MIT Press, 1995), and *Exiles and Émigrés*, exh. cat. (Los Angeles: Los Angeles County Museum of Art, 1997).

18. For an in-depth discussion of Kiesler's design for Art of This Century, see Don Quaintance, "Modern Art in a Modern Setting: Frederick Kiesler's Design of Art of This Century," in *Peggy Guggenheim and Frederick Kiesler*, pp. 206–73.

19. O'Connor and Thaw were unable to visually identify the exact submission, but they assigned an entry to the work based on the recollections of Robert Motherwell; see O'Connor and Thaw, op. cit., vol. 4, no. 1041. It is probable that Motherwell confused the submitted entry with the other collages Pollock made at the time.

20. Wysuph, op. cit., pp. 20–23.

21. Rodman, "Jackson Pollock," in Harrison, op. cit., p. 53.

22. Clement Greenberg, "Art," *Nation*, November 27, 1943, p. 621.

23. In identifying artworks that were sold during the operation of Art of This Century, I have consulted the accountant reports prepared by Bernard Reis in

the Bernard and Rebecca Reis Papers, Research Library Special Collections and Visual Resources, The Getty Institute, Los Angeles. (Portions are duplicated as the Bernard J. Reis Papers, 1934–1979, Archives of American Art, Smithsonian Institution, Washington, D.C.)

24. Clement Greenberg, "Art," *Nation*, April 7, 1945, p. 397.

25. For the financial arrangements between Guggenheim and Pollock, see Peggy Guggenheim, *Out of This Century: Confessions of an Art Addict* (New York: Universe Books, 1979), p. 315 (first contract); Jackson Pollock to Charles Pollock, April 14, 1944, quoted in O'Connor and Thaw, op. cit., vol. 4, p. 233; Jacqueline Bograd Weld, *Peggy: The Wayward Guggenheim* (New York: E. P. Dutton, 1986), p. 343 (second contract); and Harrison, op. cit., p. 22 (third and final contract).

26. By way of comparison, only two paintings from the exhibition sold. These were *The Magic Mirror* (1943, JPCR 1:85), which was purchased by San Francisco artist Jeanne Reynal and is now in the Menil Collection, Houston, and *The She-Wolf* (1943, JPCR 1:98), sold to the Museum of Modern Art, which had placed a reserve on the painting before the show opened but was unable to finalize the sale until May 1944.

27. Macpherson may have acquired *Horizontal on Black* directly from the artist, as its sale is not recorded in the accountant reports for Art of This Century. Macpherson lent the work to Pollock's second exhibition at the museum/gallery. The work is presumed lost today, and its listing—at least by this title—is not recorded in O'Connor and Thaw.

28. The sale of these works was concluded after the exhibition closed. See "Art of This Century Sales of Art Works for the Year Ended December 31, 1944," Bernard and Rebecca Reis Papers.

29. These were *The Tea Cup* (1946, JPCR 1:150), *Shimmering Substance* (1946, JPCR 1:164), and *The Blue Unconscious* (1946, JPCR 1:158).

30. William Wright, "An Interview with Jackson Pollock," in Harrison, op. cit., p. 27.

31. Jackson Pollock, "My Painting," *Possibilities* 1 (winter 1947–48), pp. 78–83, in Pepe Karmel, ed., *Jackson Pollock: Interviews, Articles, and Reviews* (New York: Museum of Modern Art, 1999), p. 17.

32. See Pepe Karmel, "Pollock at Work: The Films and Photographs of Hans Namuth," in *Jackson Pollock* (1999), pp. 87–137.

33. Jeffrey Potter, "Jackson Pollock: Fragments of Conversations and Statements," in Harrison, op. cit., p. 93.

34. Wright, "An Interview with Jackson Pollock," in Harrison, op. cit., p. 28.

35. "Concerning the Beginnings of the New York School, 1939–1943: An Interview with Peter Busa and Matta," *Art International* 11, no. 6 (summer 1967), p. 18.

36. These works were *Number 4, 1948* (pl. 50), *Number 6, 1948* (JPCR 2:209), *Number 14, 1948* (pl. 55), *Number 15, 1948* (pl. 54), *Number 19, 1948* (JPCR 2:190), *Number 20, 1948* (JPCR 2:191), and *Number 23, 1948* (JPCR 2:199), respectively; see Betty Parsons Papers and Gallery Records 1927–1985, Archives of American Art, Smithsonian Institution, Washington, D.C., microfilm 4123:1160. It is probable that Hauck purchased his work before the exhibition opened and therefore paid the artist directly, as he did again when he purchased *Number 18, 1950* (JPCR 2:278); see Betty Parsons Papers, 4123:1170.

37. Emily Genauer, "This Week in Art," *New York World-Telegram*, February 7, 1949, p. 19.

38. Kaufmann purchased *Number 12, 1949* (JPCR 2:233); Noyes, *Number 17, 1949* (pl. 60); Peck, *Number 15, 1949* (JPCR 2:236); Kimbell, *Number 28, 1949* (JPCR 2:218); and Dragon, *Number 30, 1949* (pl. 57). Numbers 9, 16A, 23, 24, 25, 26, and 29 from the exhibition checklist are identified in the Parsons ledgers as sold, although the purchasers are not identified by name; see Betty Parsons Papers, 4123:1168. Another ledger suggests that Valentine Macy may have been the purchaser of numbers 24, 25, and 29; see Betty Parsons Papers, 4123:1185–86.

39. Other early collectors were Mrs. Henry Gates Lloyd, who purchased *Male and Female* (ca. 1942, JPCR 1:87) and Lydia Winston Malbin, who purchased *Moon Vessel* (ca. 1945, JPCR 1:130).

40. The Parsons records are spotty from this exhibition, thus making it difficult to identify those works that may have sold.

Pollock Drawing: The Mind's Line

David Anfam

Drawing may conceivably be the mind's most haunting obsession. Yet is it just a question of mind?
—Paul Valéry[1]

Speed is at the bottom of it all—the hundredth of a second caught so precisely that the motion is continued from the picture infinitely: the moment made eternal.
—Hart Crane[2]

He is not drawing on the canvas so much as in the air above it.
—Hans Namuth[3]

WHY DRAWING? At face value, Jackson Pollock's attitude to this question denied one of the most traditional functions of draftsmanship. This, at least, was the bias of two well-known statements from 1950. The first: "I approach painting in the same sense as one approaches drawing; that is, it's direct. I don't work from drawings, I don't make sketches and drawings and color sketches into a final painting."[4] The second: "No Sketches/acceptance of/*what* I do—."[5] Both voice a rhetoric of immediacy familiar within the context of Abstract Expressionism. It is a mythology of the present that led Barnett Newman to declare, "I have never worked from sketches, never planned a painting, never 'thought out' a painting. I start out each painting as if I had never painted before."[6] Clyfford Still likewise asserted of his 1943 oils on paper that "each is a complete painting, not a preliminary sketch for a large one."[7] The three artists thereby set themselves against a concept of drawing established in the Renaissance, when Leon Battista Alberti (building on ancient precepts) helped to define *disegno* as belonging to the realm of mind, premeditation, measure, and "design," in opposition, it transpired, to sensuous *colore*.[8] Henceforth color/*colore* would be attributed to the seductive allure of surfaces, appealing to our mercurial bodily desires rather than to supposedly more deliberative mental instincts.[9] Thus formulated, drawing is inextricably linked to making studies—which, as noted, was anathema to the Abstract Expressionists. In reality, though, the New York artists were being polemical: drawing's affinity with the mind has also long given it a capacity to evoke the speed of thought.

Under this definition, drawing is the preeminent carrier for the sudden impulse or flash of inspiration, the swift handmaiden of the *première pensée*, which seeks to "generate creative energy and record the process of brainstorming on paper."[10] In their protean reach—from pencil jottings, via virtual carpet pages of pictograms, to poured palimpsests of commercial enamel—Pollock's works on paper upend doctrinaire attempts to separate *disegno* from *colore*, cerebral plotting from visceral making. These "drawings" encapsulate the spectrum of Pollock's thought and the extensive, even tortuous, evolution of his technical dexterity. Big canvases aside, we might say that all Pollock is here laid out, as it were, on paper.

That Pollock converted drawing into painting—transmuting line into a fluid spatial continuum—has long been a commonplace verdict.[11] For this reason, we should bypass the minefield of disentangling his "drawings" from "paintings"—beyond recognizing the basic classification implied by their materials: that is, paper as against canvas or board and, to a lesser extent, paint versus graphite, crayon, ink and watercolor/gouache.[12] Indeed, an invention such as *The Debutante* (ca. 1946, pl. 22) subverts the nominal boundaries by conjuring a collage—often associated with the manipulation of paper—from a dried "skin" of enamel house paint. Similarly, works at key junctures in Pollock's career that are unquestionably "paintings" engaged possibilities that he chose to advance in "drawings." In turn, the interplay was sometimes reversed as "drawings" broached issues that "paintings" next amplified. For example, among the earliest instances of the pouring technique is the cover of a serigraph greeting card of around 1943.[13] In short, Pollock saw the borders between painting and drawing as permeable. In this respect, he was heir to a modernist pictorial attitude stemming from Paul Cézanne, who reputedly said: "The outlines and the colors are no longer distinct from each other. To the extent that one paints, one outlines. . . ."[14] Less obvious is how the centrality of drawing to Pollock underlies its liaison with writing, thinking, and the body.

Whoever prized the quality of being "direct" as much as Pollock did would perforce be attracted to an activity that, since the caves of Lascaux and Altamira, has ranked among the primal expressive gestures of humankind, and has been described by a scholar of the subject as "making an image by direct extension of the body."[15] Furthermore, the legendary beginnings of representation spring from drawing, as recorded by Pliny the Elder in Book XXV of his *Natural History*. Pliny's germinal narrative ascribes the origins of painting to the art of tracing a shadow. There, too, Pliny distinguished between two types of drawing in terms that, millennia later, still carry an import for Pollock.

Pliny contrasted the surpassingly fine line drawn by Apelles as a token of his virtuosity to the outline made by Parrhasios that delineated contours.[16] The former embodied the direct presence of the artist's identity while the latter sought mimesis. As Pollock's use of line shifted from imaging (and incipient storytelling) in his earlier and later phases to sheer autonomy (and ambiguous abstraction) in his "classic" moment of 1947–50, so it tacitly rehearsed Pliny's two divergent modes of inscription. These tendencies are characterized as the "indexical" sign, which denotes by virtue of an existential or physical connection with its cause and the "iconic" sign, which instead bears a mimetic resemblance to its object.[17] Yet the relationship between the two is not rigid and Pollock's methods straddled them: from the impressed handprints of *Number 1A, 1948* (JPCR 2:186) back to, say, the received crucifixion dramaturgy of a gouache (pl. 8). What unites the dichotomous approaches is that they presuppose a core concern with "presence."[18] On the one hand, presence might inhere in the artist's physical stamp or other indexical traces on the canvas. On the other, it lingered in the depictive ferment of imagery—Pollock's phantasmagoria of figures, animals, flames, landscape, and so on. Whichever, drawing served to convey the pulse of the artist's mind and body onto the canvas or paper surface. For someone who believed a painting "has a life of its own,"[19] this direct transmission—with overtones of split-second timing at its crux—was everything. Vitality would otherwise be lost in the putative lag between conceiving and imaging, feeling and outpouring. No matter how slowly or fast Pollock worked, he behaved according to a model that Romanticism espoused and which Expressionism had revived in the twentieth century. It is the myth of unmediated or direct expression—that inner forces are literally ex-pressed, metaphorically squeezed out in a trice, like pigment from a tube, in the creative act.[20]

This "expressive fallacy" resounds in Pollock's words: "The modern artist, it seems to me, is working and expressing an inner world—in other words—expressing the energy, the motion and other inner forces."[21] Erroneous as the assumption is—for all expressive communication depends on cultural, semantic, and cognate channels of mediation[22]—it remained Pollock's ideology. Since the moves of Pollock's hand (and, eventually, his entire arm and physical momentum) implemented this graphic flow from mind and body to the picture plane, they pose the question of how he envisaged his inner self as against external reality. At stake was a balance between inside/outside, subjective mind and objective matter—the foundations of Pollock's entire art. These antitheses take us to his earliest works.

A dramatic contrast looms between the cultural icon of Pollock as "action painter" and the dismal truth of his personal formative years. The former is unforgettably caught in the speeding blur of Hans Namuth's photographs (fig. 8). These are unwitting progeny of a Romantic-cum-fin-de-siècle typology, whereby the priest/shaman-like dancer melds thought and expression into a total unity, as in the whirling gestures of Henri de Toulouse-Lautrec's Symbolist performer (fig. 9).[23] This fictive "Pollock" is extrovert, dynamic, and commands the space of both the canvas and his presumed ambience; the other anxiously retreats upon himself. All the biographical evidence indicates that Pollock was a frightened youth adrift in a hostile world. As his family struggled to earn a living by hardscrabble farming in a less than idyllic American West (soon to be stricken by the Great Depression), they made umpteen moves that unsettled his upbringing. Pollock's distant father considered himself a "failure," and his mother was overbearing.[24] This is the factual stuff of a *vie romancée*. The plight is encapsulated in a *Self-Portrait* (ca. 1931–35?, fig. 10). A fearful spheroid of a head stares outwards, the gaze wide-eyed yet wonky, as if to suggest a gap between internal and external foci.[25] The canvas illustrates what contemporaneous letters amplify. Pollock wrote to his brothers Charles and Frank, "People have always frightened and bored me consequently I have been within my own shell. . . ." The next year, he added: "this so-called happy part of one's life is a bit of damnable hell . . . the more I think I am thinking the darker things become."[26]

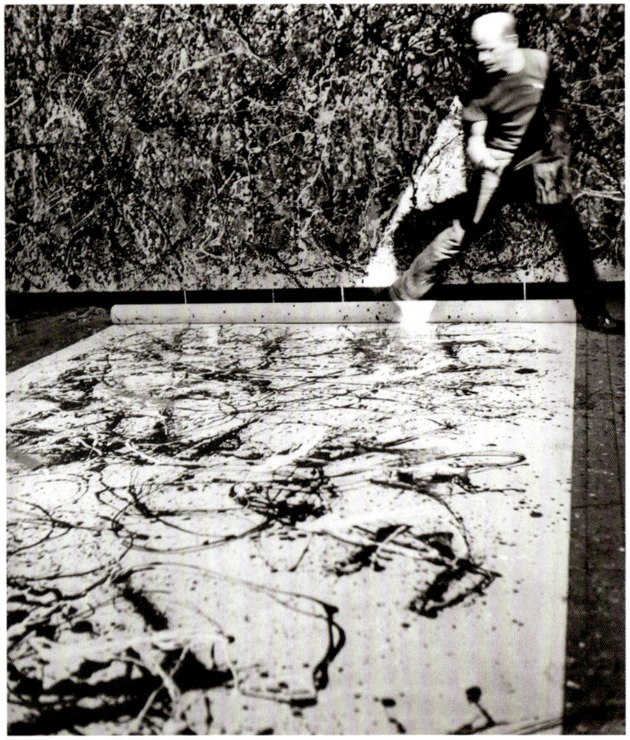

FIG. 8
Jackson Pollock painting *Autumn Rhythm: Number 30, 1950* (1950), The Springs studio, Long Island, New York, 1950. Photograph by Hans Namuth

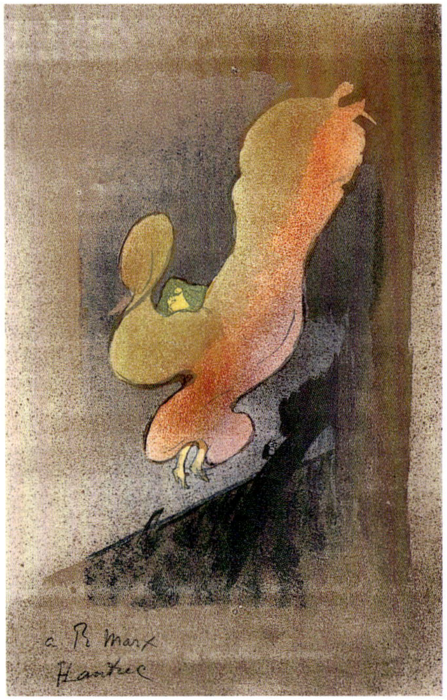

FIG. 9
HENRI DE TOULOUSE-LAUTREC
Miss Loïe Fuller, 1893
Lithograph, printed in color
14 1/2 x 10 9/16 inches (36.8 x 26.8 cm)
The Brooklyn Museum, New York

Judging by the self-portrait and his confessions, the young Pollock therefore endured an abyss of solipsism and abjection, which would have vast artistic consequences. If you believe yourself trapped in a "shell," there is likely to be both a will to burst through such an enclosure—effectively self-inflicted body armor—and, by contrast, to retreat into it when faced by external threats. Thus began a poetics of space, alternating interior and exterior, surface and depth, that infiltrated the weave of Pollock's craft.[27]

Perhaps, to take one example, Pollock's fascination with José Clemente Orozco and David Alfaro Siqueiros registers how their figures (especially Orozco's) seem to wear their musculature on the outside[28] and, correspondingly, how their ostensibly organic surfaces assume the incisiveness and shimmer of metal (evident in Siqueiros's sculpted, burnished flesh tones).[29] This transference—we naturally associate organicism with subjectivity and mechanical or metallic textures with objective things—inflects the knife-like contours that a tree acquires in a late 1930s sketchbook (pl. 5),[30] the stiff figures in studies after old masters and the dagger-like points, combating sinuous folds suggestive of plant or human innards (and drapery too), in a drawing from another pad (pl. 6). While the juxtapositions unquestionably derive from the Mexican muralists, what counts is why they should have attracted Pollock. Surely it was their conflicted dialectic. For, as the philosopher Gaston Bachelard sagely observed, "Everything about a creature that comes out of a shell is dialectical."[31]

Secondly, Pollock's youthful solipsism—consciousness trapped within its own cogitation—culminated in a volte-face. This was a somatic drive that in the great outflow of the oils/enamels on paper/canvas attained allover effects intended to respect "no limits, just edges."[32] Their *horror vacui*, in which line breeds with glittering volatility, proved the flip side of the dark stasis that had once oppressed Pollock inside his shell.

Line is also the *fons et origo* of space. An apparently paradoxical remark by the chromatic abstractionist Barnett Newman illuminates Pollock's urge to draw: "I know that if I have made a contribution, it is primarily in my drawing . . . . Instead of using outlines, instead of making shapes or setting off shapes, my drawing declares the space."[33] The same applies to Pollock's "drawing"—somehow the late 1940s oils on paper are all line *and* all space. This is their optical buzz. Whence came that electricity? An answer lurks in the kinesis of drawing. The art historian David Rosand provides, in a disparate setting, a neat rationale for the motives behind Pollock's draftsmanship:

> To make a mark or trace a single line upon a surface immediately transforms that surface, energizes its neutrality. . . . Dividing the space of its field, a line releases the allusive or generative charge of the surface—ancient Chinese calligraphers spoke of "generative paper."[34]

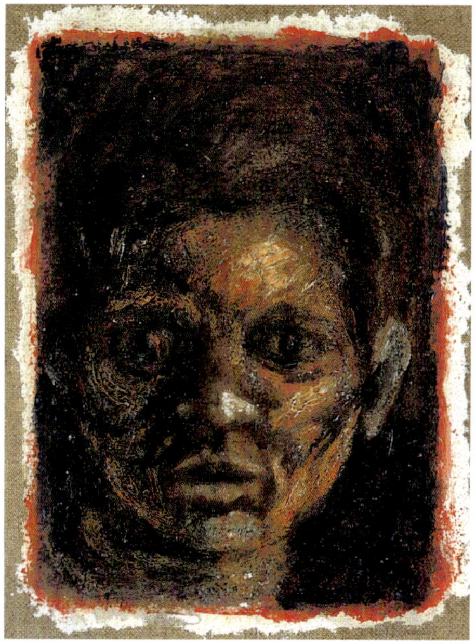

FIG. 10
JACKSON POLLOCK
Untitled (*Self-Portrait*), ca. 1931–35?
Oil on canvas, mounted on composition board
7 1/4 x 5 1/4 inches (18.4 x 13.3 cm)
Courtesy Joan T. Washburn Gallery, New York, and The Pollock-Krasner Foundation, Inc. JPCR 1:9

Probably the most reductive trend in Pollock criticism is to yoke the spectacle of his images to American landscapes.[35] That framework is complicated by Pollock's own presumptions, sparked by his mentor, Thomas Hart Benton, and subsequently abetted by Lee Krasner: his cowboy persona, a professed feeling for the "vast horizontality of the land," for the ocean, and so forth.[36] In such wishful territory, private fantasies are prone to summon artistic realities. Pollock's "West" was fabulated, a psychological antidote to unfortunate early circumstances. These, bluntly stated, must have been as akin to John Steinbeck's *The Grapes of Wrath* (1939) as to the Monument Valley splendors of John Ford's film *Stagecoach* (1939). Interestingly, Pollock's vision tapped both perspectives.

Some early drawings, *Harbor and Lighthouse* (ca. 1934–38, pl. 2) and the lithograph *Gay Head* (ca. 1936, JPCR 4:1061), impose a Western expansiveness on the intrinsically dissimilar scenery of the Eastern seaboard. Their areas interlock land and sea while the mishandling of outlines makes it hard to determine void from solid. Such a trait would be incidental were it not for the advent, a decade later, of a unique linearity. As Michael Fried argues, "There is no inside or outside to Pollock's line, or to the space through which it moves."[37] Without necessarily accepting Fried's formalist notion of "optical space" addressed to "eyesight alone," we should recognize that Pollock was not the first painter to turn graphic weakness into painterly strength.[38] Pollock's imaginary West was anyway that of the Regionalist Benton. The *locus classicus* for this "vast horizontality" without (to again paraphrase Pollock) beginning or end is Benton's *An Artist in America* (1937):

> Where does the West begin?... [In the Prairie lands.] There are definite ends to the horizon, which acts as an enclosure and sets a limit to things. In the West proper there are no limits. The world goes on indefinitely. The horizon is not seen as the end of a scene. It carries you on beyond itself into farther and farther spaces.[39]

Hence Pollock's endorsement of his abstraction in 1950 as "unframed space"[40] may have had roots in Benton's fabulated geography thirteen years beforehand. Certainly, the internalization of the Great American Outdoors was a penchant Pollock shared with Still, who recalled that "It was a grand freedom that Pollock and I felt in the West, looking over the mountains, being able to move any number of miles."[41] Another corollary is less noticed and bears especially upon the works on paper.

From the initial landscapes onward, Pollock filled his designs with increasing obsessiveness. The first tondos are dense; the "psychoanalytic" drawings of around 1939–40 pack their shards together like a violent jigsaw (pl. 17); by the mid-1940s, sheets are covered with tracery almost from one edge to another (pls. 38 and 42); and, in the intensest pourings (pl. 61 and JPCR 4:1021), the infinite activity has a manic touch that, were it not superbly calculated, would invoke the mazes of psychotic art.[42] Consequently, given Pollock's assimilation of a mythic American spaciousness, it seems logical to relate his methods to a particular propensity in the national culture: an existential need for the artistic imagination to inject a perceived void with labyrinthine fabrications. In tracing this tendency, the structuralist literary critic Tony Tanner demonstrates that it is not just nature that abhors a vacuum but also numerous American artists.[43]

Tanner's standpoint may be helpful in situating Pollock's webs in a framework less narrow than, for instance, either Clement Greenberg's formulation of the Cubist-derived "allover" composition or sundry bids to tag them to the claustrophobic film noir discourse of the 1940s.[44] On the contrary, American ruminations on space that populate its vacancy with gossamer webs run from Jonathan Edwards in the eighteenth century to Walt Whitman's "noiseless patient spider" that

> Mark'd how to explore the vacant vast surrounding,
> It launch'd forth filament, filament, filament, out of itself,
> Ever unreeling them, ever tirelessly speeding them.
>
> And you O my soul where you stand,
> Surrounded, detached, in measureless oceans of space,
> Ceaselessly musing, venturing, throwing, seeking the spheres to connect them.[45]

In light of Pollock's early solipsism and ensuing faith that his painting arose from the unconscious,[46] it is instructive that such writers' emblems posit—in advance of Freudian and Jungian paradigms of interiority—an equation between the inner brain or soul and the space without. When contemplating Pollock's most finely tuned calligraphic meshes, such as the big *Lavender Mist* (1950, JPCR 2:264) and analogous works on paper where the scale is breathtakingly minute, an even clearer precedent arises. Henry James's essay "The Art of Fiction" (1884) invokes a web, which is internalized, so that experience becomes the atmosphere of mind. There are few more telling prefigurations of Pollock's classic lineation:

> What kind of experience is intended, and where does it begin and end? Experience is never limited and it is never complete; it is an immense sensibility, a kind of huge spiderweb of the finest silken threads suspended in the chamber of consciousness, and catching every airborne particle in its tissue. It is the very atmosphere of the mind; and when the mind is imaginative—much more when it happens to be that of a man of genius—it takes to itself the faintest hints of life, it converts the very pulses of the air into revelations.[47]

Returning from James's "chamber of consciousness" to Pollock's "shell" of the self also reveals a dark side that left an enduring legacy. Later, Greenberg—stimulated by F. O. Matthiessen's groundbreaking book *American Renaissance* (1941)—identified this mood as "Gothic."[48] Yet it is less well known that Benton's distortions were already deemed "Gothic" in the 1930s.[49] The

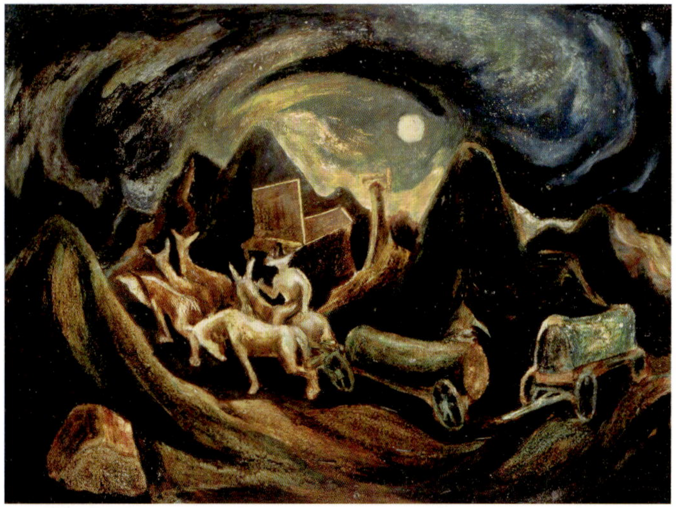

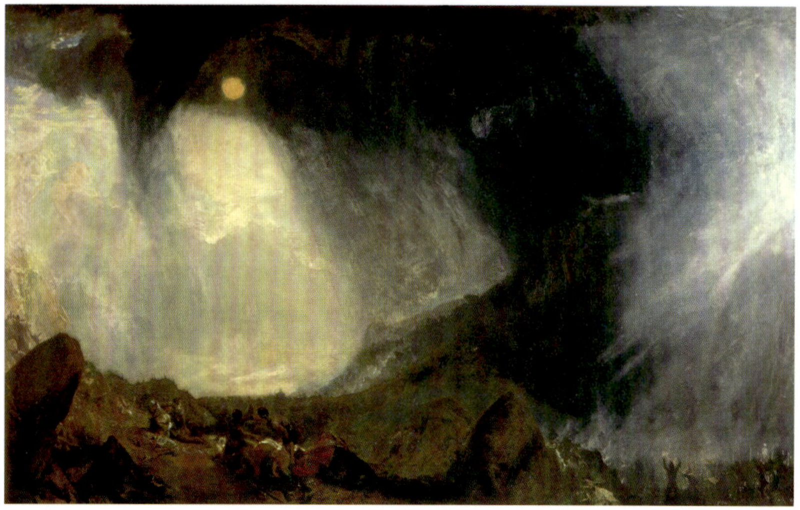

judgment yields a clue to the second angle to Pollock's early mindset—its wellspring in the "Western Gothic" genre.

"Western Gothic" has never been fully codified and requires explanation. In brief, it is an offshoot of that already portmanteau entity, "the Gothic" itself—the dark underside to the Edenic American West as a place of new frontiers, vigorous expansion, and boundless optimism. A potted history of Western Gothic might start with Zane Grey's novels with their stark psychologized landscapes,[50] proceed through the death-on-a-pale-horse menace of Jack Palance's villain in the film *Shane* (1953), continue with the lonesome revenant of Clint Eastwood's *High Plains Drifter* (1973)[51] and conclude with Annie Proulx's recent, brooding *Wyoming Stories* (1999). Proulx summarizes the genre's flight into fantasy with the quip of a Wyoming farmer: "Reality's never been of much use out here."[52] Should the comparisons sound far-fetched, recall that the young Pollock absorbed this sort of low-cultural milieu and had a taste for the "spooky" myths of the West—"wild stallions, white wolves, lost gold mines and mysterious unattended campfires."[53] These trappings, Pollock's guilt-ridden, haunted mentality, and such details as the creepy supernal horse of *Bowl* (ca. 1939, JPCR 4:925) belong to the Western Gothic lineage, brazenly exemplified by a popular song such as "Ghost Riders in the Sky":

> Then cowboy change your ways today or with us you will ride
> Tryin' to catch this devil-herd. . . . Across these endless skies[54]

Western Gothic is the vein of several early Pollock scenes: *Going West* (ca. 1934–35, fig. 11), the lithograph *Lone Rider* (ca. 1934–35, JPCR 4:1056) and *Landscape with Rider II* (1933, JPCR 1:6). In the last two, a cowboy confronts a steer carcass; they have been called "a nocturnal meditation on death."[55] Tellingly, in the lithograph *Landscape with Steer* (ca. 1935–37, JPCR 4:1064–65), Western Gothic stage props—lurid fires, angular demonic cattle—segue seamlessly into the tumultuous schemes of Siqueiros. Elsewhere, in pages from a late 1930s sketchbook (pl. 7), the jumbled anatomies parallel the equally Western Gothic milieu of Still's contemporary paintings.[56] But *Going West* contains other telltale ingredients.

The justified emphasis on Benton and Albert Pinkham Ryder (himself an exemplar of the American Gothic persuasion)[57] as primary influences on Pollock tends to obscure a further source for *Going West*: J.M.W. Turner's *Snow Storm: Hannibal and His Army Crossing the Alps* (1812, fig. 12). They share a benighted atmosphere, leftward propulsion, mountainous scenery, two pyramidal rocks at lower left, a glowing disk on high, diminutive protagonists pitted against the macrocosm, and a fascination with the vortex—a phenomenon that Pollock mined in the

FIG. 11
JACKSON POLLOCK
Going West, ca. 1934–35
Oil on composition board
15 1/8 x 20 3/4 inches (38.3 x 52.7 cm)
Smithsonian American Art Museum, Washington, D.C. JPCR 1:16

FIG. 12
J.M.W. TURNER
Snow Storm: Hannibal and His Army Crossing the Alps, 1812
Oil on canvas
57 1/2 x 93 1/2 inches (146 x 237.5 cm)
Clore Collection, Tate, London

late 1940s.[58] No other single precursor contains all the above features.[59] Like the labyrinth, the vortex whirls together outermost limits and an innermost focus.

An iconography now emerges that, during the years ahead, will be repeated especially in the works on paper. It is a configuration based on a circular template. Apparently, for Pollock this nexus embodied a complex amalgam of psychological and pictorial forces—inside/outside, motion/rest, micro- and macrocosm. Starting with the spheroid head in *Self-Portrait*, the shape migrates to the tondos of various graphics (e.g., JPCR 3:394 and 3:452r) and the centrifugal *Going West*.[60] Elsewhere, it seems equated with the womb, as in *Bowl*, where the tondo cradles a baby at its center,[61] *Birth* (ca. 1941, JPCR 1:77), a stream of circular nodes, and the fetus of *The Child Proceeds* (1945, JPCR 1:145).[62] Jungian interpretations would doubtless regard this *idée fixe* as a symbol of integration, a union of opposites. Yet it arises in Pollock's vocabulary almost right away and before the many Jungian yin-and-yang and mandala emblems from the late 1930s onwards (e.g., pls. 13 and 14).[63] Furthermore, if we accept that the womb is among the guises into which the spheroid-tondo-vortex leitmotif metamorphoses, it links with Pollock's Gothic abjection at the outset. The psychologist Melanie Klein proposed that the mother's womb is the first abode that the baby occupies: it can be conceptualized as a site of safety as well as of destruction, one "to be attacked with all the sadistic armoury."[64] Julia Kristeva in *Powers of Horror* (1980) develops Klein's insight, writing that the mother's body/womb is among the earliest "things" that the child abjects.[65]

While Pollock's psychologically charged imagery promises a rich mine for Kleinian and Kristevan takes, it is not my aim here to pursue them, nor to indulge psychobabble about the artist's hazardous birth and other problems.[66] My point instead is that Pollock's Gothic and abject inclinations catalyzed many developments through the later 1940s. They include: an upsurge of destruction with sadistic undertows, as in the heads and animals inspired by Pablo Picasso's *Guernica* phase that appear to tear themselves apart (pls. 10 and 16); the advent of a distinctive line—child-like, febrile, and messy—again indebted

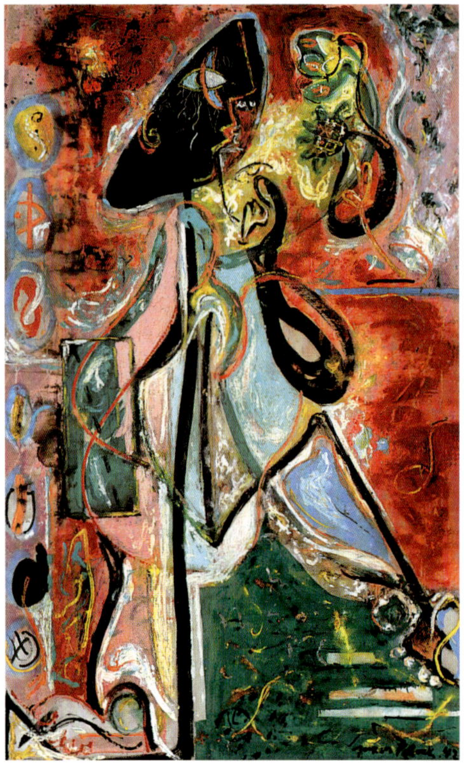

FIG. 13
JACKSON POLLOCK
The Moon-Woman, 1942
Oil on canvas
69 x 43 1/16 inches (175.2 x 109.3 cm)
Peggy Guggenheim Collection, Venice
JPCR 1:86

to Picasso's *Dream and Lie of Franco* (1937) as well as to André Masson, which intimates a subject increasingly out of control and under trial (pl. 24 and JPCR 3:661);[67] and the progressive stress on materiality—be it chalk, ink, crayon, splatter, or collage fragments (pl. 34). The last trend, which climaxes in Pollock's apotheosis of the liquidity of paint, can still be traced to the sensibility of abjection—fixated upon the body's material baseness as it regresses to infantile compulsions to master, play with, and let go its fluids.[68] A collapsed demon, whose tongue spews forth like vomit (pl. 9), personifies this ghastly *jouissance*. The wonder is that Pollock channeled such disruptiveness into the strictest aesthetic order. How aptly his notes set "organic intensity" next to "states of order."[69] The works on paper are the laboratory for such extremes.

Yet a major canvas heralds Pollock's shrewdly organized foray into subconscious depths. *The Moon-Woman* (1942, fig. 13) introduces whiplash calligraphy for its figure; Pollock perfected

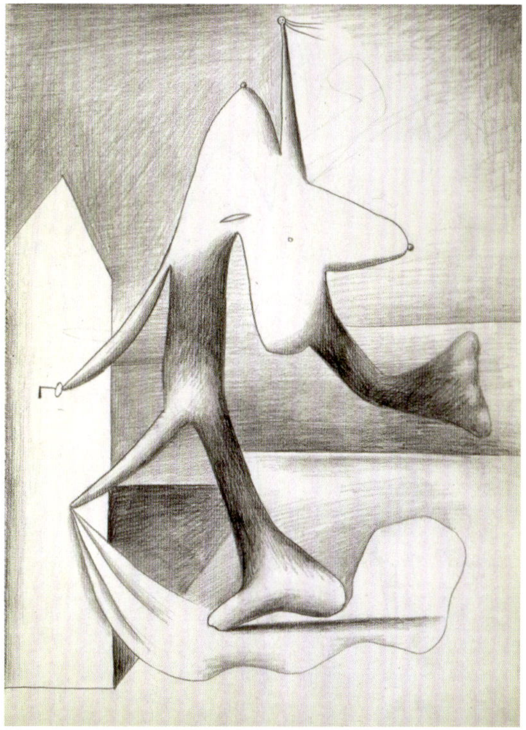

the departure in drawings during the next three years. By 1944 these start to combine explosiveness, rich coloration and filigree patterns, reaching a peak in 1945–46 (pls. 42 and 44 and JPCR 4:990)—developments indebted to Vasily Kandinsky. However, it is *The Moon-Woman* that initiates Kandinsky's clashing hues (here green and red) and splashy brushwork.[70] Moreover, *The Moon-Woman* recalls a 1927 Picasso drawing (fig. 14).[71] The moon woman's ovoid head (an eye-slash echoing a mouth-slash on the earlier creature's swollen anatomy), her one leg erect and the other thrust back, a sky-blue horizon line above right center and the vertical stele at extreme left alike find correspondences in the Picasso. Did Pollock also intuit that the bather's key can be understood—particularly according to standard Surrealist and Jungian usage—as a trope for unlocking hidden secrets?[72] If so, the ruse augured Pollock's emergent model of pictorial process as an unlocking of unconscious energies.

Further testimony to Pollock's strategies is the sketches after El Greco and other old masters (pl. 3). His reliance on reproductions as a starting point for the drawings carries wider consequences. Images are always flattened in print, while leafing through illustrations in books or magazines is liable to foster a chain of perceptual associations between diverse subjects. The first fact must have assisted Pollock's avowed difficulties with drawing by translating actual volumes into virtual schemata. The second could have prompted him to equate the physical succession of images—as one page turns to another at the flick of a wrist—with the mobility of thought (especially as the not very literate Pollock probably scanned texts with some awkwardness[73]). Thus, at a formative stage, Pollock may have begun to visualize the mind and, by extension, the unconscious, as somewhat like the intermingled pages of a book.

Akin to the imaginative totality of a codex, the early 1940s works on paper are a compendium of literal flatness—note the foursquare rectangles of *[Drawing with Two Signatures]* and Untitled (ca. 1941, pl. 13; and 1943, pl. 19) as well as the stark black grounds (pl. 25 and JPCR 3:705)—and conceptual spaciousness, as in the Kandinsky-inspired whirlpools typified by Untitled (1943, pl. 24). Signifiers progressively slip from resemblance—to body parts, beasts, totems[74]—into cryptic abstract strokes. One particularly unusual work of 1943, a so-called *Abstract Painting* (1943, pl. 20), appears to confirm Pollock's conflation of psychic and textual dimensions. Evoking the wartime ideogram known as "Kilroy was here!"—a head with eyes and hands peering over the top of a blank wall—it nods towards graffiti, an age-old mode of inscription signaling subconscious urges. By setting mirror-inverted writing and amorphous paintwork on a sheet of purple paper (the "wall"), it also aligns illegible scripts with the absent space of the figure (the proverbial "Kilroy" had vanished before his graffiti was found).[75] To ascribe Pollock's maneuvers here solely to Surrealist *écriture automatique* is to forget that the metaphor of the mind/self as writing tablet is as ancient as Plato and as modern as Sigmund Freud's "mystic writing-pad."[76] Regardless of whether Pollock knew Freud's idea (its gist—a wax slab, covered with paper and transparent

FIG. 14
PABLO PICASSO
Bather and Cabana, summer 1927
Pencil on paper
12¼ x 9¼ inches (31 x 23.5 cm)
Musée Picasso, Paris

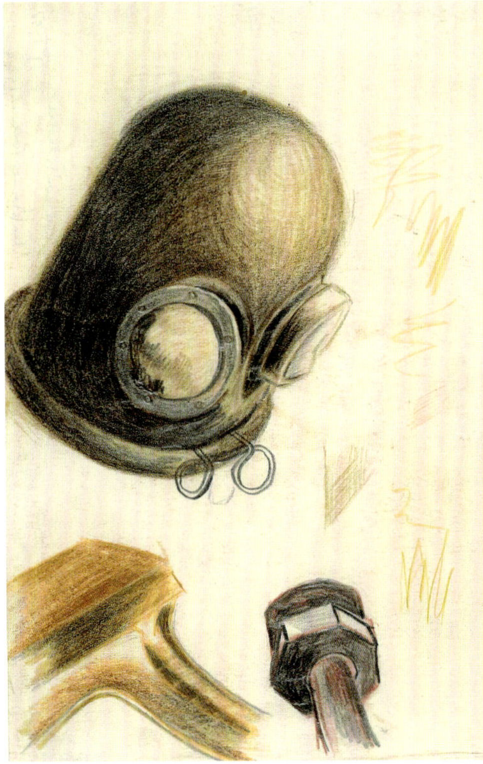

FIG. 15
JACKSON POLLOCK
Untitled (*Sandblaster's Goggled Hood*), 1938
Colored pencils and pencil on paper
8 3/8 x 5 3/8 inches (21.3 x 13.7 cm)
The Metropolitan Museum of Art, Gift of Lee Krasner Pollock, 1982.
JPCR 3:387

celluloid, capable of endless intercalation—could have been transmitted to him by, among others, John Graham),[77] it neatly anticipates the interminable layerings, memory traces, and erasures that became the hallmark of the drawings from 1943 onwards.[78]

Another one-off piece, *The Mask* (ca. 1943, pl. 18), likewise unites assorted themes. Its weird "mask" (a template for constructing dolls' heads) clearly descends from an earlier study of a sandblaster's protective helmet (fig. 15). This 1938 sketch has several noteworthy aspects. The helmet is a new variant of an old impasse: Pollock's encasing "shell" of consciousness.[79] Its descendant, the "mask," is surrounded by linear chaos. In turn, it is the figural prototype of the masking—the concealment of areas—that infiltrates the next two years, anticipating Pollock's avowed "veiling" of imagery during 1947–50.[80] Also, the sandblaster's clunky helmet highlights the proximity of "Gothic" to the grotesque, a tenor that dominates the convolutions that Pollock's line acquired after 1943.[81] "Gothic" and "grotesque" are categories that hinge upon a transgression of boundaries and a predilection for excess.[82] How better to understand the profusion of calligraphy during 1944–50—multiplying and twisting every which way—than as a breathtaking venture into transgressive excess? Lastly, Pollock's recourse to a *Life* magazine photograph for the 1938 drawing hints that he was perhaps more aware of life around him than is commonly supposed.[83] This is a suitable theme with which to conclude: it connects the achievement for which Pollock will be forever celebrated—the pourings of 1947–50—and the preceding decade or so, upon which I have deliberately concentrated. There is a valid reason for this emphasis.

Lee Krasner averred that "all of Jackson's work" grew from the decade from around the mid-1930s.[84] Might we speculate whether he took more than just the inspiration of his own work from then? Always, Pollock was keen to "express" his "age." In 1950, he said: "It seems to me that the modern painter cannot express this age, the airplane, the atom bomb, the radio, in the old forms of the Renaissance or of any other past culture. Each age finds its own technique."[85] We have heard this refrain before—nowhere more insistently than from those who faced the First Machine Age in Pollock's formative epoch of the 1930s. Compare these words:

> Different times and different countries have their own art. Modern is only a relative term. . . . Art of today must be created today. It must express the life about us. Ours is a complex age. . . . Invention, machinery, industry, science and commerce are characteristic of today. . . . *Materials*—these new ideas demand new materials.[86]

It is an anonymous teenager writing in a high school notebook in Minneapolis in 1937. Why should Pollock in 1950 echo the otherwise completely unrelated schoolgirl's phrases? Because they are alike stock responses to one thing: confronting modernity in the United States in the 1930s, the age of so-called Depression Modern. Possibly, elements in Pollock's classic abstractions are vestiges of Depression Modern prerogatives taken to limits where they no longer recognize themselves.

Few images read "faster" than such pourings as *Number 13,*

1949, *Number 19, 1948*, and Untitled (1949, pl. 61; 1948, JPCR 2:190; and 1951, JPCR 4:1021). Our eyes empathize with the ductile fleetness of their lines.[87] Why speed? "Speed" was a byword in the American 1930s, from the marvels of flight to radio's instantaneous transcendence of time and space. The globe or concentric circles—recall Pollock's lengthy preoccupation with this cipher culminating with *Tondo* (1948, fig. 20)—were frequent symbols of its encompassing universality.[88] "The tempo of life is speeded," declared cultural commentators in 1933.[89] Speed joined transparency and the dynamic use of line (the linear continuity of "streamline moderne") pervading the American aesthetic of the era—which Pollock cannot have missed.[90] The immediate comparison that an Untitled sheet (ca. 1938–41, pl. 6) makes with Orozco belies its striking congruence with the design principles—blending organic arabesques with mechanistic or geometric forms—epitomized by the radiator grilles of Manhattan's Chanin Building (fig. 16). Both reflected similar "moderne" stylistic imperatives.[91] Similarly, Pollock's purported harmony with the rhythms of nature contains a distant ripple effect from when designers supposed that "by integrating our own work rhythmically we are repeating the structural scheme of the universe in which we live."[92] Even Pollock's shimmering colors during 1947–50—aluminum paint, black and white, cool grays, subtle bright or buff accents—retain the faintest whiff of the suave chrome and opalescent hues of American Art Deco.[93]

Crucially, Pollock associated his "age" with photography:

> The modern artist is living in a mechanical age and we have a mechanical means of representing objects in nature such as the camera and photograph. The modern artist, it seems to me, is working and expressing an inner world—in other words—expressing the energy, the motion, and other inner forces.[94]

Since the 1920s, photography had proved the medium par excellence to arrest speeding motion and invisible energies—as the poet Hart Crane's lines about Alfred Stieglitz's prints confirm (see the epigraph to this essay). Evidence indicates that photography was an interface between Pollock's art and his

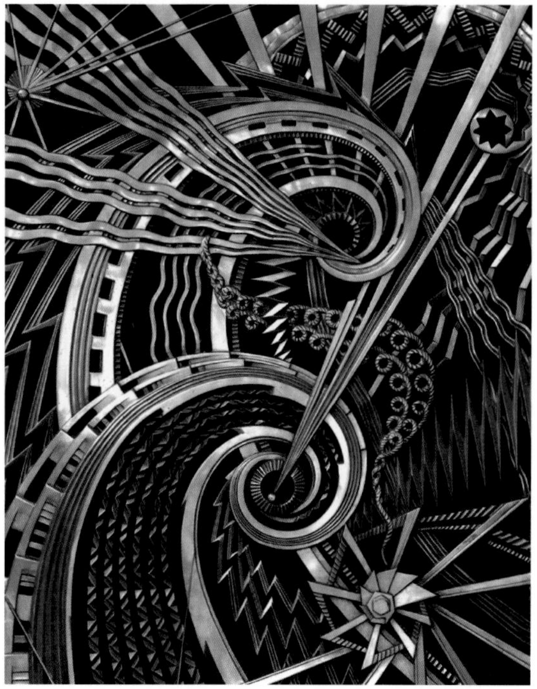

FIG. 16
Radiator grill designed by René Chambellan, Chanin Building, New York, 1928. Photograph by Andrew Bordwin (*Tsunami*, 1993)

"experience of our age."[95] Appropriately, the photograph automatically telescopes three-dimensional dynamics into two-dimensional hieroglyphics.

"Action photography" could be the missing factor in the vast Pollock literature. Photographic portrayals of motion in the late nineteenth century start with pioneers such as Étienne-Jules Marey and Eadweard Muybridge.[96] In the 1930s, this tradition blended with others, such as László Moholy-Nagy's "photograms" exploring abstract kinetic patterns and photojournalism's blurry snaps of humanity in extreme situations.[97] By the early 1940s in the United States, manifold trends—multiple exposure, chronophotography, stroboscopic shots, and wartime "action" snaps—permeated everyday imagery,[98] not least via the pages of *Life* (which Pollock perused in the late 1930s).[99] Such images—at once often blending furious activity into overall gestalts of light and shade while quintessentially evoking modern, Einsteinian space-time relations[100]—were a materialization of Pollock's core objectives:

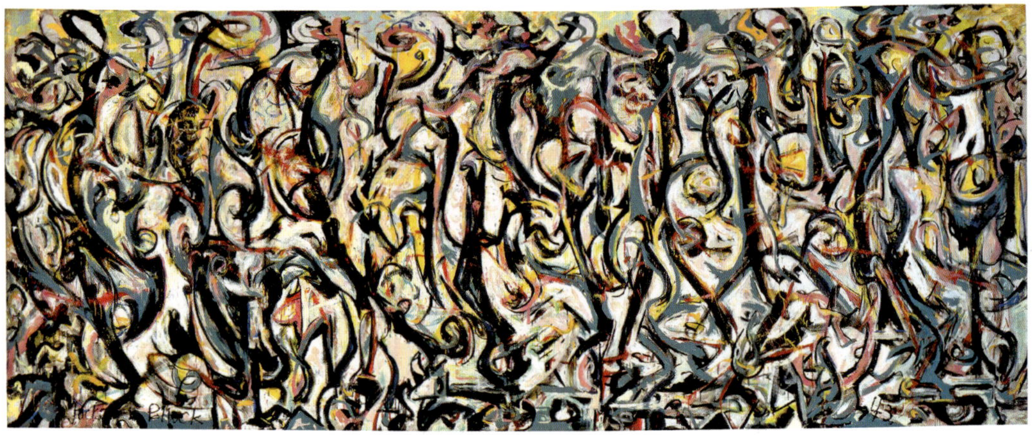

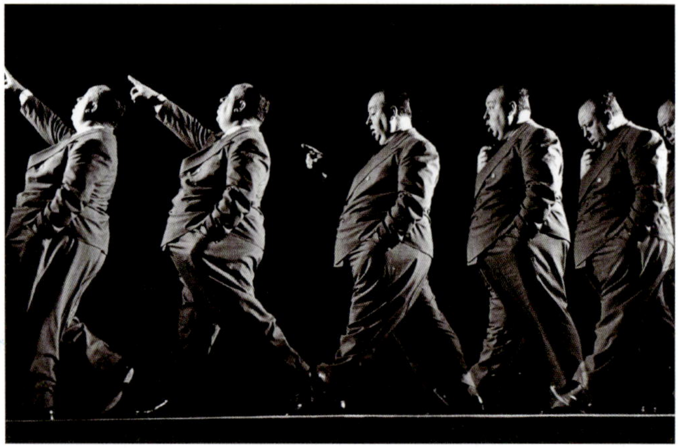

FIG. 17
JACKSON POLLOCK
Mural, 1943
Oil on canvas
7 feet 11 3/4 inches x 19 feet 9 1/2 inches
(243.2 x 603.2 cm)
University of Iowa Museum of Art,
Iowa City. Gift of Peggy Guggenheim, 1948.
JPCR 2:259

FIG. 18
Director Alfred Hitchcock during the filming of *Shadow of a Doubt*, 1943.
Photograph by Gjon Mili

States of order—
Organic intensity—
energy and motion
made visible—
memories arrested in space[101]

The likelihood that Pollock noticed action photographs in *Life*—which had a vast U.S. circulation in the 1940s and an equally high "pass-along" rate—is increased by the specific similarities between *Burning Landscape* (1943, JPCR 1:95) and an aerial photograph of the bombing of Düsseldorf published that year in the magazine.[102] Pollock's markings duplicate the photograph's billowing smoke clouds and wavy light trails caused by burning incendiaries.[103] Such photographs, in short, yielded readymade, indexical traces of time and energy, less "illustrations" (to rephrase Pollock) than graphic "equivalents" to lived experience.[104] Further evidence supports the theory that Pollock knew them.

Mural (1943, fig. 17) constitutes a turning point in the rendition of energic movement since here Pollock begins to shift from mimetic to indexical draftsmanship, as brushstrokes career across the picture plane.[105] *Mural*'s looping repetitions will haunt the pourings of the late 1940s. What haunts *Mural*? One likely catalyst was the *Action Photography* exhibition held at the Museum of Modern Art, New York, during August–September 1943, precisely when *Mural* was conceived.[106] Indeed, Pollock's friend, Herbert Matter, was among the photographers included.[107] A print in the show by Gjon Mili (fig. 18) particularly adumbrates the frieze-like flux of *Mural*:[108] Alfred Hitchcock is shown in multiple exposures striding horizontally with outflung gestures.[109]

In any event, the 132 works at MoMA encompassed every brand of action photography; its wall texts read like a running commentary on Pollock's ongoing concerns. For instance, Barbara Morgan (who moved in Abstract Expressionist circles and had photographed Arshile Gorky in 1940) was described as "interpreting universal rhythms through an individual dancer."[110] Another panel announced: "By substituting photography for our eyes and memories, speed has been tamed and the invisible made visible."[111] If this were not enough to attest to Pollock's seminal exposure to action photography, other clues increase the chances of that encounter.[112] Mili's prolonged-exposure photograph of light transformed into line (fig. 19)—published in 1945 in *Life*[113]—presages the floating, luminous white cat's cradles that Pollock weaved some two or three years later (pl. 53 and JPCR 2:209). So, too, do photographs in another MoMA show, *In and Out of Focus* (1948), which Matter even designed and installed.[114] There, again, Louis Faurer's metamorphic, silhouetted figures paralleled Pollock's wavy shadow presences in ink wash (JPCR 4:1019) and the shredded personages of *Triad* (1948, pl. 51).[115] Finally, the rapidly burgeoning vogue for aerial photographs during World War II exerted a profound impact on the general conceptualization of space in the mid-1940s, especially in the United States.[116] It is hard not to discern at least some legacy of this quantum leap from one orientation to another as subliminally underlying Pollock's momentous decision to place his canvases and papers on the floor so that he worked on them from above.[117] Such a vantage point was replete with the sort of perspectives—alternately commanding and clipped —that are inherent in aerial photography. The exceptional *Tondo* seems to distill the globe itself into a panoptic eyeball, cosmos, and microcosm in one.[118]

This brings us, in closing, to the extraordinary kaleidoscope of sources, traditions, and methods in Pollock's 1947–50 pourings—a distillation of oppositions that subtends the countless interpretations that they have sustained. The contexts that these works invite are just as multifarious, whether they be the fascination in the 1940s with illegible scripts and graffiti—the runes of a world gone awry—as seen in contemporary representational works such as Bernard Perlin's *Orthodox Boys* (1948, fig. 21), the doctrine of utterance as an energy field that the poet William Carlos Williams propounded the same year,[119] or the older, pragmatic American belief in art as action.[120] Pollock's scope speaks for itself: from monochrome (pl. 55) to incandescent hues (JPCR 2:229); from latent figuration (JPCR 3:786) to utter nonobjectivity (JPCR 2:190); from coarse gestures (JPCR 2:200) to gossamer finesse (pl. 57); and from rigid lines (pl. 61) to those that seem to trail and wind into infinity (pl. 56). All suggest a measure of entrancement, a visual "reign of wonder" on the part of the beholder over how so much has been reduced to so small an arena.[121] Here, with calculated naïveté, the literally little and the virtually vast are collapsed into a single perceptual plane.[122] The ethos behind these pourings on paper is prophesied by Whitman: "I believe a leaf of grass is no less than the journey work of the stars."[123] Or, as Bachelard wryly remarked about "intimate immensity": "If a poet looks through a microscope or a telescope, he always sees the same thing."[124]

Is this amazingly mutable line that constellates such myriad allusions and possibilities the line of the mind, the eye, or the

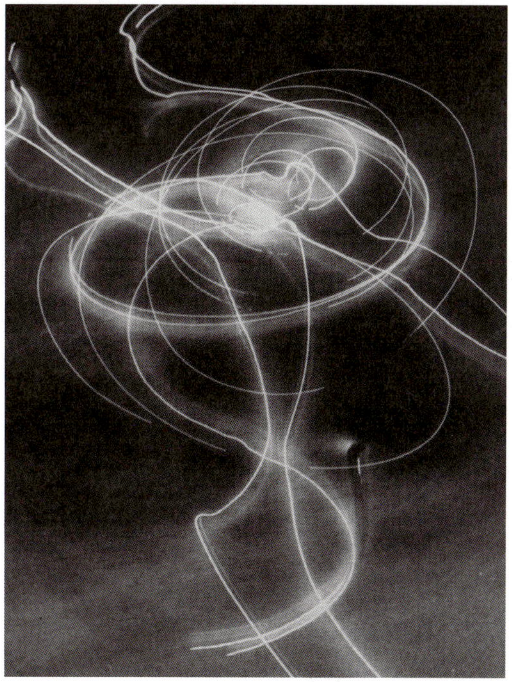

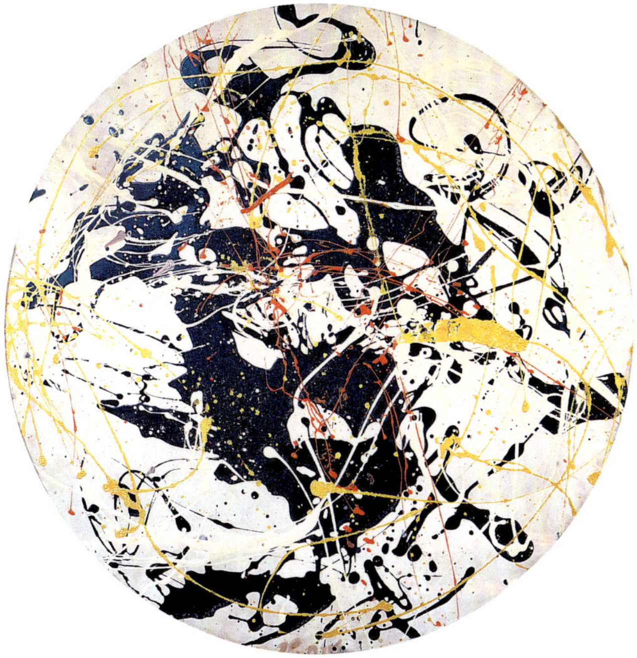

FIG. 19
Figure skater Carol Lynne, 1945.
Photograph by Gjon Mili

FIG. 20
JACKSON POLLOCK
Tondo, 1948
Oil and enamel on metal
Diameter: 23 1/8 inches (58.7 cm)
Collection of Adèle and Willard Gidwitz, Illinois.
JPCR 2:208

hand? Namuth's revelation that Pollock was "not drawing on the canvas so much as in the air above it" implies vistas in the mind's eye. Yet these virtuoso traces also betray great physical discipline. Of course, as Valéry knew when meditating on Edgar Degas's drawing, there need be no contradiction between the two:

> But the hand is very indirectly governed by the eye. Many "relays" come in between; notably that of memory. Every glance at the model, every line traced by the eye, at once becomes a recorded memory, and it is from this record that the hand will have to derive its law of movement on the paper. . . . The artist approaches, withdraws, leans over . . . his whole body behaving like an instrument of the eye, becoming entirely a means for aiming, pointing, controlling, reducing to focus.[125]

Valéry's scenario fits the equilibrium between the contesting claims of memory, imagination and manual verve that Pollock attained during 1947–50. From this watershed, his final graphics wend their way down to a more fragmentary state in which staccato tempi become semaphores of the erratic return of repressed presences seeping through from below (pl. 78).[126] Some sheets indeed arose—like residues or after-images—from paper placed beneath other drawings (pl. 69).[127] Formlessness contends with the tug of long-forgotten geometric ordonnances. As the paper's absorbency confounds surface and space, so indeterminacy and, sometimes, opacity, rule.[128] Previously, "flow" was the keynote of Pollock's draftsmanship; now it ends in the ominous spread of blots.[129] They are the final punctuation marks in the handwriting of the self.[130]

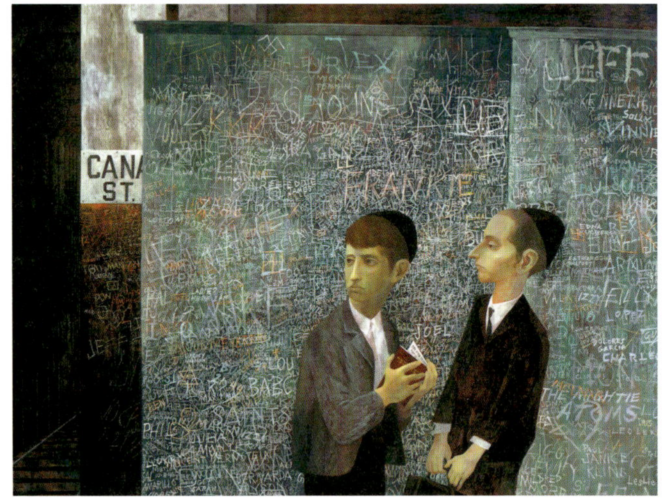

FIG. 21
BERNARD PERLIN
Orthodox Boys, 1948
Tempera on board
30 x 40 inches (76.2 x 101.6 cm)
Tate, London

NOTES

In preparing this essay, I especially acknowledge Fred Bearman, Claude Cernuschi, Helen Harrison, Kent Minturn, Justin Roebuck, and Walter Wells.

1. Paul Valéry, *Degas. Danse. Dessin* (Paris: Gallimard, 1938), p. 137.

2. Hart Crane (1923) in Langdon Hammer and Brom Weber, eds., *O My Land, My Friends: The Selected Letters of Hart Crane* (New York and London: Four Walls, Eight Windows, 1997), p. 149.

3. Hans Namuth, "Photographing Pollock—A Memoir" in Namuth, *Pollock Painting* (New York: Agrinde, 1980), n.p.

4. Jackson Pollock, "Interview with William Wright," (late 1950) in Pepe Karmel, ed., *Jackson Pollock: Interviews, Articles, and Reviews* (New York: The Museum of Modern Art, 1999), p. 22 [henceforth abbreviated as Karmel 1999].

5. Pollock, handwritten statement, in Karmel 1999, p. 24.

6. Barnett Newman (1962) in Richard Shiff, "Performing an Appearance: On the Surface of Abstract Expressionism," in Michael Auping, ed., *Abstract Expressionism: The Critical Developments* (London: Thames and Hudson, 1987), p. 95.

7. Clyfford Still in Thomas Kellein, ed., *Clyfford Still 1904–1980: The Buffalo and San Francisco Collections* (Munich: Prestel, 1992), p. 149.

8. David Rosand, *Drawing Acts: Studies in Graphic Expression and Representation* (Cambridge: Cambridge University Press, 2002), pp. 5–6, 24ff.

9. See David Batchelor, *Chromophobia* (London: Reaktion Books, 2000).

10. "Drawing" in Jane Turner, ed., *Dictionary of Art*, vol. 9 (New York: Macmillan, 1996), p. 213. Interestingly, this sounds almost as much a description of Surrealist automatism as of old masterly practice.

11. Bernice Rose, *Jackson Pollock: Drawing into Painting* (New York: Museum of Modern Art, 1979).

12. That the Pollock catalogue raisonné overrode this distinction by including enamel pourings and other works on paper among both "Paintings" and "Drawings" reflects Pollock's radical conflation of the two. The criterion used was instead the actual medium—differentiating poured enamel and gouache from pencil, crayon, pen, and ink. The rationale was that the latter media account for what the "editors feel are *essentially* drawings." See Francis V. O'Connor and Eugene V. Thaw, *Jackson Pollock: A Catalogue Raisonné of Paintings, Drawings, and Other Works*, vol. 3 (New Haven and London: Yale University Press, 1978), p. vii [henceforth abbreviated as JPCR]. Nevertheless, for example, cat. nos. 783 and 786 in the "Drawings" volume are enamels on paper. This indicates less any methodological confusion than how Pollock's radicalism undercuts such separations.

13. JPCR 4:1088. I am grateful to Dr. Harry Cooper for returning my attention to this work, now at the Fogg Art Museum, Harvard University.

14. Cézanne, quoted in Maurice Merleau-Ponty, "Cézanne's Doubt," trans. Hubert L. Dreyfus and Patricia Allen Dreyfus, in Thomas Baldwin, ed., *Maurice Merleau-Ponty: Basic Writings* (New York: Routledge, 2004), p. 279.

15. Rosand, op. cit., p. xxi.

16. Ibid., pp. 6–7.

17. C. S. Pierce coined the terminology. My source is Roger Cardinal, *Expressionism* (London: Paladin Books, 1984), pp. 29–30. Shiff, op. cit., p. 98, further explicates it (though this discussion largely omits the "symbolic" sign, the third component of Pierce's much-used trichotomy).

18. With strong, paradoxical overtones of semiotic absence because the indexical mark has been cut away from the human marker. See Rosalind Krauss, *The Optical Unconscious* (Cambridge, Mass.: MIT Press, 1993), p. 260.

19. Pollock, "My Painting," *Possibilities* (New York) no.1 (Winter 1947–48), in Karmel 1999, p. 17.

20. See Cardinal, op. cit., p. 16.

21. Pollock (late 1950) in Karmel 1999, p. 21.

22. As demonstrated by, among others, E. H. Gombrich in "Expression and Communication," in *Meditations on a Hobby Horse* (London: Phaidon Press, 1963), pp. 56–69.

23. Frank Kermode, "The Dancer," in *Romantic Image* (London: Ark Paperbacks, 1967), pp. 49–91, charts the typology of the figure—with numerous trenchant parallels to Pollock's undeclared theories. In short, Namuth's photographs of Pollock recapitulate a Romantic ideology of the creator internalizing natural energies and then externalizing them in the outreach of his/her art. Cf. Kermode, op. cit., p. 53: "In a sense, the body does the thinking."

24. For relevant biographical data, see Steven Naifeh and Gregory White Smith, *Jackson Pollock: An American Saga* (New York: Clarkson N. Potter, 1989).

25. This rarely remarked detail—Pollock's right eye veers to the left while the other stares ahead—again unknowingly echoes a Romantic prototype. This is the gaze that looks out on the world juxtaposed to that which sees within. A prime example is Caspar David Friedrich's *Self-Portrait with Cap and Visor* (May 8, 1802, Hamburger Kunsthalle), wherein the one eye is blindfolded.

26. Letter to Charles and Frank (October 22, 1929) and to Charles (January 31, 1930) in Helen Harrison, ed., *Such Desperate Joy: Imagining Jackson Pollock* (New York: Thunder's Mouth Press, 2000), pp. 8, 9.

27. For a thought-provoking reading of this topic, see Francis V. O'Connor, "Down to the Weave. A Commentary on a Selection of Key Works," in Harrison, op. cit., pp. 177–94.

28. John Golding, *Visions of the Modern* (Berkeley: University of California Press, 1994), pp. 338–39: "One of the features of Orozco's art is the way in which his figures all seem to be in some way flayed; they wear their skeletons on the outside, like armour, although it is an armour that is useless, and he mostly seems to see humanity as doomed."

29. Pollock's *Self-Portrait* can hardly postdate Siqueiros's *Echo of a Scream* (1937, Museum of Modern Art, New York). Yet a definite resemblance obtains between the modeling of the head(s) in the latter—like a dark brassy sphere—

and Pollock's. See also Jürgen Harten, *Siqueiros/Pollock, Pollock/Siqueiros* (Düsseldorf: Kunsthalle/Dumont, 1995).

30. Of course knives cut, rendering the internal external. Consider the implications of the tense anatomical oppositions in Pollock's Untitled *(Naked Man with Knife)* (ca. 1938–41, JPCR 1:60). The conclusion of this trend is the pictorial gash-cum-vaginal orifice of *The Deep* (1953, JPCR 2:372).

31. Gaston Bachelard, *The Poetics of Space* (Boston: Beacon Press, 1969), p. 108. Bachelard, p. 91, characterizes nests and shells as "images that bring out the primitiveness in us."

32. Pollock (undated) in Harrison, op. cit., p. 93.

33. Barnett Newman (1962) in John P. O'Neill, ed., *Barnett Newman: Selected Writings and Interviews* (New York: Alfred A. Knopf, 1990), p. 251.

34. Rosand, op. cit., pp. 1–2.

35. Typified by Bryan Robertson, *Jackson Pollock* (New York: Harry N. Abrams, Inc., 1960). A much more cogent version is: Robert Rosenblum, *Modern Painting and the Northern Romantic Tradition* (London: Thames and Hudson, 1972).

36. Pollock (February 1944) in Karmel 1999, p. 15.

37. Michael Fried (1965) in Karmel 1999, p. 98.

38. Recall Caravaggio's early difficulties with portraying forms in even illumination and his ensuing development of dramatic chiaroscuro. Conversely, in the twentieth century, Marcel Duchamp's limitations as a painter nurtured his conceptualist strengths.

39. Thomas Hart Benton, *An Artist in America* (New York: R. M. McBride and Company, 1937), pp. 199–200.

40. Pollock (August 5, 1950) in Karmel 1999, p. 19.

41. Still quoted in David L. Shirey, "Man of the Arts," *Newsweek* (New York) December 22, 1969, p. 105. Like Pollock, Still was of mixed Scots-Irish ancestry.

42. While hard to describe, their tempi and delicacy are of a different, more muscular order, to Mark Tobey's "white writing."

43. Tony Tanner, *Scenes of Nature, Signs of Man* (Cambridge: Cambridge University Press, 1987), pp. 25–45.

44. Clement Greenberg, "'American-Type' Painting," (1955) in *Art and Culture* (Boston: Beacon Press, 1961), p. 218. Michael Leja, *Reframing Abstract Expressionism: Subjectivity and Painting in the 1940s* (New Haven, Conn.: Yale University Press, 1993), pp. 319–23.

45. Quoted in Tanner, op. cit., p. 26.

46. Pollock (1947) in JPCR vol. 4, p. 241.

47. Henry James, "The Art of Fiction" in John Auchard, ed., *The Portable Henry James* (New York: Penguin Books, 2004), p. 434. Far from being a prerogative of twentieth-century "Modern Man" and noir discourse, such *topoi* and metaphors thus stem from a much older, and frequently idealist, tradition. The magazine, *The Tiger's Eye*, often signposted these pre-modern and/or American Transcendentalist taproots of Abstract Expressionism.

48. Greenberg, "The Present Prospects of American Painting and Sculpture," (October 1947) in John O'Brian, ed., *Clement Greenberg: The Collected Essays and Criticisms*, vol. 2 (Chicago: University of Chicago Press, 1986), pp. 164–66. F. O. Matthiessen, *American Renaissance: Art and Expression in the Age of Emerson and Whitman* (New York: Oxford University Press, 1941). It is almost inconceivable that Greenberg would not have known Matthiessen's acclaimed study; the critic's portrayal of the "Gothic"—first essayed in a 1944 review of Thomas Eakins—parallels the latter's on numerous points. Furthermore, this—more than Leja's "Modern Man" paradigm—is a key point of influx of notions of dark subjectivity into the discourse of Abstract Expressionism.

49. Baker Brownell, *Art is Action: A Discussion of Nine Arts in a Modern World* (New York: Harper and Brothers, 1939), p. 181: "In Benton, on the other hand, there is a deliberate angularity and stubbornness of line, a Gothic emphasis and witchcraft." Interestingly, given Pollock's sources, a discussion of the Mexican muralists immediately follows.

50. See Richard W. Etulain, *Re-Imagining the Modern American West* (Tucson: University of Arizona Press, 1996), p. 29.

51. Not to mention the American Indian spirits of the film *Poltergeist* (1982).

52. Annie Proulx, *Close Range: Wyoming Stories* (London: Fourth Estate, 1999), epigraph.

53. Deborah Solomon, *Jackson Pollock: A Biography* (New York: Simon and Schuster, 1987), p. 65; Ellen G. Landau, *Jackson Pollock* (New York: Harry N. Abrams, Inc., 1989), p. 32.

54. Stan Jones, "Ghost Riders in the Sky" (1949). Although such a song postdates Pollock's Western years, it taps a hotchpotch of popular sources and images that he surely encountered then.

55. Landau, op. cit. pp. 34–35.

56. See David Anfam, "Clyfford Still's Art: Between the Quick and the Dead," in *Clyfford Still: Paintings, 1944–1960.* (Washington, D.C.: Hirshhorn Museum and Sculpture Garden, 2001), pp. 24–28. Compare especially Still's paintings of around 1935–36 such as Untitled *(Indian Houses, Nespelem)* and Untitled *(Two Figures)* with, for example, JPCR 3:461r. Like Pollock, Still looked to Orozco.

57. As only recently clarified by Sarah Burns, *Painting the Dark Side: Art and the Gothic Imagination in Nineteenth-Century America* (Berkeley: University of California Press, 2004), pp. 221–45.

58. Indeed, Turner's vortex was among his most acclaimed and imitated innovations. See Barry Venning, *Turner* (London: Phaidon Press, 2003), p. 124.

59. If O'Connor's ingenious reading of the brighter area of the sky as a head overlooking the muleteer is valid, it brings *Going West* still closer to the celestial spooks of the "Ghost Riders in the Sky" ilk. See Francis V. O' Connor, "Pollock (Paul) Jackson," in Jane Turner, ed., op. cit., vol. 25, p. 166.

60. The props in *Camp with Oil Rig* (ca. 1930–33) derive from Benton, but the impression of the earth's curvature does not. I take it as another expression of Pollock's fixation with the circular form.

61. Described by Pollock as "the story of my life." See Naifeh and Smith, op. cit., p. 323.

62. The sickle-shaped Mimbres pottery bowl creature whose form appears in *The Guardians of the Secret* (1943, JPCR 1:99) and other paintings repeats this motif.

63. From the outset, Pollock was a God-seeker. Successive creeds—Marxism, theosophy, Krishnamurti's spiritualism, Jungianism—merely filled that vacuum. His remark, "Way I see it, we're part of the one, making it whole" (in Harrison, op. cit., p. 37) summarizes this fundamentally unrequited pantheism.

64. Melanie Klein, "A Contribution to the Theory of Intellectual Inhibition" (1931), in *Love, Guilt and Reparation and Other Works. Writings of Melanie Klein*, vol. 1 (London: Hogarth Press, 1975), p. 241.

65. See Julia Kristeva, *Powers of Horror: An Essay on Abjection*, trans. Leon S. Roudiez (New York: Columbia University Press, 1982), passim; Noëlle McAfee, *Julia Kristeva* (New York: Routledge, 2004), pp. 47–48.

66. Jeremy Lewison, *Interpreting Pollock* (London: Tate Gallery Publishing, 1999), rightly critiques overly psychological and Jungian stances towards Pollock.

67. The notion of the body-in-process/under trial is Kristeva's.

68. This is Kristeva's "semiotic" mode as opposed to the mental control of the "symbolic" order.

69. Pollock (late 1950) in Karmel 1999, p. 24.

70. Although Kandinsky's influence on Pollock is often dated to 1944–45, *The Moon-Woman* is arguably one of its first points of entry. *The Moon-Woman*'s palette and painterly morphologies are similar to works such as Kandinsky's *Black Lines* (1913, Solomon R. Guggenheim Museum, New York).

71. Reproduced in *Cahiers d'art* (Paris) no. 3–10, 1938, p. 85.

72. A 1946 canvas was titled, albeit perhaps not by Pollock, "The Key," while the key in *Full Fathom Five* (1947, JPCR 1:180) is placed exactly at the crotch of the submerged figure. See James Coddington, "No Chaos Damn It," in Kirk Varnedoe and Pepe Karmel, eds., *Jackson Pollock: New Approaches* (New York: Museum of Modern Art, 1999), p. 103.

The Jungian paraphernalia with which some interpreters have loaded Pollock's allusion to a "moon woman" should not obscure a less far-flung possible point of reference. Namely, that William Baziotes's *The Mirror at Midnight* (ca. 1942) was inspired by the moon-mad woman of Charles Baudelaire's prose poem, "Favors of the Moon." It is not extravagant to suspect that Baziotes could have alerted Pollock to this source.

73. Pollock (undated) in Harrison, op. cit., p. 88: "I can read by sensing a book."

74. Pollock's pattern making in the early 1940s sometimes recalls linear illustrations in those of his favored book, D'Arcy Thompson's *On Growth and Form* (Cambridge: Cambridge University Press, 1917). For example, compare the doodle-like curves of the "Subgroup III" drawings in Claude Cernuschi, *Jackson Pollock: Psychoanalytic Drawings* (Durham, N.C.: Duke University Press, 1992), pp. 59, and those in Thompson, pp. 72–73.

75. The mirror-inversion is particularly notable: see Harten, op. cit., p. 194. Could Pollock have known the most famous mirror-writing in Western art, Leonardo da Vinci's? If so, Leonardo's drawing of a child in the womb (ca. 1510–12, Royal Library, Windsor Castle) becomes an obvious precursor for the fetus of *Bowl*.

76. See Eric Jager, *The Book of the Heart* (Chicago: University of Chicago Press, 2000); Sigmund Freud, "A Note upon the 'Mystic Writing-Pad,'" in *The Standard Edition of the Complete Psychological Works of Sigmund Freud* (London: Hogarth Press, 1961), pp. 226–32.

77. The first English translation of Freud's paper was in 1940. Freud's emphasis on the role of time in the memory's peregrinations is especially apposite.

78. Cf. Freud, op. cit., pp. 230–31: "I do not think it is too far-fetched to compare the celluloid and waxed paper cover with the system *Pcpt.-Cs.* [perception and consciousness] and its protective shield, the wax slab with the unconscious behind them, and the appearance of the writing with the flickering-up and passing-away of consciousness in the process of perception."

79. The shell proved a frequent object of D'Arcy Thompson's analyses. Another remark of Thompson's (op. cit., p. 37) is also pure Pollock: "The living cell is a very complex field of energy."

80. Pollock: "I choose to veil the imagery," quoted by Lee Krasner (1969) in Karmel 1999, op. cit., p. 36.

81. For the notion of the grotesque in this context, I am indebted to Claude Cernuschi's manuscript for a forthcoming monograph on Pollock.

82. See Fred Botting, *Gothic* (London: Routledge, 1996), pp. 1–20. Compare Pollock's famous declaration (to Hans Hofmann), "I am nature," with Botting's verdict about "Gothic" ideology, p. 12: "Nature, wild and untameable, was as much within as without."

83. See Nan Rosenthal, "The Pollock Sketchbooks: An Introduction," in Rosenthal, Katharine Baetjer, and Lisa Mintz Messinger, *The Jackson Pollock Sketchbooks in the Metropolitan Museum of Art* (New York: Metropolitan Museum of Art, 1997), p. 25.

84. Krasner, op. cit., in Karmel 1999, p. 35.

85. Pollock (late 1950) in Karmel 1999, p. 20.

86. Quoted in Martin Greif, *Depression Modern: The Thirties Style in America* (New York: Universe Books, 1975), p. 32. The schoolgirl continues by lauding the transparency of glass—inadvertently prophesying Pollock's 1950 painting on that material, *Number 29, 1950* (JPCR 4:1036).

87. For how we read such images, see the analysis in terms of cognitive psychology in Claude Cernuschi, *"Not an Illustration but the Equivalent": A Cognitive Approach to Abstract Expressionism* (Madison, Wisc.: Fairleigh Dickinson University Press and Associated University Presses, 1997), pp. 56–64.

88. Jeffrey L. Meikle: "Domesticating Modernity: Ambivalence and Appropriation, 1920–40," in Wendy Kaplan, ed., *Designing Modernity: The Arts of Reform and Persuasion 1885–1945* (London: Thames and Hudson, 1995), pp. 153–54.

89. Malcolm M. Willey and Stuart A. Rice, "The Agencies of Communication" (1933), quoted in Jeffrey L. Meikle, *Twentieth Century Limited: Industrial*

Design in America, 1925–1939 (Philadelphia: Temple University Press, 1979), p. 9.

90. In a lecture, "Pollock, and America, too," at the conference *Abstract Expressionism: A Universal Language* (New York: SUNY Stony Brook/Pollock-Krasner House and Study Center, May 18, 2004), Stephen Polcari proposed analogies between Pollock and 1930s design. Polcari argued that Pollock adopted the "getting America going again" attitude during the stagnation of the Depression—in effect, a kind of aesthetic boosterism. By contrast, Meikle's theory (in Meikle 1995, op. cit., pp. 143–44) that "streamline moderne" was an ideology that domesticated, and thus neutralized, the traumas of a disruptive modernity—in which, as Karl Marx wrote, "all that is solid melts into air"—offers a more cogent platform for grasping the complexities of Pollock's evolution.

91. The honed, rhythmic idioms of the Mexican muralists now look, in a sense, as much a part of Art Deco painting as does the architecture, such as the RCA Building (New York, 1934), for which their works were on occasions created. The same applies to some of Pollock's acutely rhythmic-jazzy zigzag imagery, for instance, the spiky ca. 1939–40 *Untitled* sheet (JPCR 3: 542), which unintentionally recalls the angular chandelier and its shards in Alastair Duncan, *American Art Deco* (New York: Harry N. Abrams, Inc., 1986), p. 69.

92. Jay Hambridge (1940), quoted in Meikle 1979, op. cit., p. 45.

93. See the eau-de-nil, ivory and metallic hues—allied to filigreed designs and organic motifs—of many artefacts and building decorations illustrated in Duncan, op. cit. Even Ruth Reeves's textile design (1931, p. 142) foreshadows *Untitled (Drawing with Two Signatures)* (ca. 1941, pl. 13). From industrial design colors (1930s) to Pollock's industrial paints (1940s) would also comprise a logical transition.

94. Pollock (late 1950) in Karmel 1999, p. 21.

95. Pollock (undated) in ibid., p. 24.

96. See Marta Braun, "The Expanded Present: Photographing Movement," in Ann Thomas, *Beauty of Another Order: Photography in Science* (New Haven, Conn.: Yale University Press, 1997), pp. 150–237. Given the perennial dialectic between movement and the body, it is noteworthy that Marey was a physiologist.

97. Most famously exemplified by Robert Capa's immensely well-known shots of the Spanish Civil War and the Normandy landings. Namuth had photographed the Spanish conflict. See Hans Namuth and Georg Reisner, *Spanisches Tagebuch 1936* (Berlin: Nishen, 1936).

98. Witness the vast fame that Harold Edgerton's stroboscopic shots attained during the 1940s. See Gus Kayafas, ed., *Stopping Time: The Photographs of Harold Edgerton* (New York: Harry N. Abrams, Inc., 1987). Revealingly, the editors of the 1961 edition of *On Growth and Form* saw fit to illustrate Thompson's text with an Edgerton photograph.

99. A second drawing copies a *Life* (July 8, 1938) cover. See Rosenthal, op. cit., pp. 22–23.

100. Sigfried Giedion, *Space, Time and Architecture: The Growth of a New Tradition* (Cambridge, Mass.: Harvard University Press, 1941) was illustrated with two stroboscopic speed photographs by Edgerton (pp. 368, 577).

101. Pollock (late 1950) in Karmel 1999, p. 24. The other paradigm in which memory traces were arrested in space was of course Freud's "'mystic' writing-pad."

102. *Life* (New York), September 27, 1943, p. 18, captioned: "The R.A.F. photographed burning incendiaries and great billow of smoke over Düsseldorf on June 11–12."

103. Cf. Landau, op. cit. p. 245, n. 16, who reads a motif in *Burning Landscape* as a reference to "the parabolic trajectory of either an aerial bomb or another disabled aircraft."

104. Pollock (late 1950) in Harrison, op. cit., p. 24: "Experience of our age in terms/of painting—not an illustration of—(but the *equivalent*.)"

105. That movement inheres in line is a supposition as ancient as Plato's apothegm, "A line is a point in motion." Cf. Aristotle, *De Anima* 1.4 (409a).

106. August 18–September 19, 1943. There was no catalogue, but the Museum of Modern Art's archive retains a checklist; Edward Alden Jewell, "Display of Photos Opens Here Today," *New York Times*, August 18, 1943, p. 15, also reviewed the show. After a considerable gestation period, Pollock completed *Mural* by November 9, 1943. See Francis V. O'Connor, "Jackson Pollock's *Mural* for Peggy Guggenheim: Its Legend, Documentation, and Redefinition of Wall Painting," in Susan Davidson and Philip Rylands, eds., *Peggy Guggenheim and Frederick Kiesler: The Story of Art of This Century* (Venice: Peggy Guggenheim Collection, 2004), pp. 154–55.

107. Matter had visited Pollock's studio in 1941, attended the opening of the artist's first solo show in 1943 at Art of This Century, and so on. Matter's photographs of dancers in motion cannot be discounted as another cue for Pollock's gestural dance around the canvas once placed on the floor from 1947 onwards.

108. The only commentator to almost uncover the allusion by relating *Mural* to multiple exposure photography (by Thomas Eakins) is Lewison, op. cit., p. 33.

109. The photograph was no. 37 in the show. This was surely not *Mural*'s only source, but it looks a prime one, especially as the painting's ovoids echo Hitchcock's rotund physique. Likewise, the conspicuous loops at the upper left edge suggest the director's outthrust arm and hand.

110. The stress on the dance-like character of Pollock's movements when "in action" accords with the supposition that dance overcomes the Cartesian dualism of mind versus body. See Jamake Highwater, *Dance: Rituals of Experience* (Oxford: Oxford University Press, 1992), pp. 25–26.

111. Museum of Modern Art Press Release no. 43813–45, p. 3. Other phrases in the wall texts have a resonance that bears on Pollock. For example: "It [the stroboscope] *isolates* action and holds it motionless" and "the extraordinary revelations of physical and emotional action made possible by action photography have influenced the arts, the sciences, the industries, and even the amusements of our time." As Pollock moved into imagery suggesting the cosmos or celestial phenomena in 1947, so too did *Action Photography* progress to astronomical shots of nebulae. Even Pollock's *Shimmering Substance* (1946, JPCR 1:64) was adumbrated by the museum's label for Matter, who "uses dance and multiple exposure to create a strangely shimmering fantasy."

112. Pollock praised the photographs of Herbert Matter and Stieglitz: see Harrison, op. cit., p. 92.

113. *Life*, March 26, 1945, p. 106. The cover of this issue featured another Mili "light writing" photograph of the skater Carol Lynne.

114. April 7–July 11, 1948. The show included "Five mural-size color transparencies . . . made especially for this exhibition." (Museum of Modern Art Press Release no. 4845–19). Throughout these years, Pollock voiced his ambition to create murals.

115. Faurer reduced his figures to black shadows in some photographs (for example, *Win, Place and Show: 3rd Avenue El at 53rd St., New York* (1946–48), in a parallel move to Pollock's cut-out black figuration in, say, Untitled *(Shadows: Number 2, 1948)* (JPCR 4:1034).

116. Susan Schulten, *The Geographical Imagination in America, 1880–1950* (Chicago: University of Chicago Press, 2001), p. 134: "But the experience of the 1940s was in other respects unique, for what was now required was a reconceptualization of space itself." If the connection between the cartographic view-from-above and Pollock seems surprising, recall that *Life* devoted a 1942 feature to cartography and that Still painted a *Map of Europe* (1940–41, Private collection). The astonishing aerial photograph of 160,000 German POWS in *Life* (May 14, 1945, pp. 30–31)—a double-page spread—also bears an uncanny resemblance to the allover compositional mode.

117. Rosalind Krauss rightly regards the shift to the horizontal plane as Pollock's most radical departure. She also argues that aerial photography influenced Namuth's images of Pollock but, curiously, does not connect that tradition to the artist. Krauss, "Reading Photographs as Texts," in Namuth, op. cit., n.p. Krauss makes the vital point that Namuth must have seen Mili's *Space Drawings* photographs of Picasso outlining contours with light before doing his own film of Pollock. Krauss, op. cit., p. 302.

118. An impression enhanced by how the paintwork becomes increasingly attenuated at the peripheries, creating subtle implications of spheroid space (as if the peripheral lines were very distant from the central ones). See Maurice Roche, "Action Writing," in *Jackson Pollock* (Paris: Centre Georges Pompidou, Musée national d'art moderne, 1982), pp. 153–58. Cartographic projections of the globe, widely published in U.S. newspapers, had assumed exceptional importance during World War II. See Schulten, op. cit., pp. 204–38 ("War and the Re-Creation of the World 1939–1950").

119. William Carlos Williams, "The Poem as a Field of Action" (1948) in *Selected Essays of William Carlos Williams* (New York: Random House, 1954), pp. 280–91. The poet Charles Olson—aware of Pollock's methods—would next amplify the somatic basis of artistic creation with his emphasis on breathing in the spoken process of "composition by field" (1950) that constitutes his concept of "projective verse."

120. Brownell, op. cit., reiterates the "art as action" theme ad infinitum, reflecting a pragmatic-cum-Marxist or John Dewey–inspired faith in activism at all levels that was rife during the 1930s and to which Pollock would have been exposed. Among its homegrown forbears is Ralph Waldo Emerson's dictum that "to think is to act."

121. See Tony Tanner, *The Reign of Wonder: Naivety and Reality in American Literature* (London: Cambridge University Press, 1965). Tanner, p. 36, quotes Emerson in a coincidental but vivid paraphrase of Pollock's *Tondo*: "The world globes itself in a drop of dew."

122. Again, the typical polarizations of a God-seeker. Listen to William Blake, "Auguries of Innocence" (ca. 1803), l.1–4: "To see a World in a Grain of Sand/ And a heaven in a Wild Flower,/Hold infinity in the palm of your hand/And Eternity in an hour."

123. Whitman, quoted in Tanner, op. cit., p. 77. Compare Pollock to Julien Levy, quoted in Landau, op. cit., p. 159: "You can hear the life in the grass, hear it growing."

124. Bachelard, op. cit., p. 184. For a coda to these ideas, see also T. J. Clark, "Pollock's Smallness," in Varnedoe and Karmel, op. cit., pp. 15–31.

125. Paul Valéry, *Degas Manet Morisot*, trans. David Paul (London: Routledge and Kegan Paul, 1960), p. 38. Valéry's analysis of the spatialization of time in relation to the line in *Leonardo, Poe, Mallarmé*, trans. Malcolm Cowley and James R. Lawler (Princeton: Princeton University Press, 1972), pp. 24–25, has special relevance to Pollock's drawing.

126. Perhaps a last inversion—in practice if not deliberate intention—of the surface-to-depth transferences of Freud's "mystic writing-pad."

127. Vic Muniz's "Action Photographs" of the late 1990s enact an ironic commentary on Pollock's engagement with materials and Namuth's interposition—by photography—of a new tissue of meanings that have infiltrated Pollock's interpretative afterlife. Muniz's zany fabrications are photographs of re-creations done in Bosco chocolate syrup of Namuth's photojournalism. See David Campany, *Art and Photography* (London: Phaidon Press, 2003), p. 149.

128. "Rice paper" is a misnomer, as no rice is involved in its manufacture. The Japanese papers used by Pollock are comprised predominantly of fibers taken from the inner bark of native *kozo*, a member of the paper mulberry family.

129. The *Collins English Dictionary*'s definitions, which catch the relevant, contending psychological senses of "blot," are instructive: "to soak up (excess) . . . to absorb . . . to darken or hide completely . . . obscure." Moreover, another informal definition—"to spoil one's reputation"—nicely adverts to Pollock's edgy retort to his own prior virtuosity in this phase.

130. The phrase is Rosand's, op. cit., p. 61, apropos of Leonardo. But a study of Pollock's manifold signature styles—such as the 1998 Museum of Modern Art retrospective enabled—proves that he deftly inscribed himself into the images in as many different ways as, say, Hitchcock made his mini-appearances in his own films.

PLATES

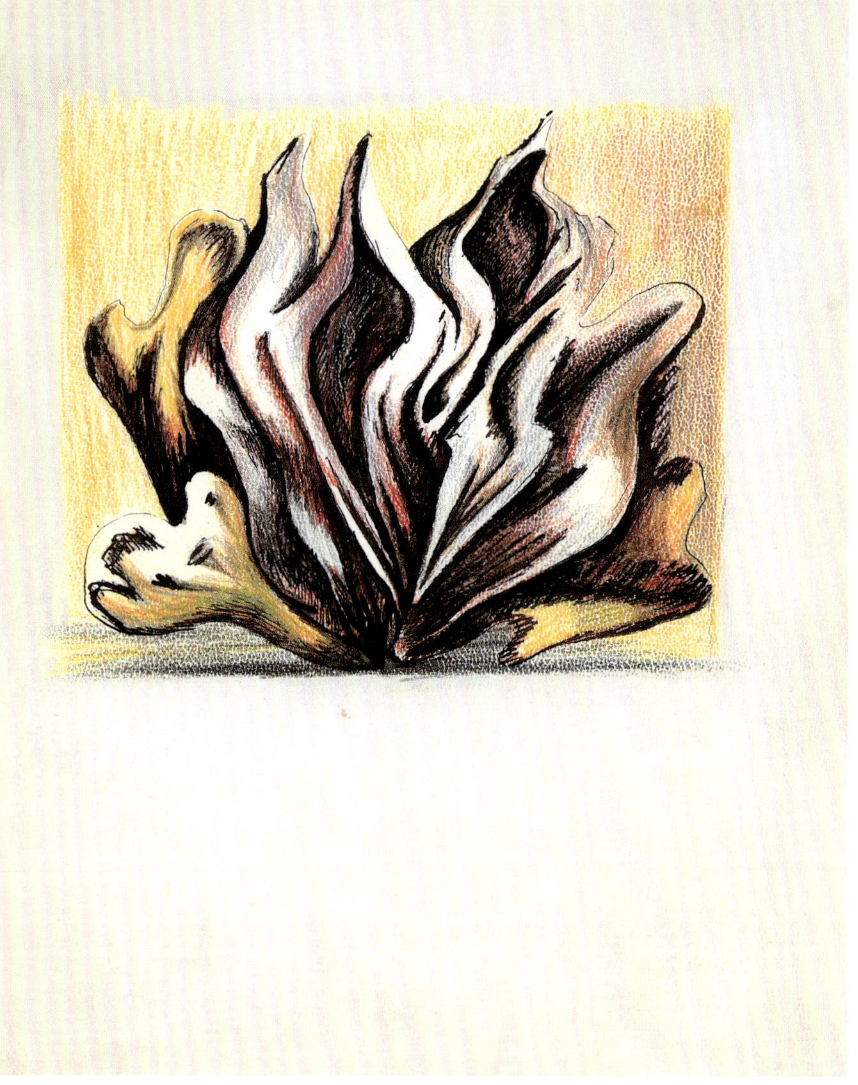

1
Untitled, ca. 1934–38
Colored pencils, pen, and India ink on paper
$11^{7}/_{8}$ x $8^{7}/_{8}$ inches (30.2 x 22.5 cm)
The Metropolitan Museum of Art, New York.
Gift of Lee Krasner Pollock, 1982 (1982.147.4)
JPCR 3:392

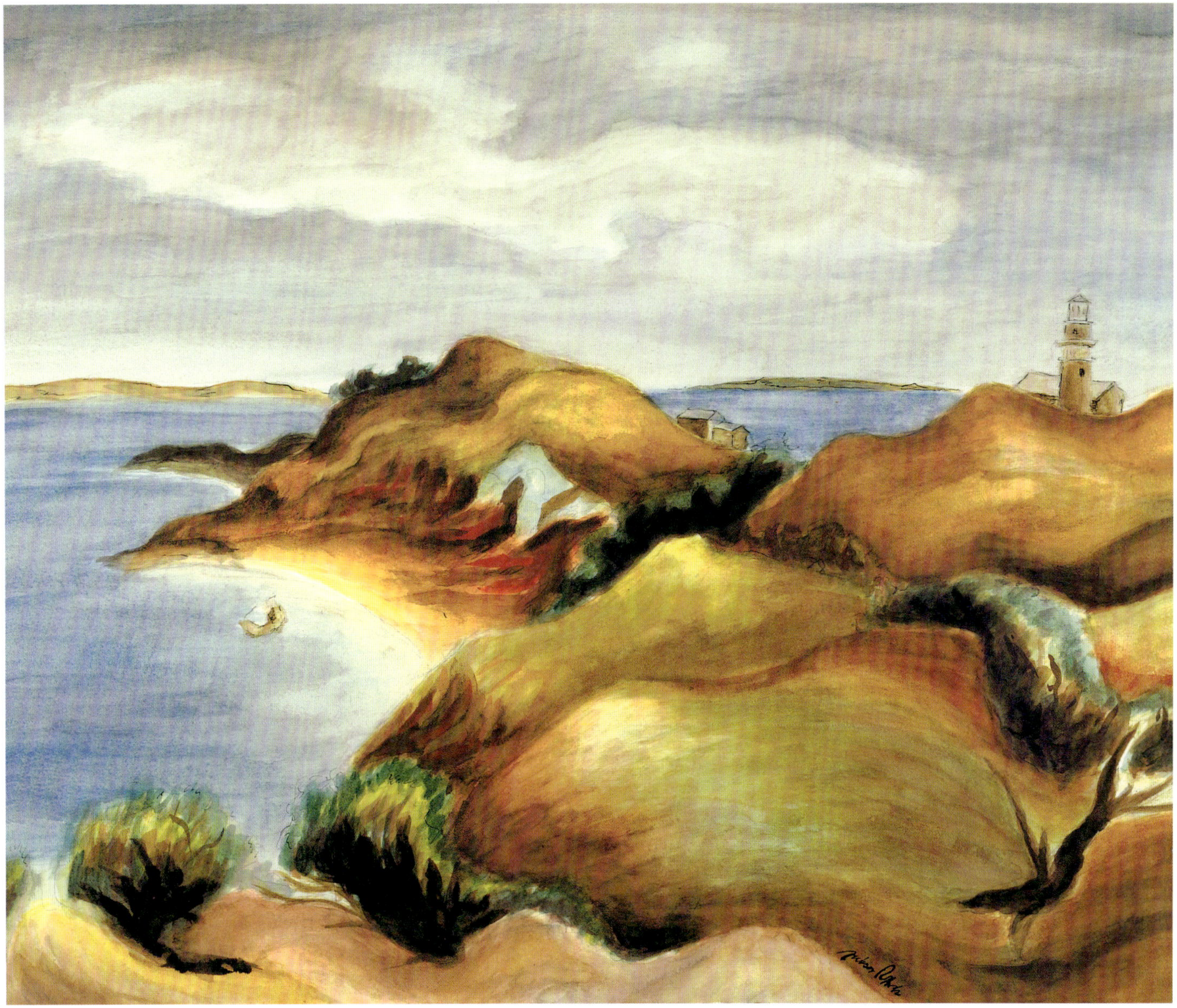

2
Harbor and Lighthouse, ca. 1934–38
Watercolor on paper
$19\frac{1}{4}$ x 23 inches (48.9 x 58.4 cm)
The Robert B. Mayer Family Collection, Chicago
JPCR 4:934

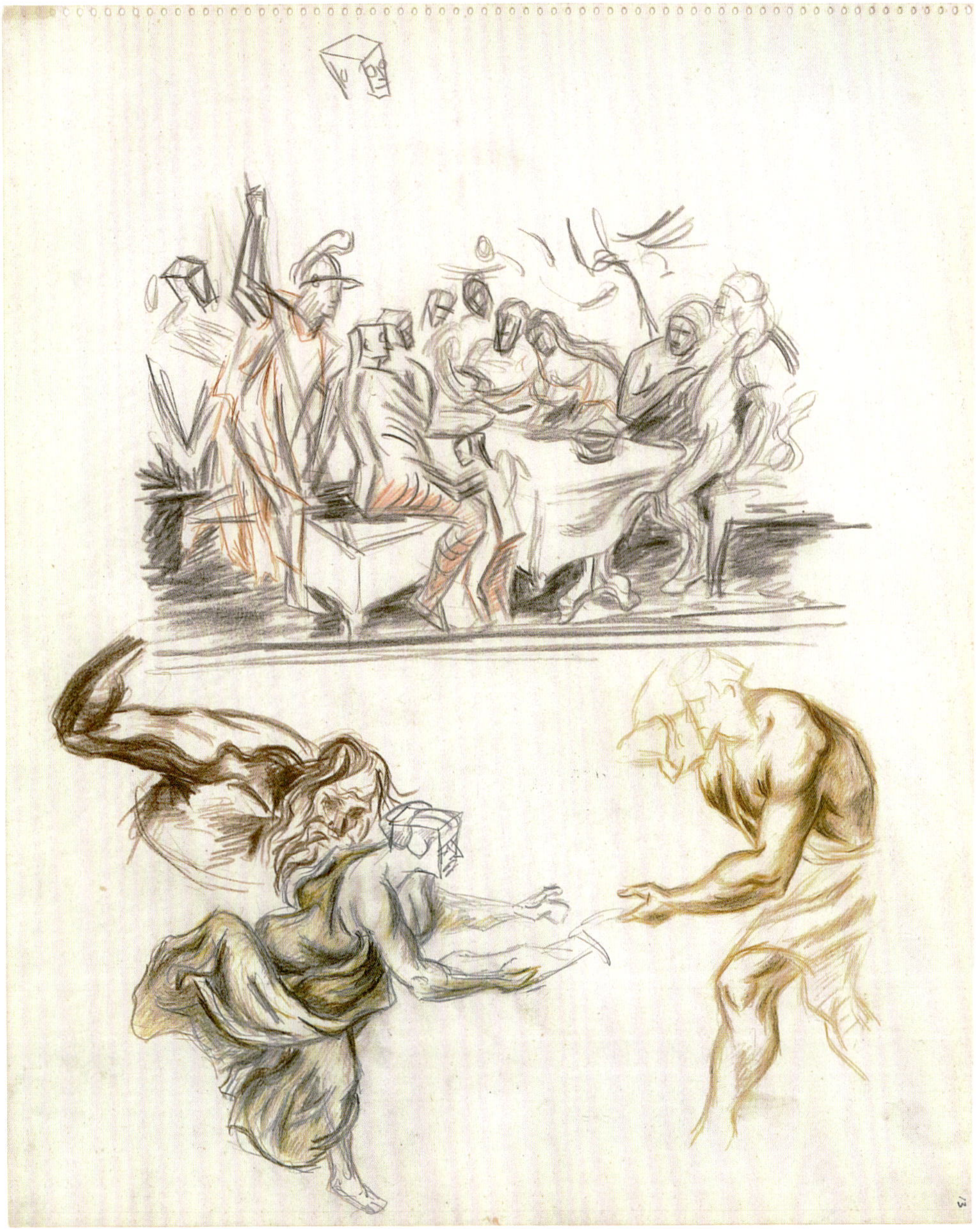

3
Untitled [2nd Sketchbook, folio 13], ca. late 1937–38
Pencil and colored pencils on paper
17 x 13¾ inches (43.2 x 34.9 cm)
The Metropolitan Museum of Art, New York.
Purchase, Anonymous Gift, 1990 (1990.4.39)
JPCR 3:440 r

4
Untitled (*Figure in a Landscape*), ca. 1938–39
Colored pencils on paper
11⅜ x 14⅜ inches (18.8 x 36.5 cm)
The Metropolitan Museum of Art, New York.
Gift of Lee Krasner Pollock, 1982 (1982.147.39)
JPCR 3:397

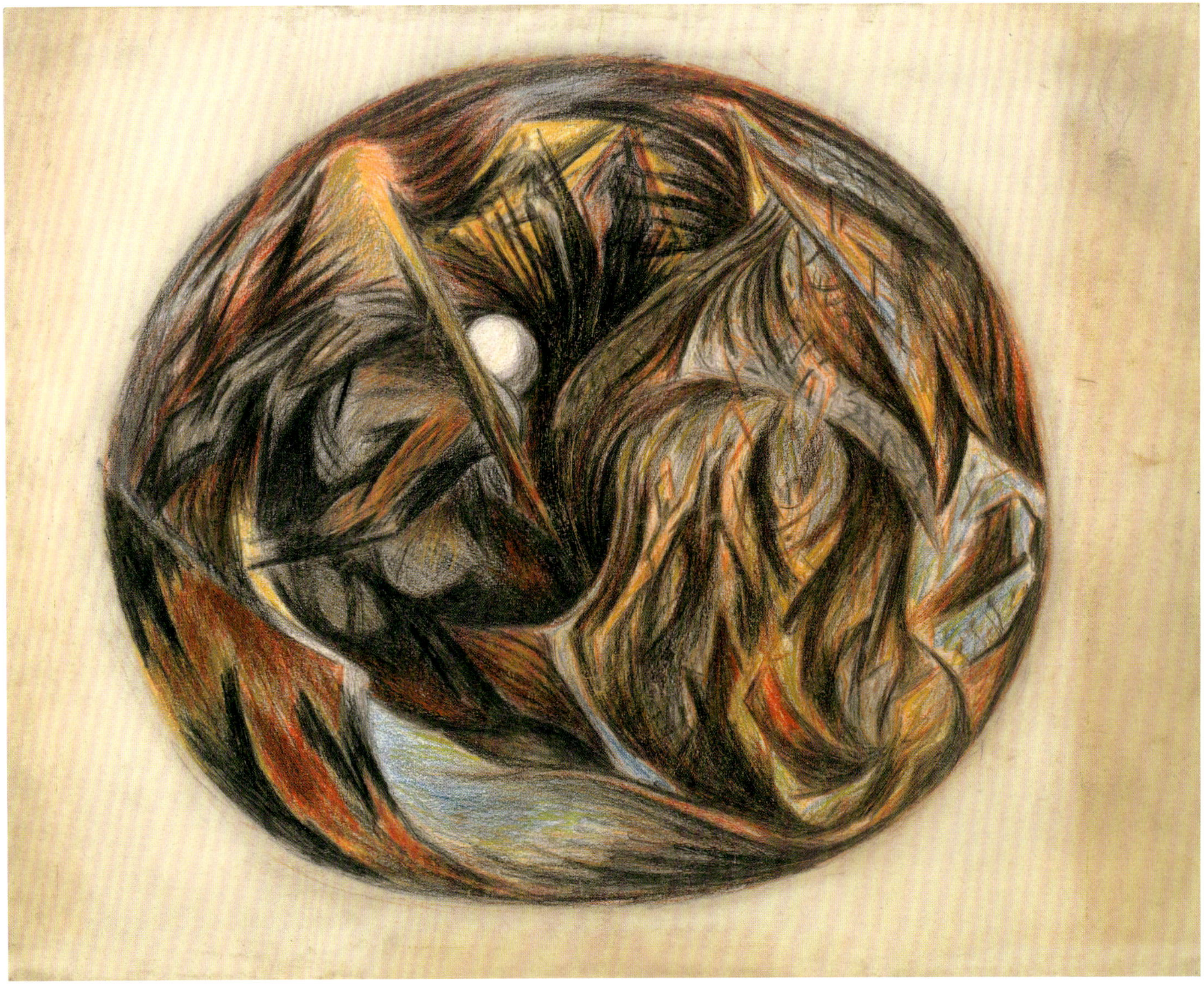

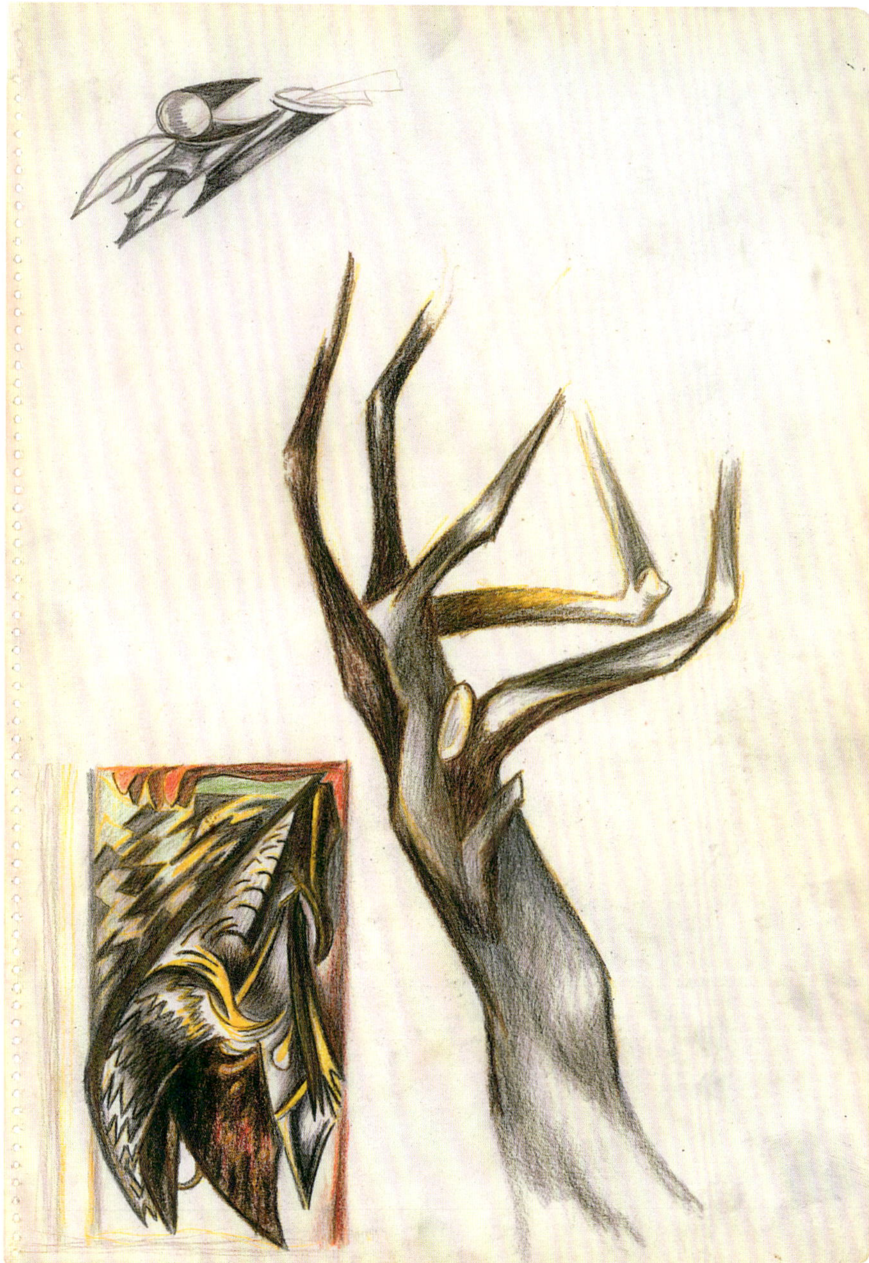

5
Untitled [3rd Sketchbook, folio 13], ca. 1938–41
Pencil and colored pencils on paper
14 1/4 x 10 inches (36.2 x 25.4 cm)
The Metropolitan Museum of Art, New York.
Purchase, Anonymous Gift, 1990 (1990.4.65)
JPCR 3:472r

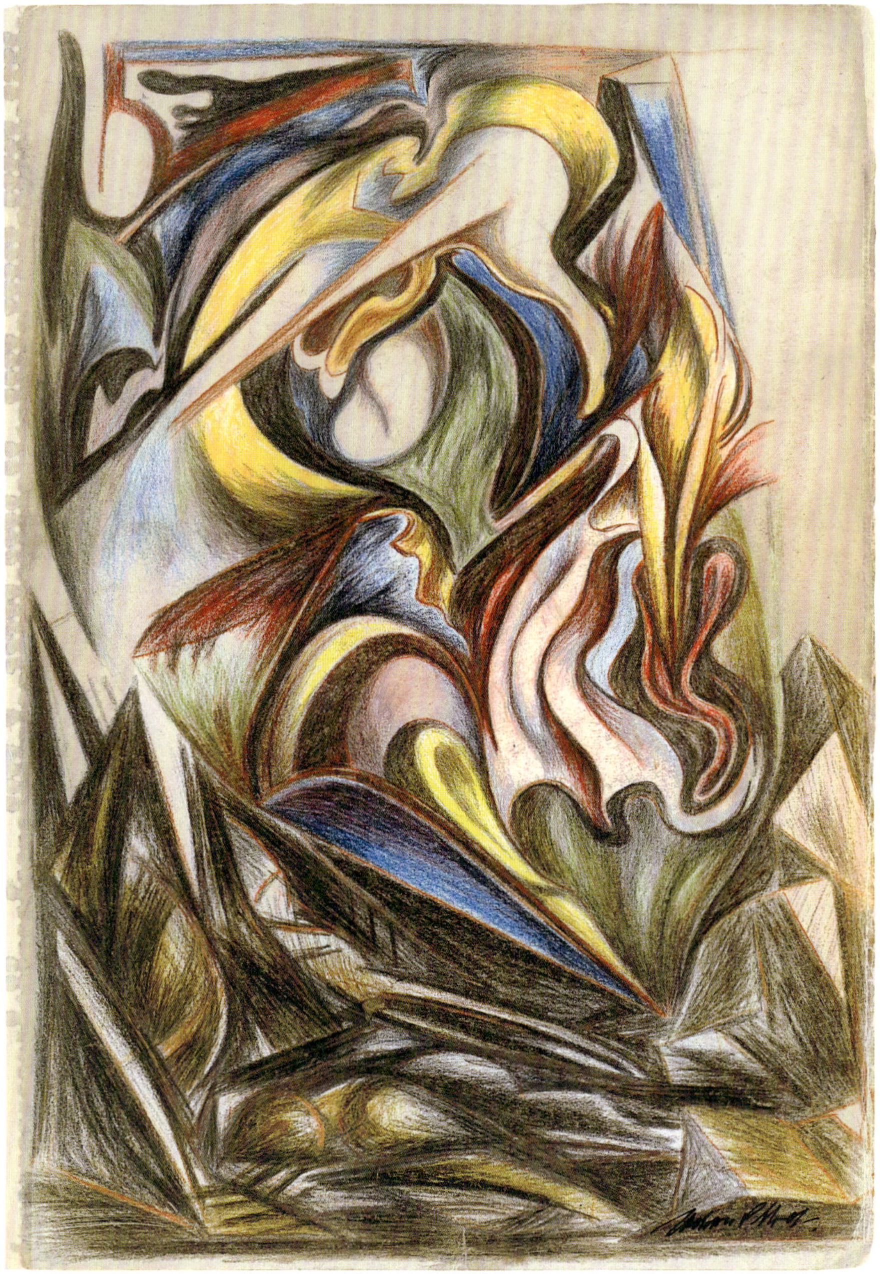

6
Untitled [3rd Sketchbook, folio 4], ca. 1938–41
Pencil and colored pencils on paper
14 1/4 x 10 inches (36.2 x 25.4 cm)
The Metropolitan Museum of Art, New York.
Purchase, Anonymous Gift, 1990 (1990.4.56)
JPCR 3:463r

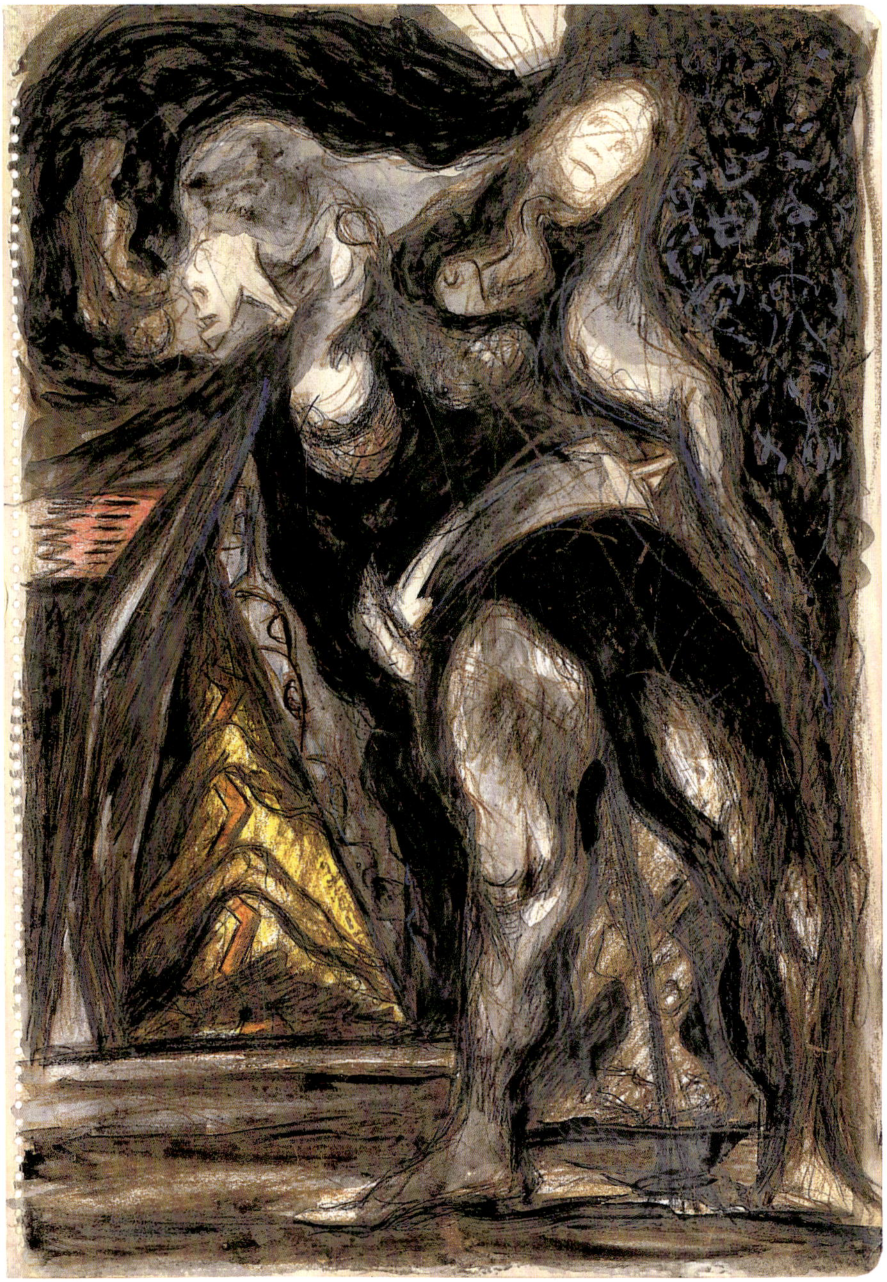

7
Untitled [3rd Sketchbook, folio 15], ca. 1938–41
Pencil, colored pencils, and gouache on paper
14 1/4 x 10 inches (36.2 x 25.4 cm)
The Metropolitan Museum of Art, New York.
Purchase, Anonymous Gift, 1990 (1990.4.67)
JPCR 3:474r

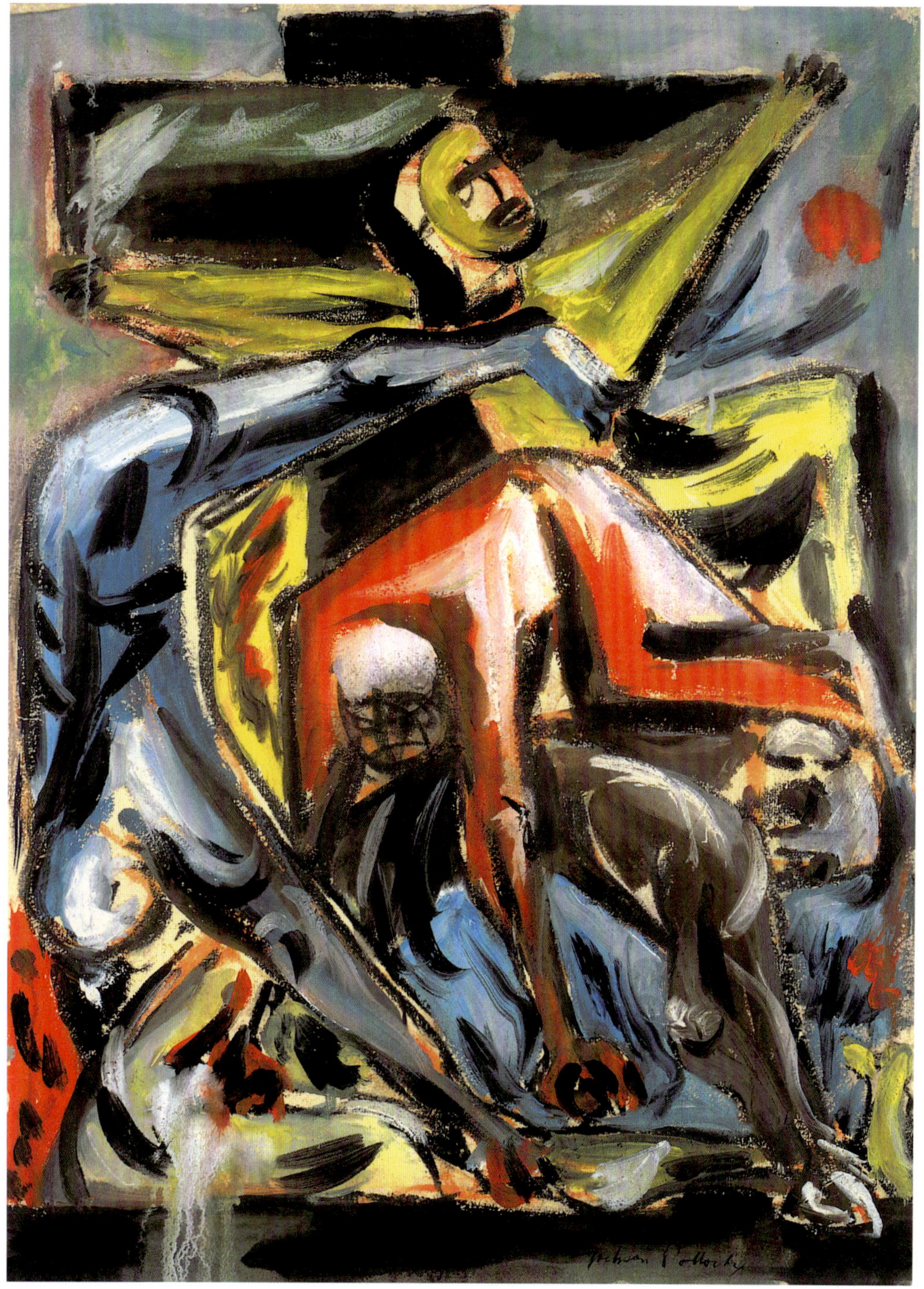

8
Untitled, 1939–40
Gouache on paper
$21\frac{1}{2}$ x $15\frac{1}{2}$ inches (54.6 x 39.4 cm)
Gagosian Gallery
JPCR 4:940

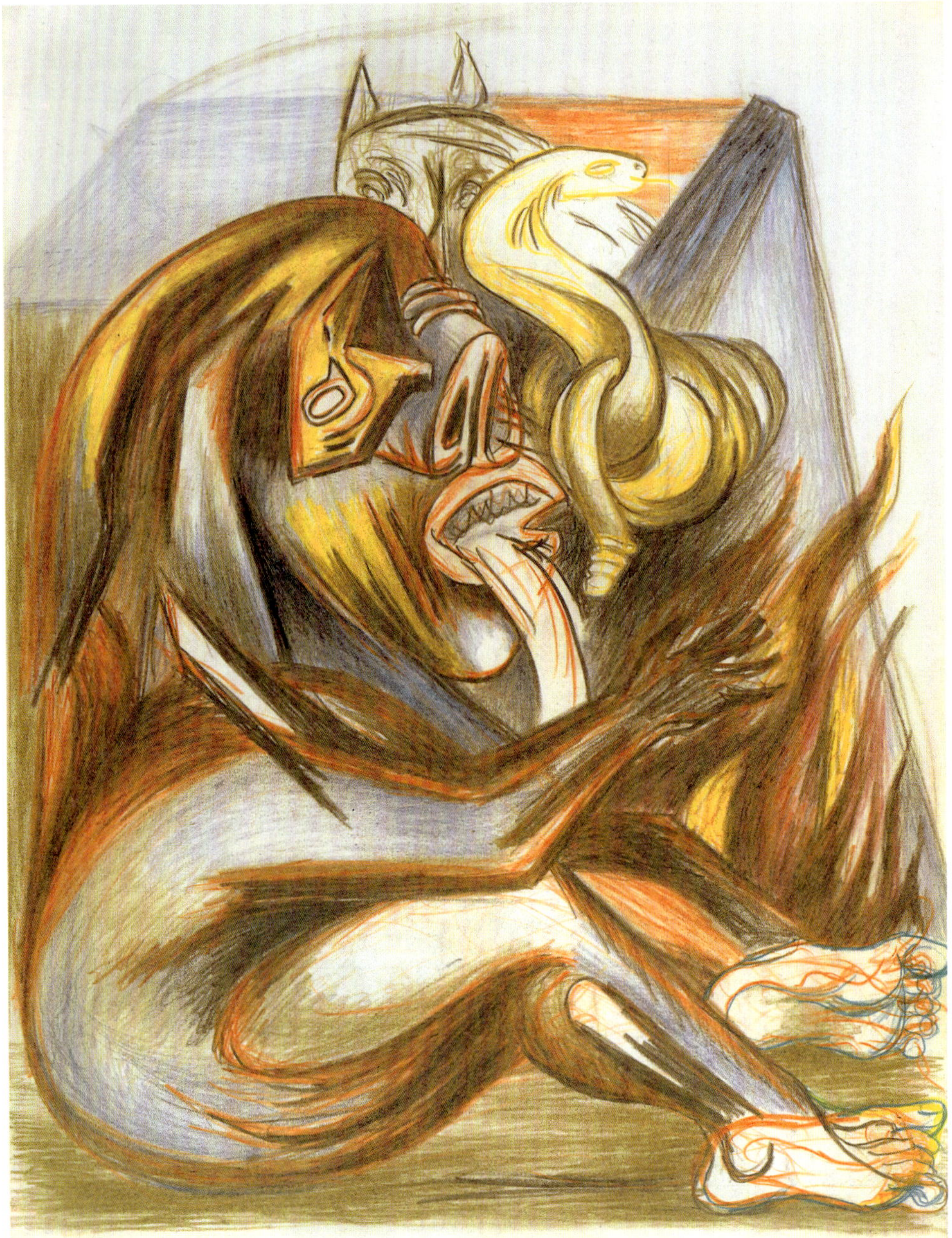

9
Untitled, ca. 1939–42
Colored pencils and pencil on paper
14 x 11 inches (35.6 x 27.9 cm)
The Whitney Museum of American Art, New York.
Purchased with funds from the Julian B. Engel Purchase Fund and the Drawing Committee (85.18)
JPCR 3:557

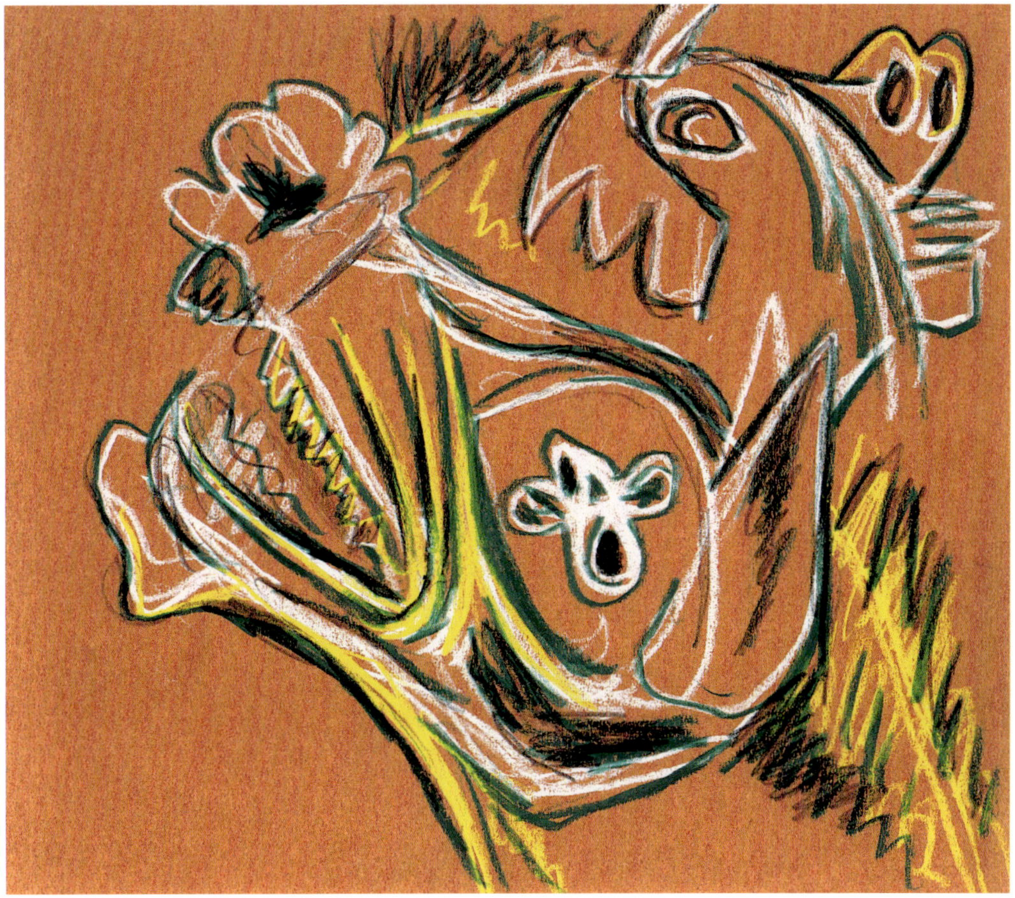

10
Untitled, 1939
Colored pencils and pencil on rust paper
6 x 7 1/8 inches (15.2 x 18 cm)
University of New Mexico Art Museum, The University of New Mexico, Albuquerque. Gift of Vernon Nikkel Clovis, New Mexico, in memory of Frank F. Nikkel, Anna Zielke Nikkel, Ruth Nikkel, Irene Hutchinson, and Martha Nikkel Critelli (89.10.5)
JPCR 3:500

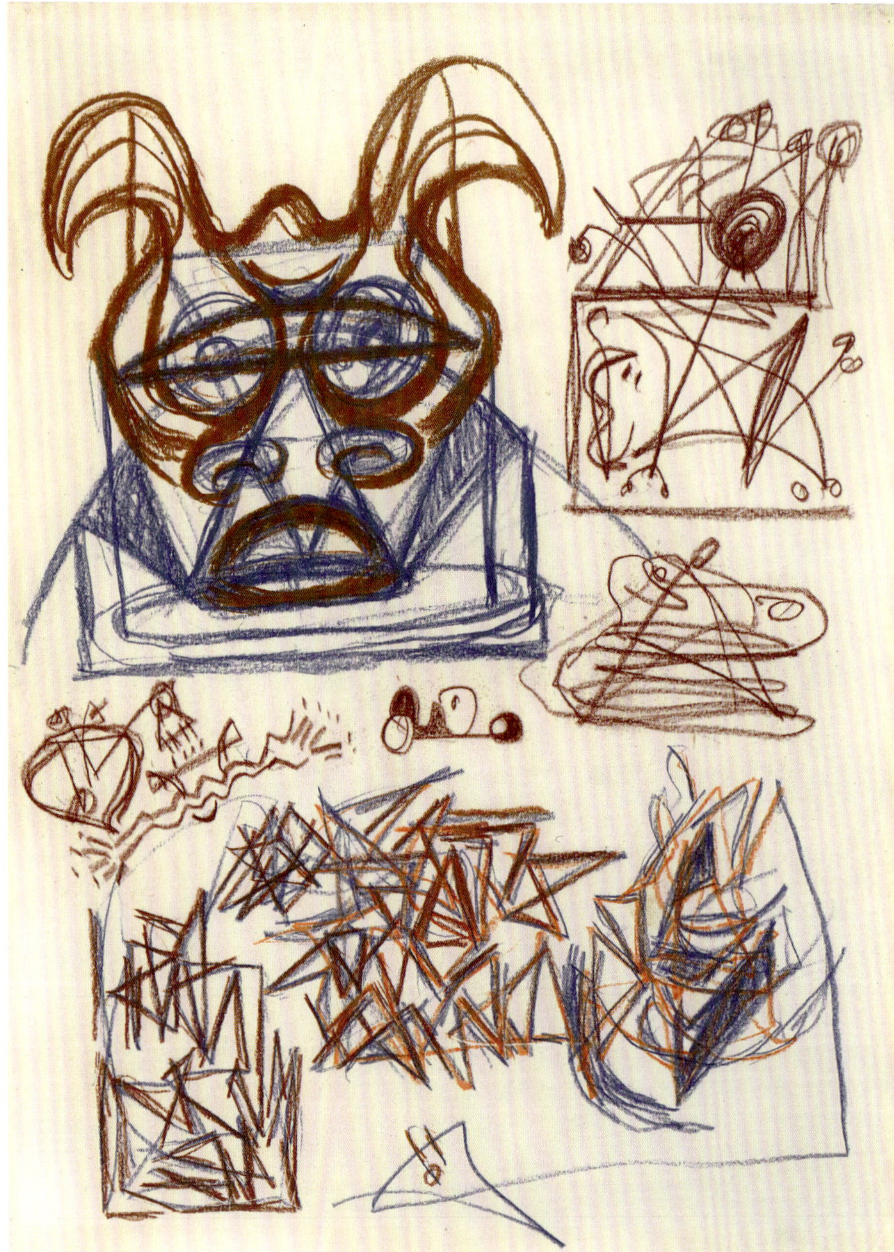

11
Untitled, ca. 1939–40
Colored pencils on paper
15 x 11 inches (38.1 x 27.9 cm)
Collection of Saul and Ellyn Dennison, Bernardsville, New Jersey
JPCR 3:538v

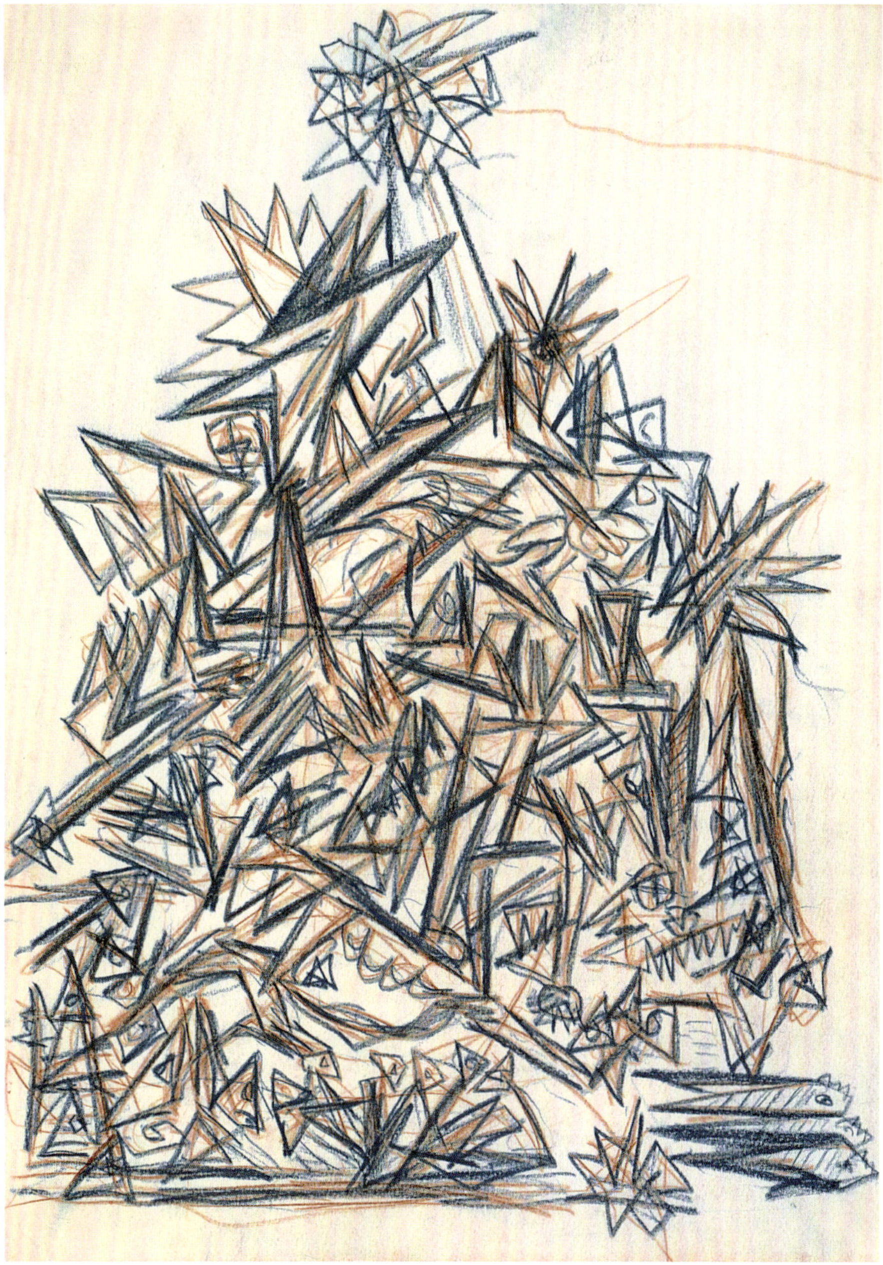

12
Untitled, ca. 1939–40
Colored pencils and crayon on paper
15 x 11 inches (38.1 x 27.9 cm)
The Menil Collection, Houston
JPCR 3:542

13
[Drawing with Two Signatures], ca. 1941
Gouache and pen and ink on paper
22 9/16 x 23 1/16 inches (57.3 x 58.6 cm)
Private collection
JPCR Supplement 15

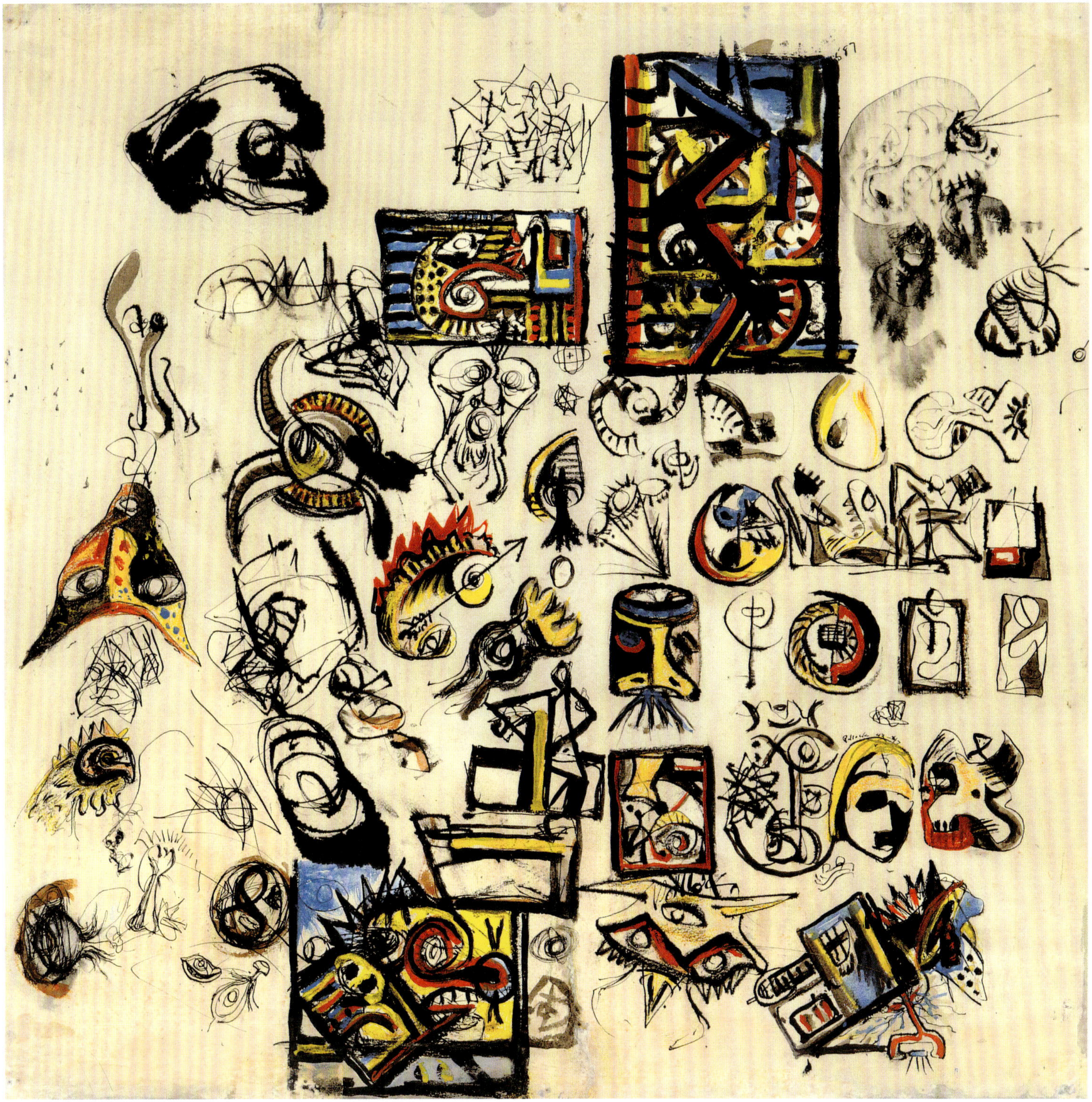

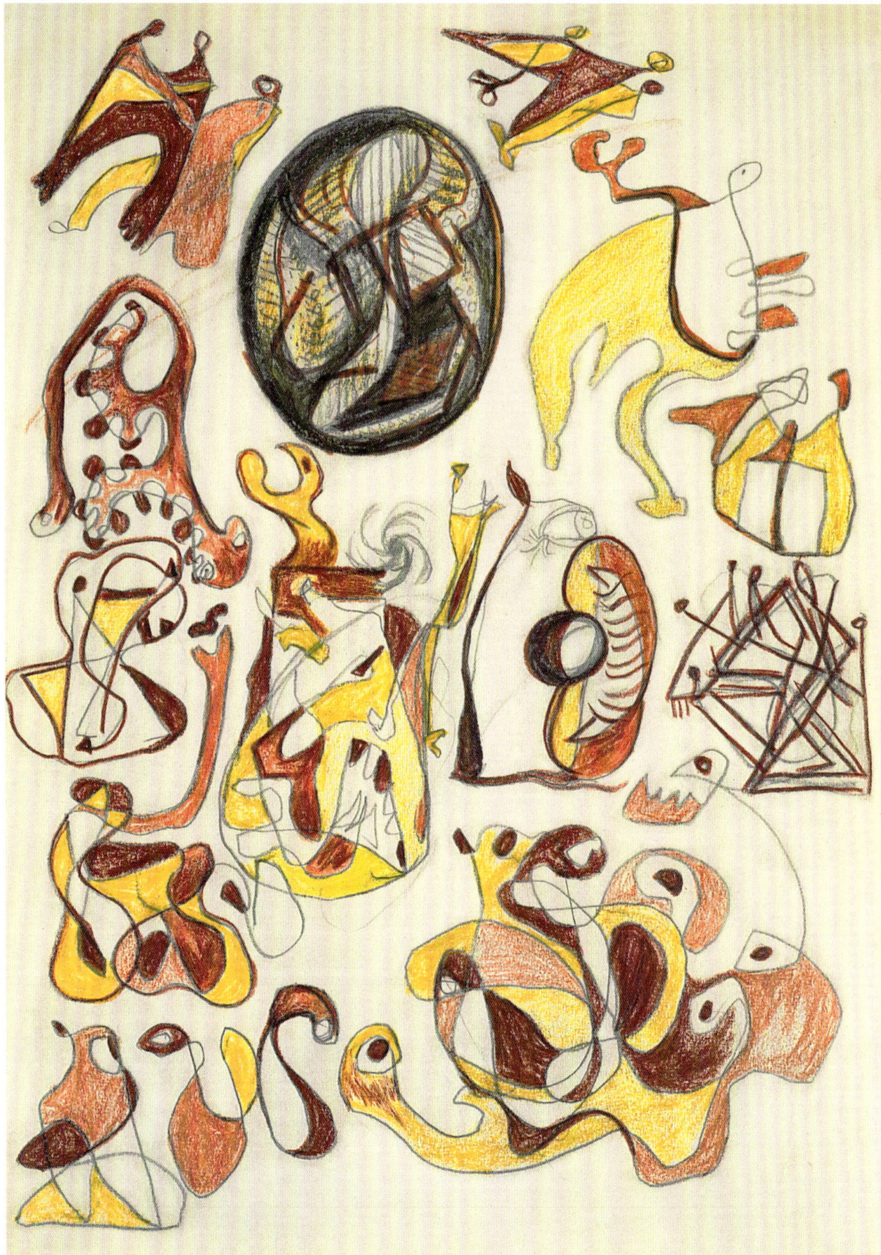

14
Untitled, ca. 1939–42
Colored pencils and pencil on paper
$15^{1/16}$ x 11 inches (38.2 x 27.9 cm)
Collection of Blake Byrne, Los Angeles
JPCR 3:626

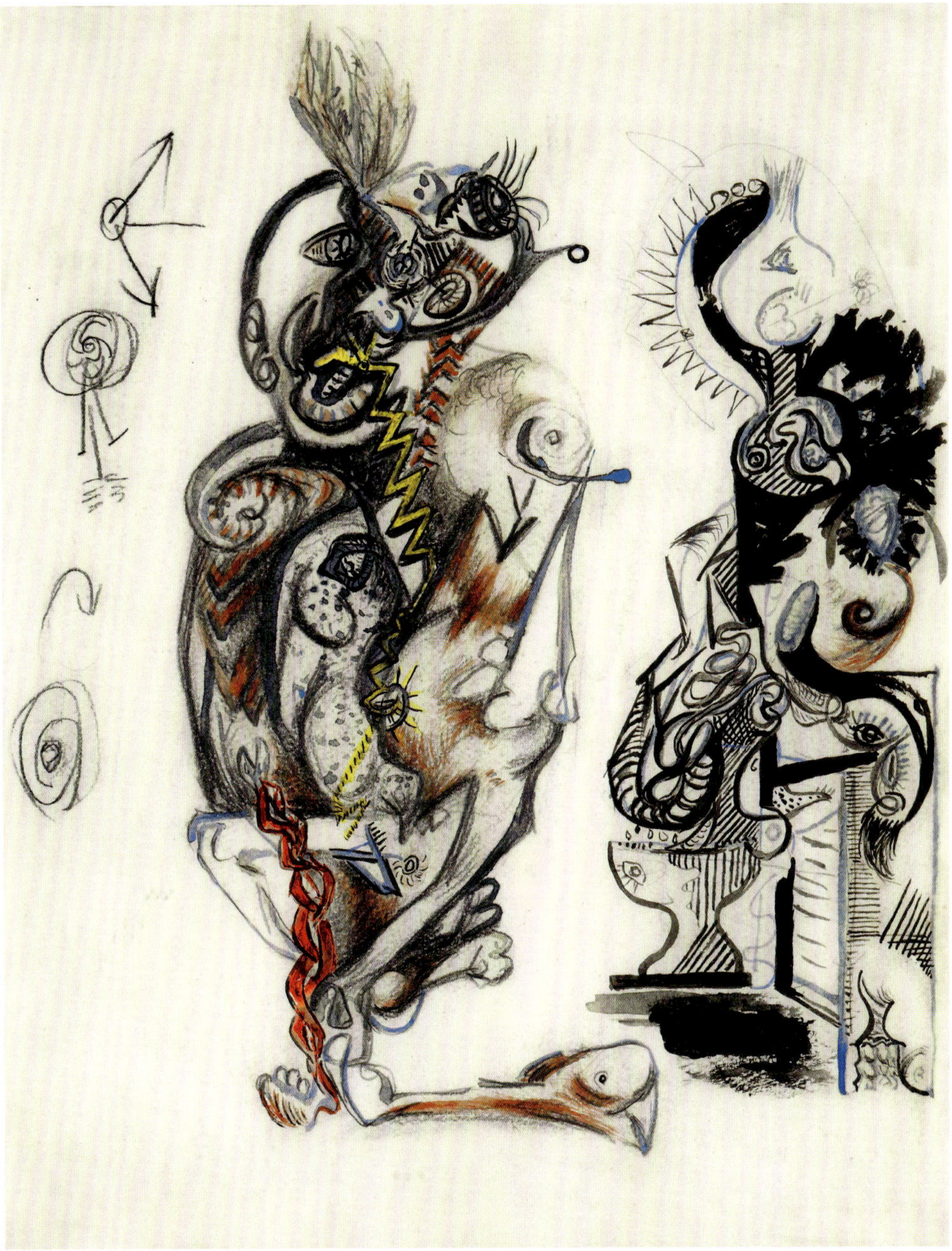

15
Untitled, ca. 1939–42
Ink, watercolor, and pencil on paper
$13^{1}/_{8}$ x $10^{3}/_{8}$ inches (33.3 x 26.3 cm)
Collection of Dr. John T. and Molly P. Chiles
JPCR 3:593

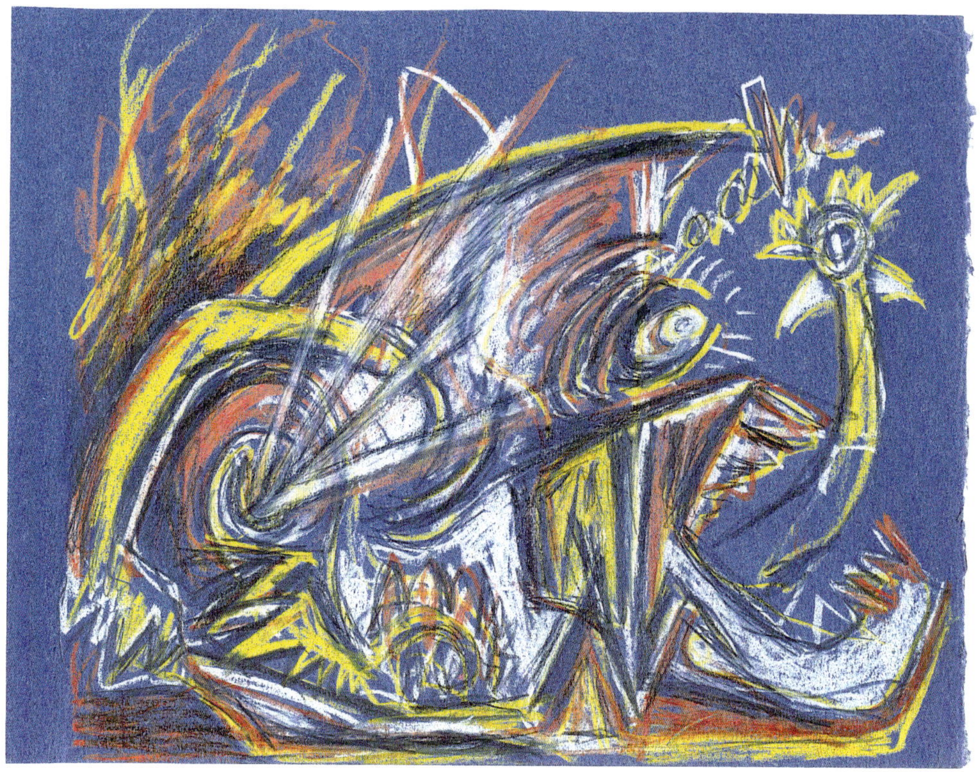

16
Untitled, ca. 1939–40
Colored pencils and pencil on blue paper
6 x $7^{5/8}$ inches (15.2 x 20 cm)
The Menil Collection, Houston
JPCR 3:502

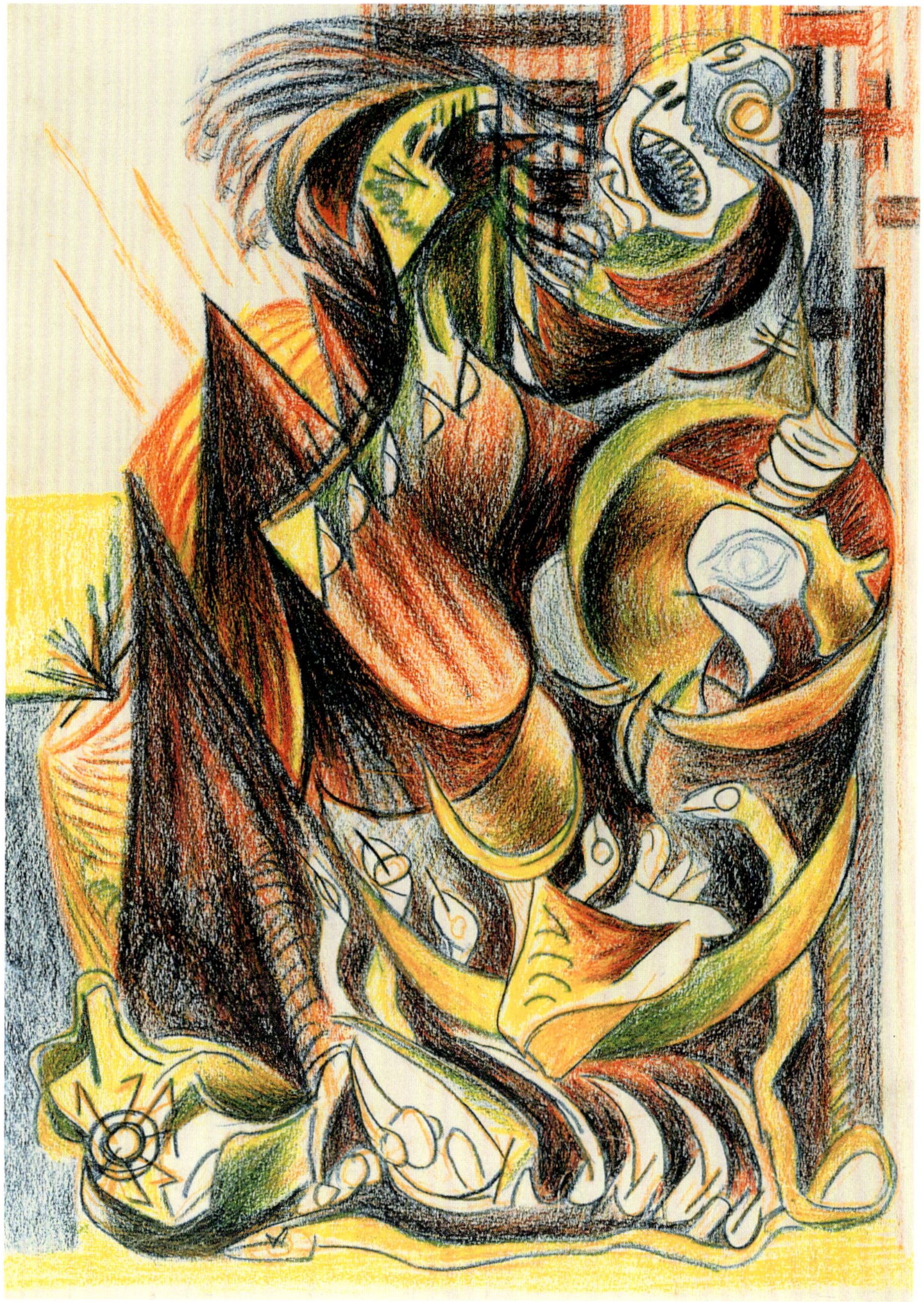

17
Untitled, ca. 1939–40
Colored pencils on paper
15 x 11 inches (38.1 x 27.9 cm)
Collection of Robert Aichele
JPCR 3:546

18
The Mask, ca. 1943
Gouache, oil, pen and ink, and fabric on paper
$29\frac{7}{8}$ x $21\frac{7}{8}$ inches (75.9 x 55.6 cm)
Private collection
JPCR Supplement 24

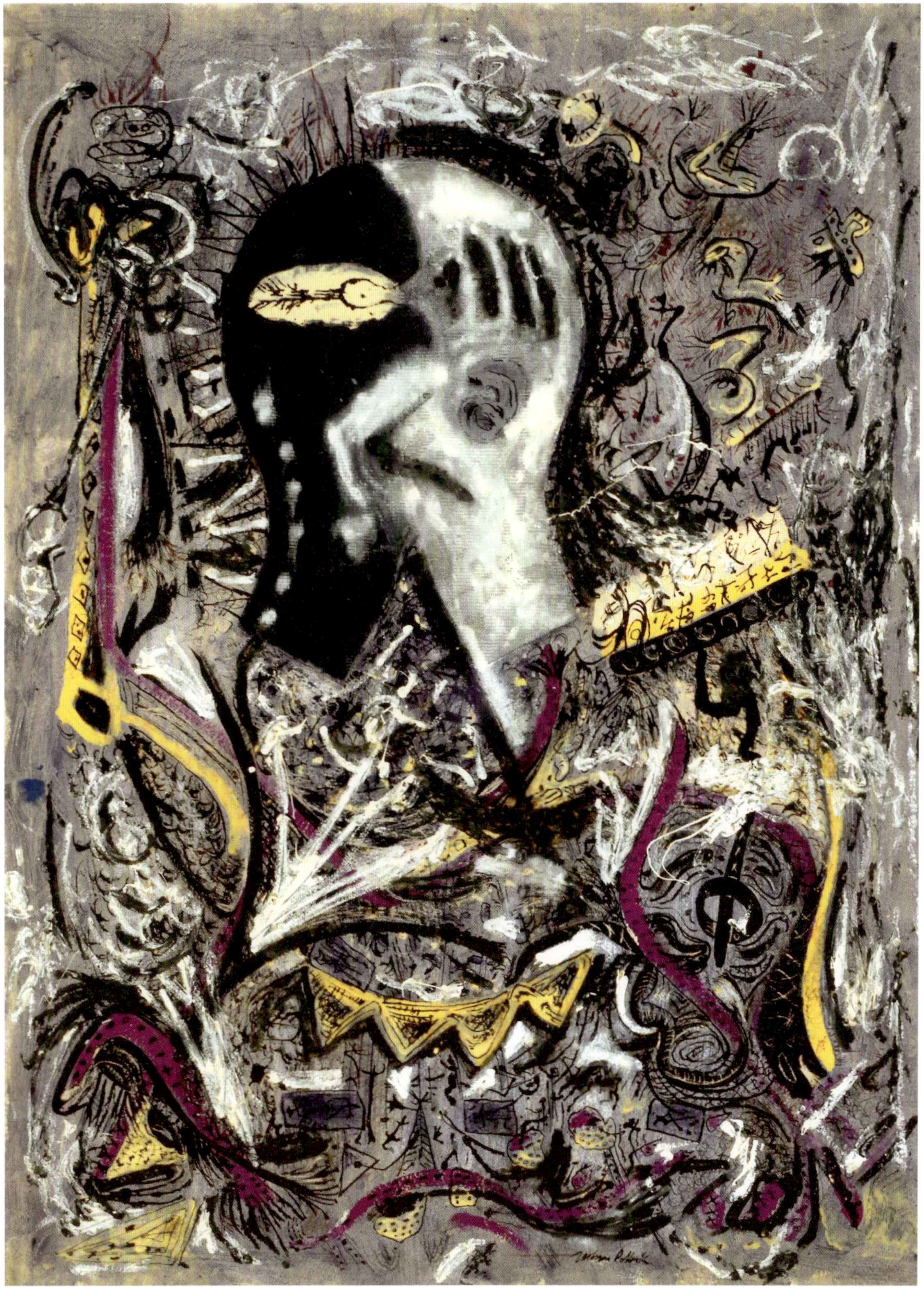

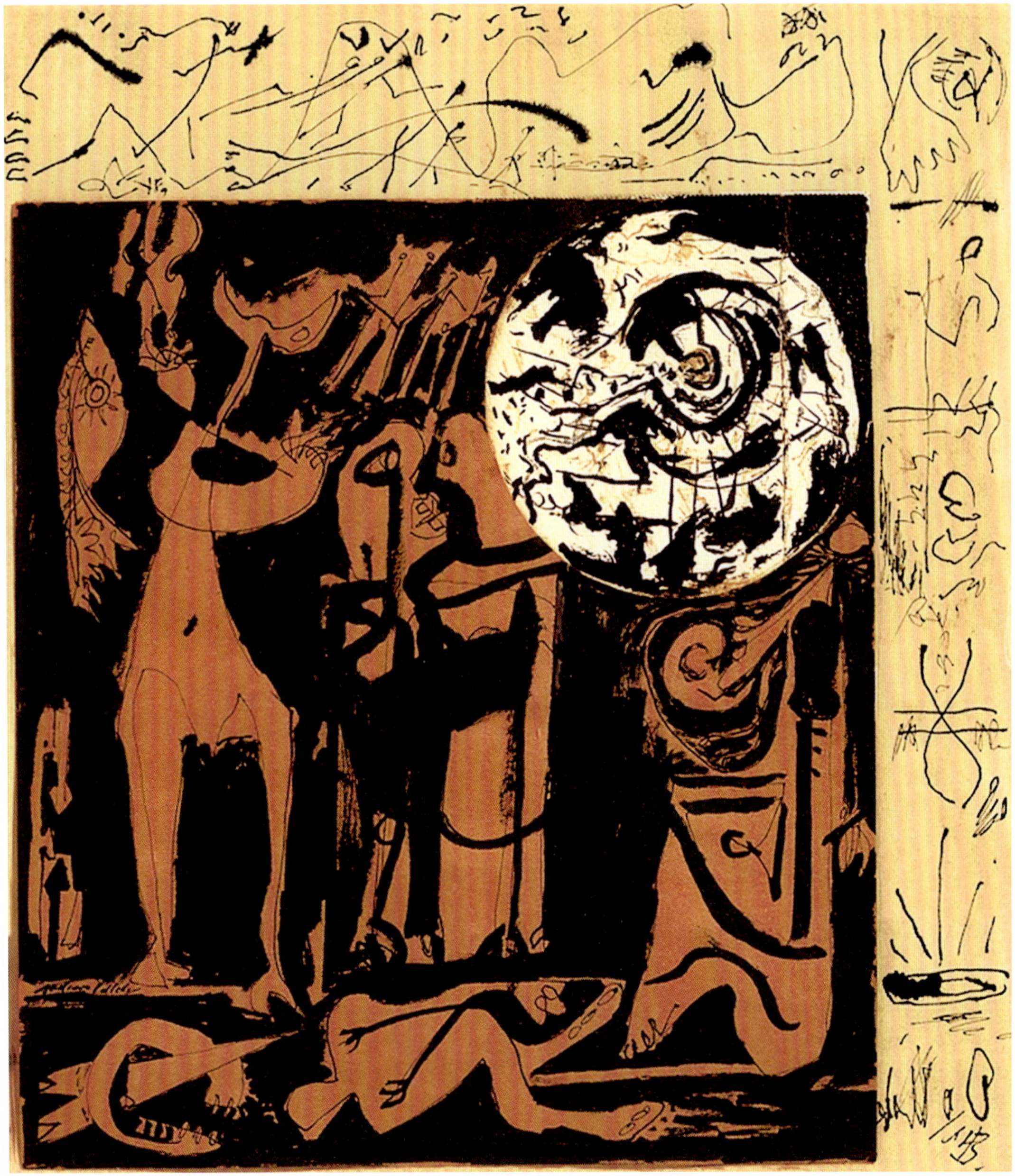

19
Untitled, 1943
Pen and ink, colored pencils,
and watercolor on colored paper
$15\frac{3}{8}$ x $13\frac{1}{2}$ inches (39.4 x 34.6 cm)
The Museum of Contemporary Art, Los Angeles.
Bequest of Marcia Simon Weisman
JPCR 4:1023

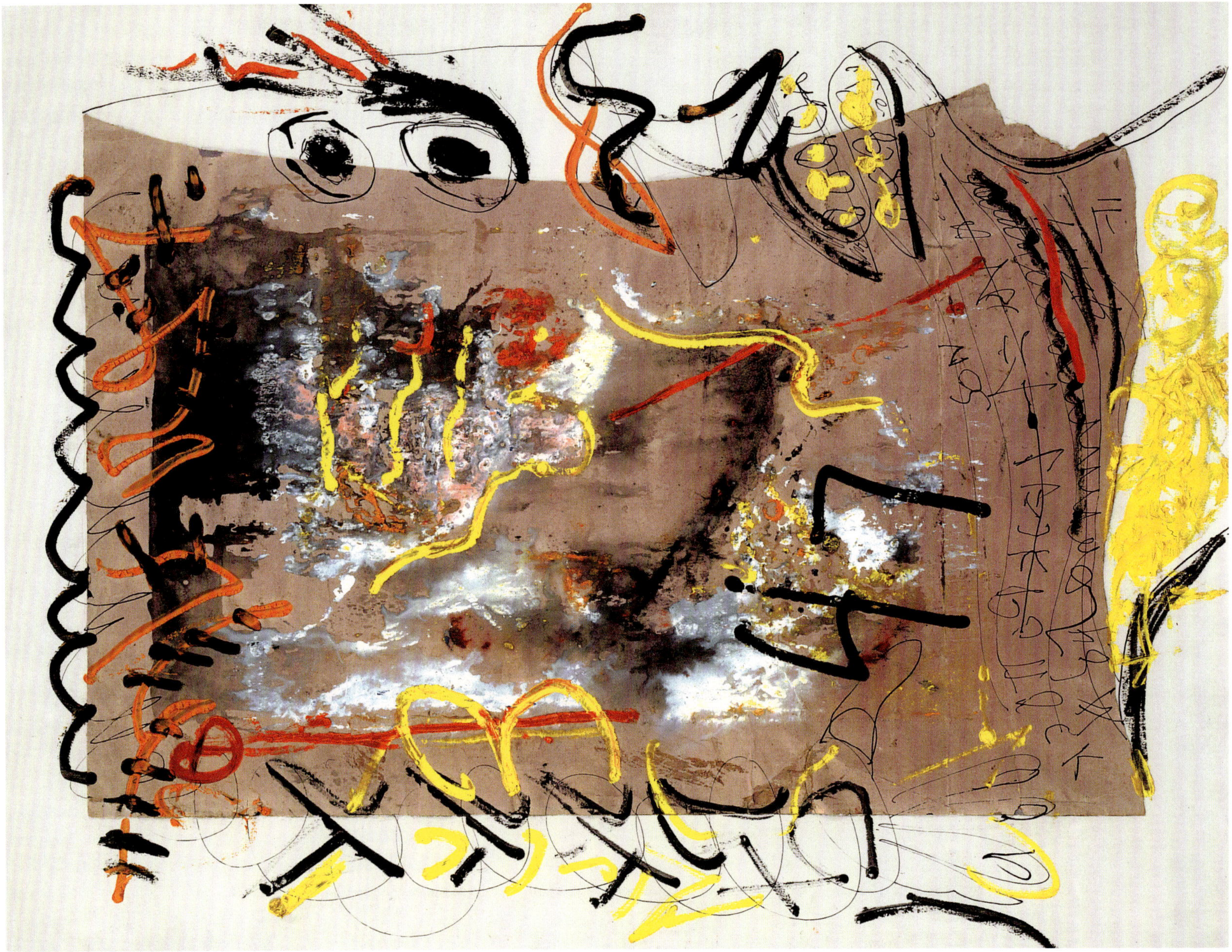

20
Abstract Painting, 1943
Oil, ink, and pink paper on paper
$15^{3}/_{4}$ x 21 inches (40 x 53.3 cm)
Courtesy Robert Miller Gallery, New York
JPCR 4:1024

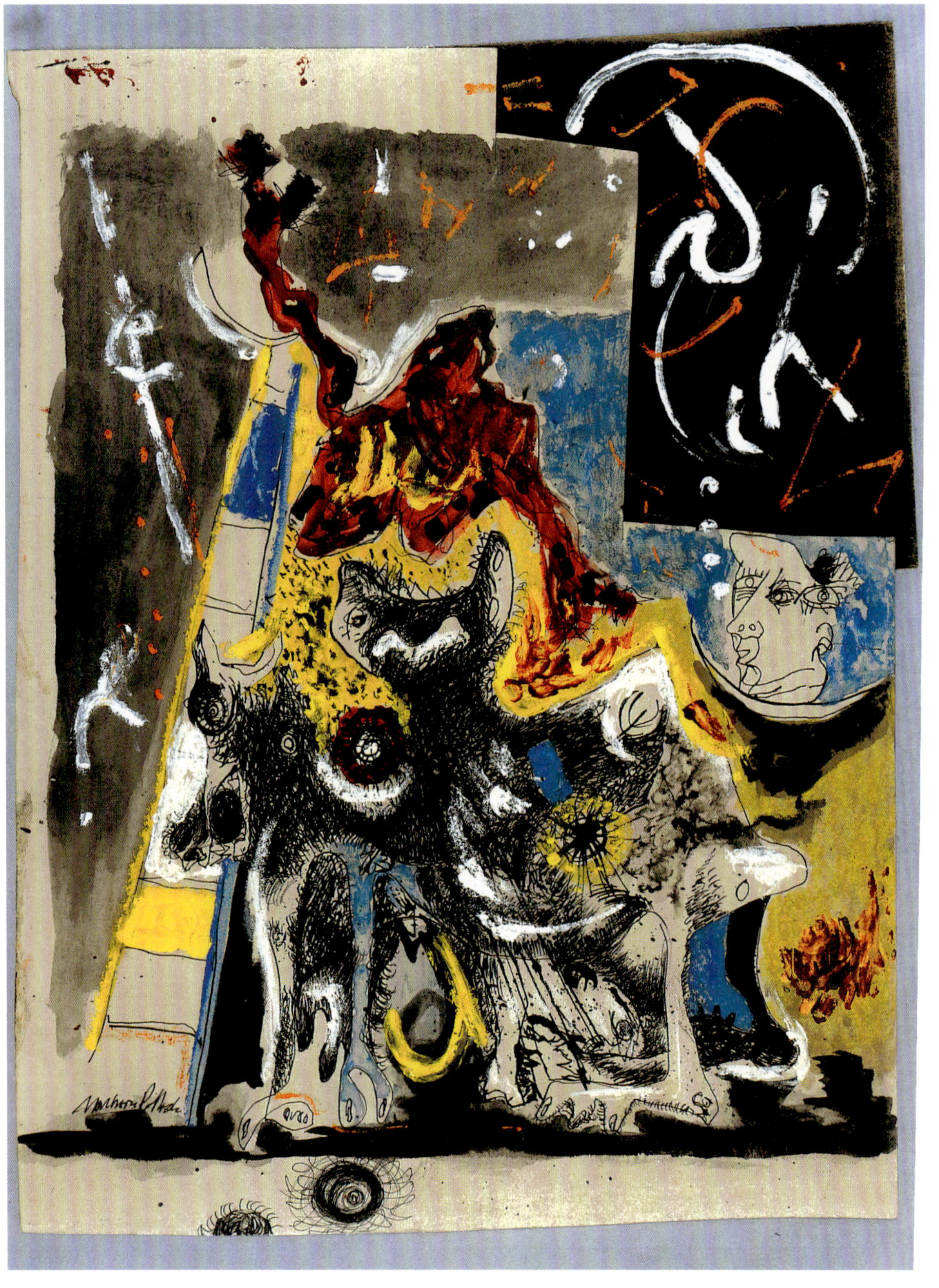

21
Untitled, ca. 1943
Ink, gouache, and watercolor on
cut papers mounted on blue paper
16 x 12 inches (40.6 x 30.5 cm)
The Kasser Art Foundation, Montclair, New Jersey
JPCR 4:1025

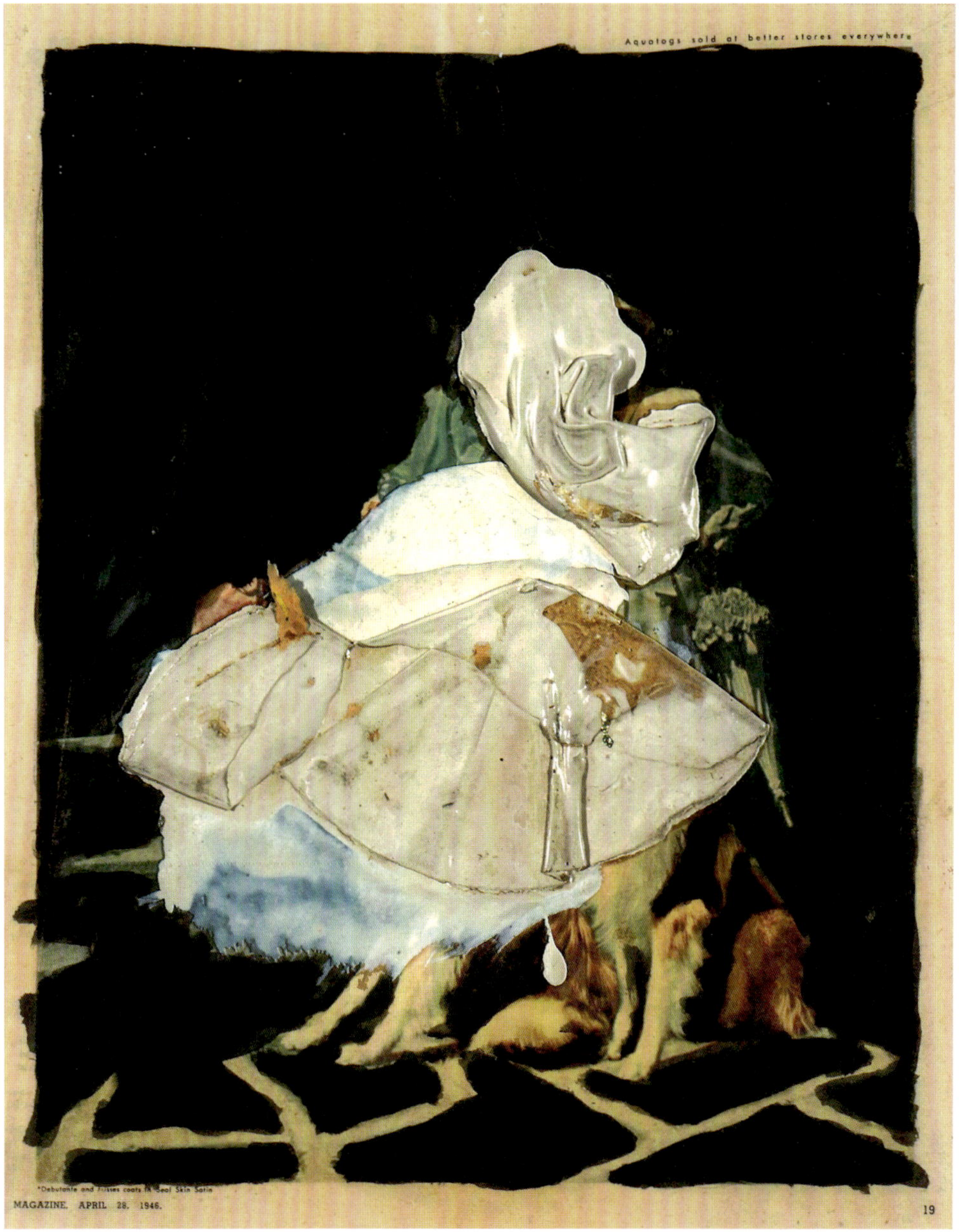

22
The Debutante, ca. 1946
Ink and dried enamel paint can "skin" on magazine reproduction
13½ x 11½ inches (34.3 x 29.2 cm)
Private collection
JPCR 4:1027

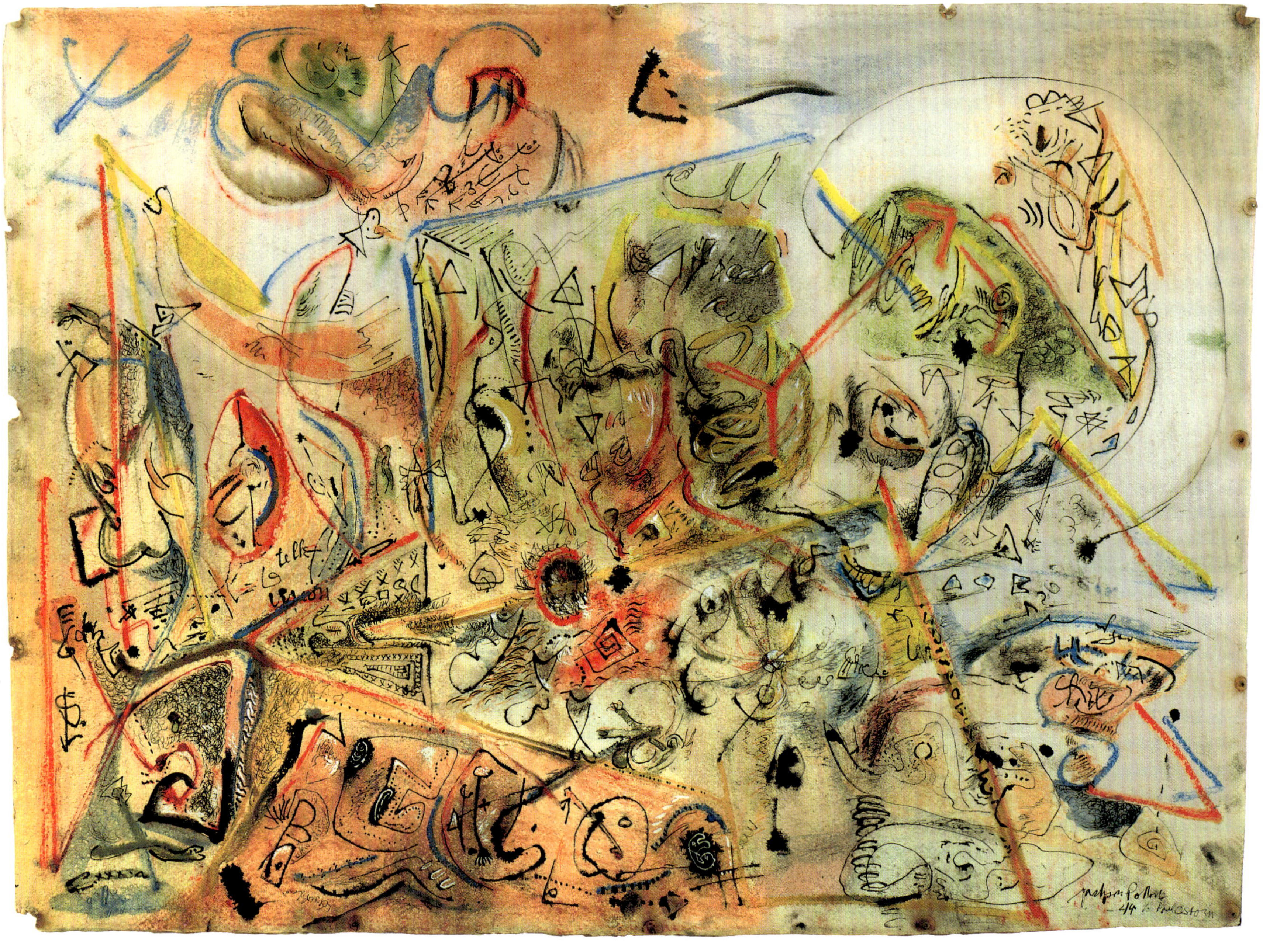

23
Untitled, 1944
Gouache, ink, and wash on paper
$22^{1/2}$ x $30^{5/8}$ inches (57.1 x 77.8 cm)
Private collection
JPCR 3:723

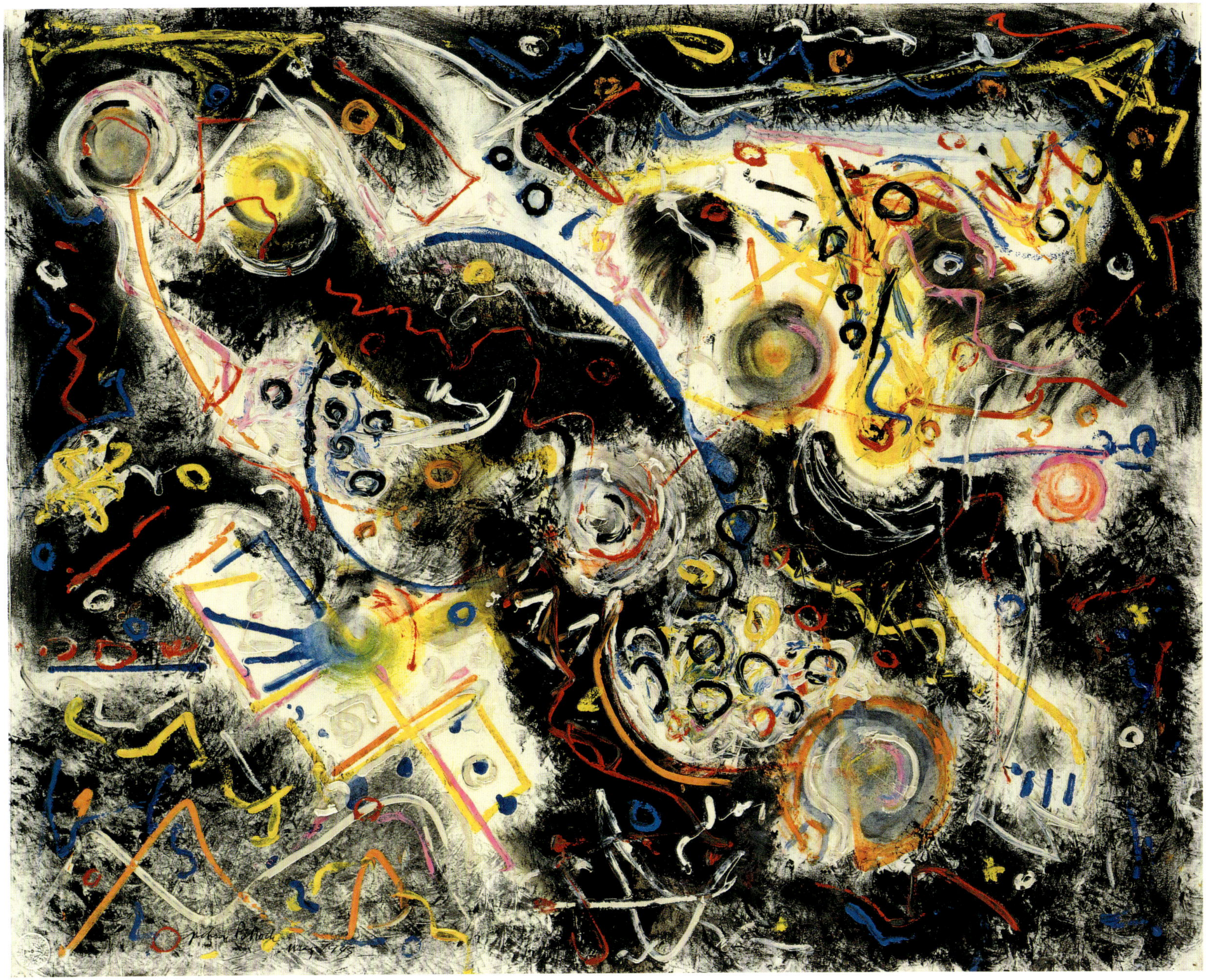

24
Untitled, 1943
Gouache on paper
$22^{7}/_{8}$ x $28^{7}/_{8}$ inches (58.1 x 73.3 cm)
The Menil Collection, Houston
JPCR 4:973

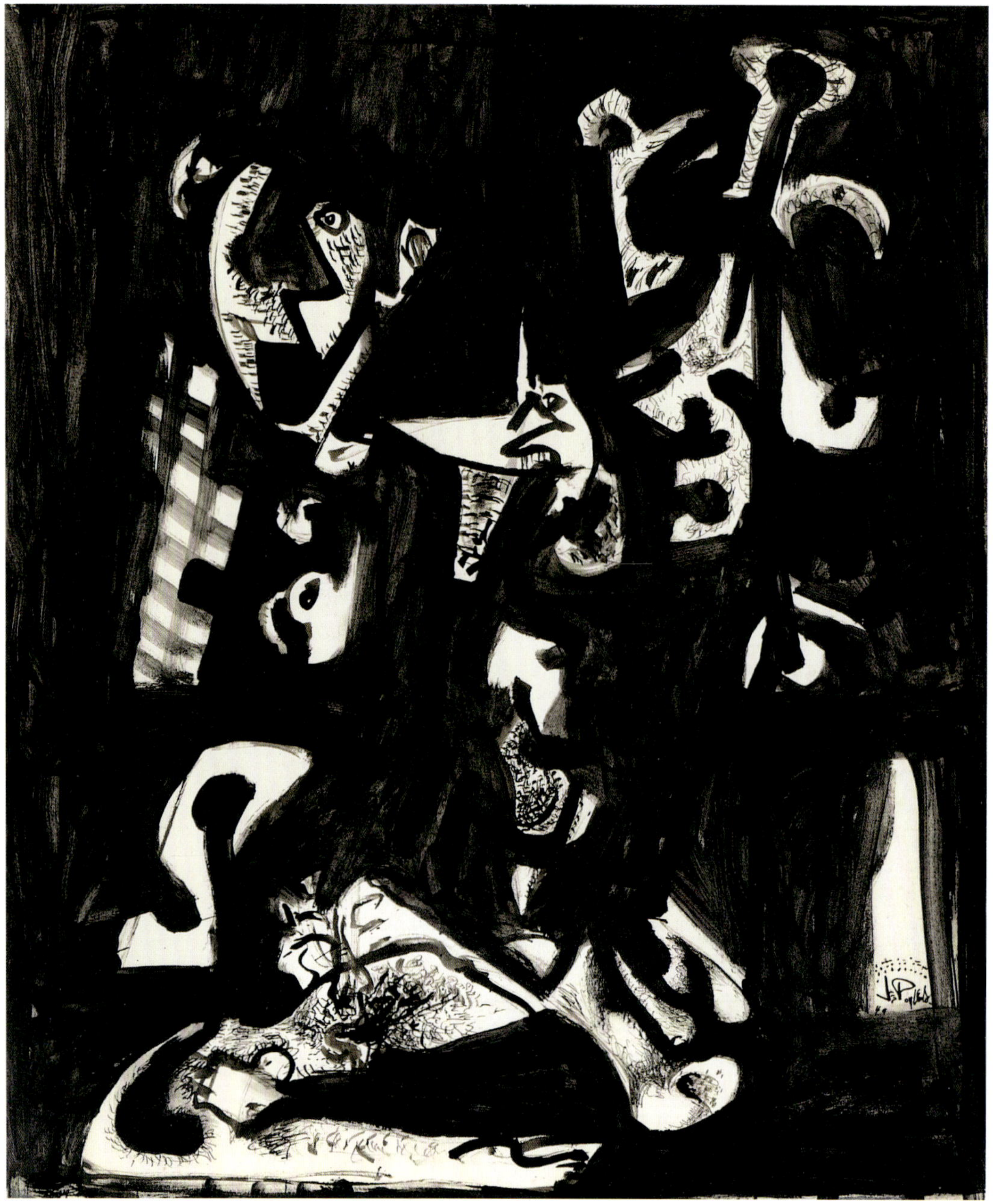

25
Untitled, 1944
Ink and gouache on paper
$13^{1}/_{8}$ x $11^{1}/_{8}$ inches (33.7 x 28.3 cm)
The Whitney Museum of American Art, New York.
Purchased with funds from the Julian B. Engel Purchase
Fund and the Drawing Committee (85.20)
JPCR 3:706

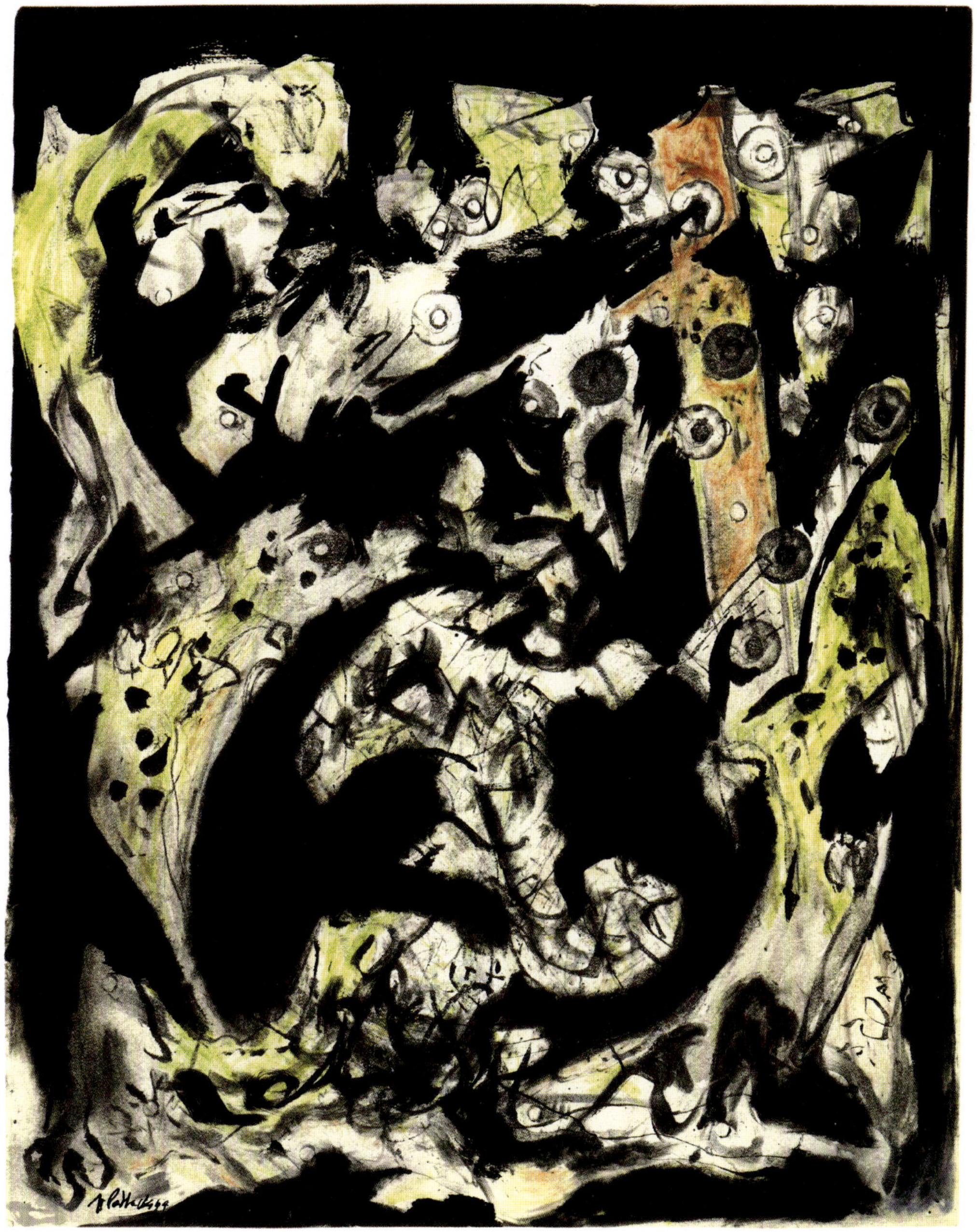

26
Untitled, 1944
Ink and watercolor on Japanese paper
12 1/2 x 10 1/8 inches (31.8 x 25.7 cm)
The Museum of Modern Art, New York.
The William S. Paley Collection
JPCR 4:977

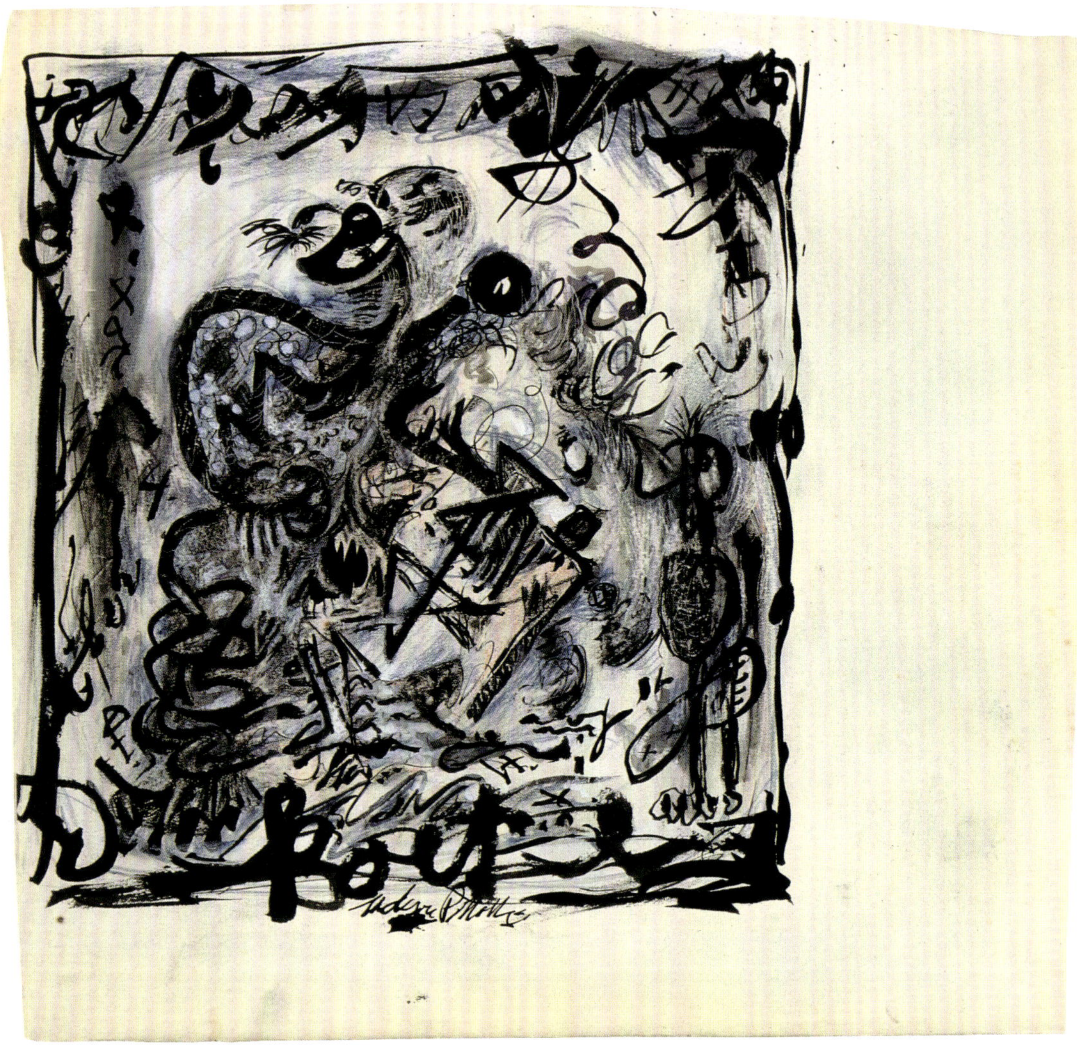

27
Untitled *[Poet]*, ca. 1944
Brush, pen and ink, gouache, colored pencils, and sgraffito on paper
9 1/4 x 8 7/16 inches (23.5 x 21.5 cm)
The Baltimore Museum of Art. Gift of Mr. and Mrs. Morton E. Rome (1978.135)
JPCR 4:984

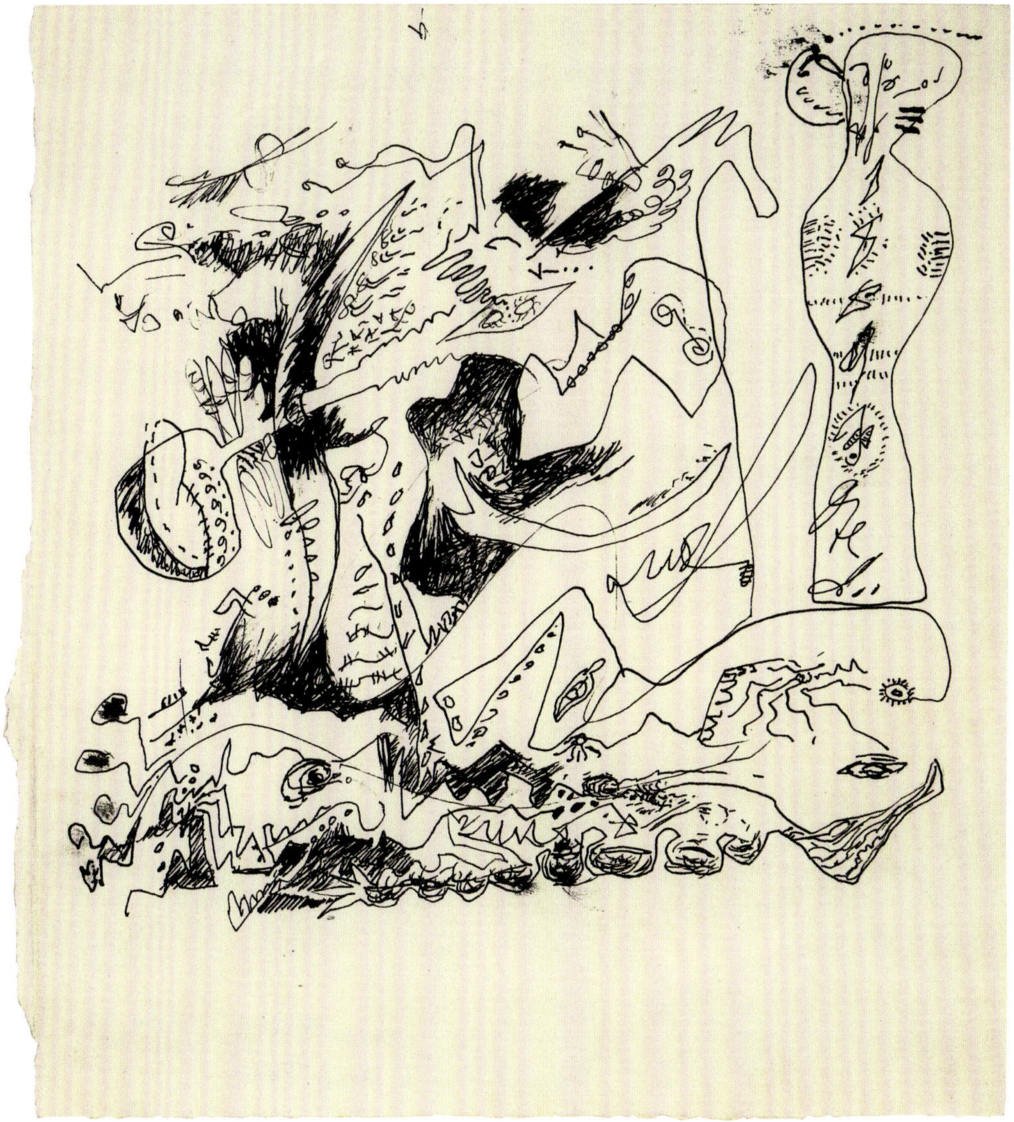

28
Untitled, ca. 1943
Pen and ink on paper
10½ x 9¾ inches (26.7 x 24.8 cm)
National Gallery of Art, Washington, D.C.
Alisa Mellon Bruce Fund (1985.62.1)
JPCR 3:674

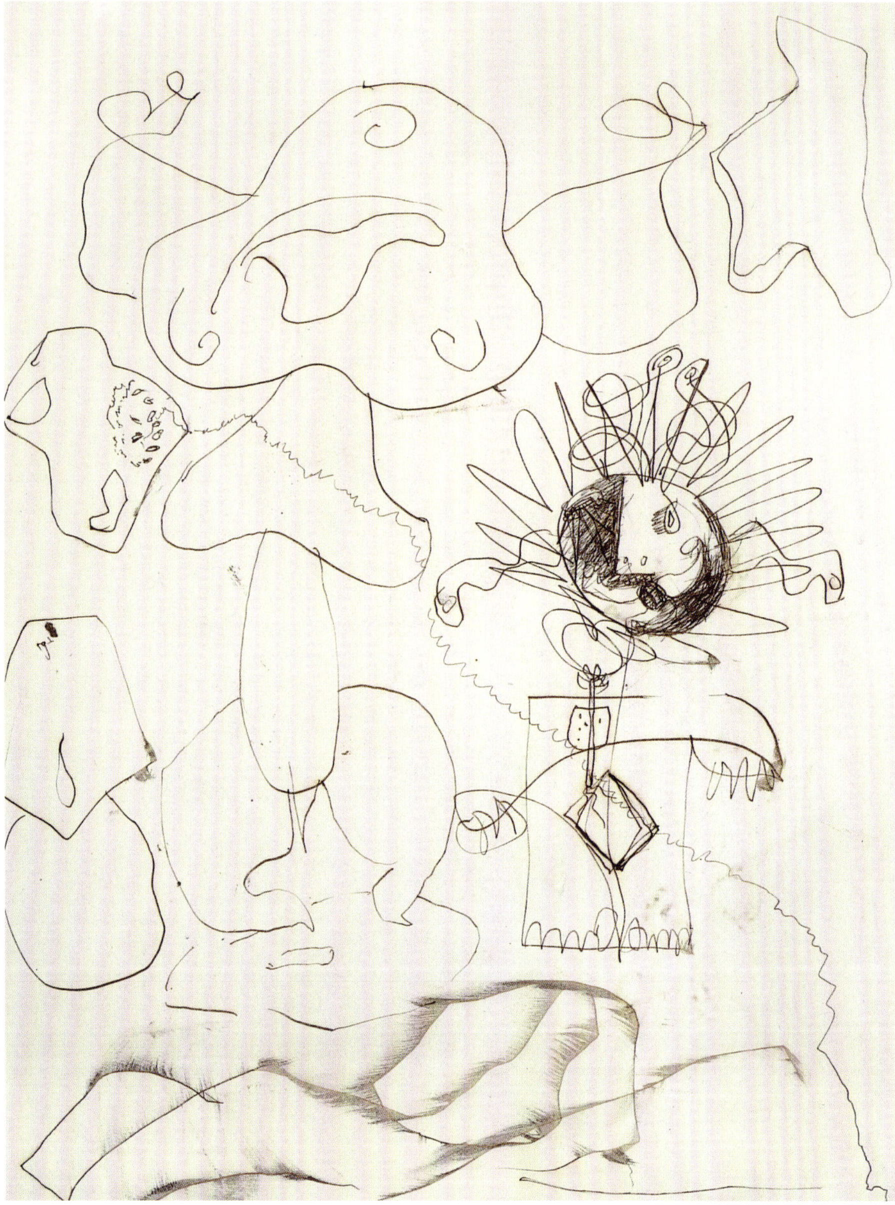

29
Untitled, ca. 1943
Pen and ink and colored pencil on paper
18 x 14 inches (45.7 x 35.6 cm)
Courtesy Joan T. Washburn Gallery, New York,
and The Pollock-Krasner Foundation, Inc.
JPCR 3:667r

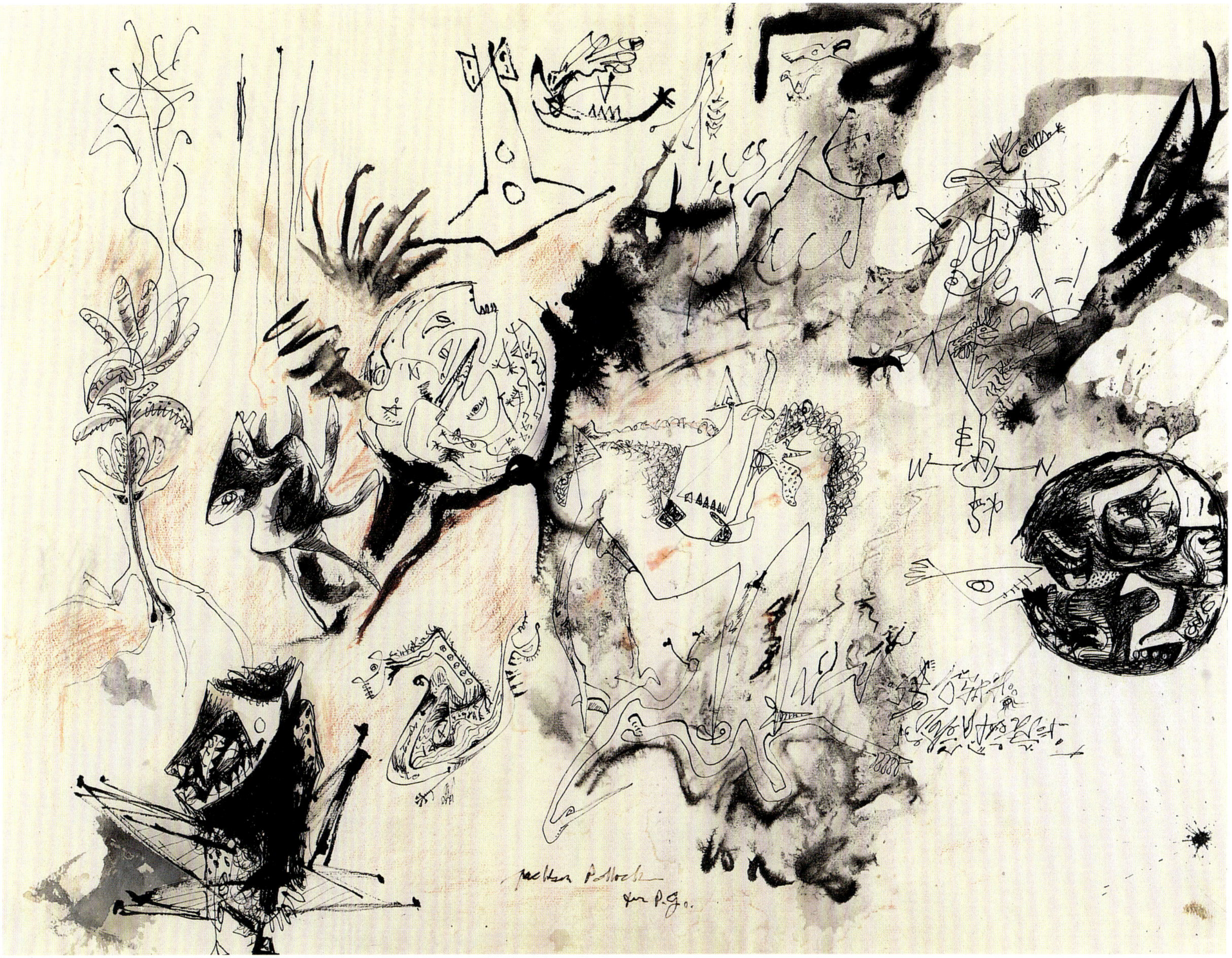

30
[Drawing for P.G.], ca. 1943
Pen and ink, wash, gouache, and red pencil on paper
18 3/4 x 24 3/4 inches (47.6 x 62.9 cm)
The Pierpont Morgan Library, New York. The Thaw Collection
JPCR Supplement 17

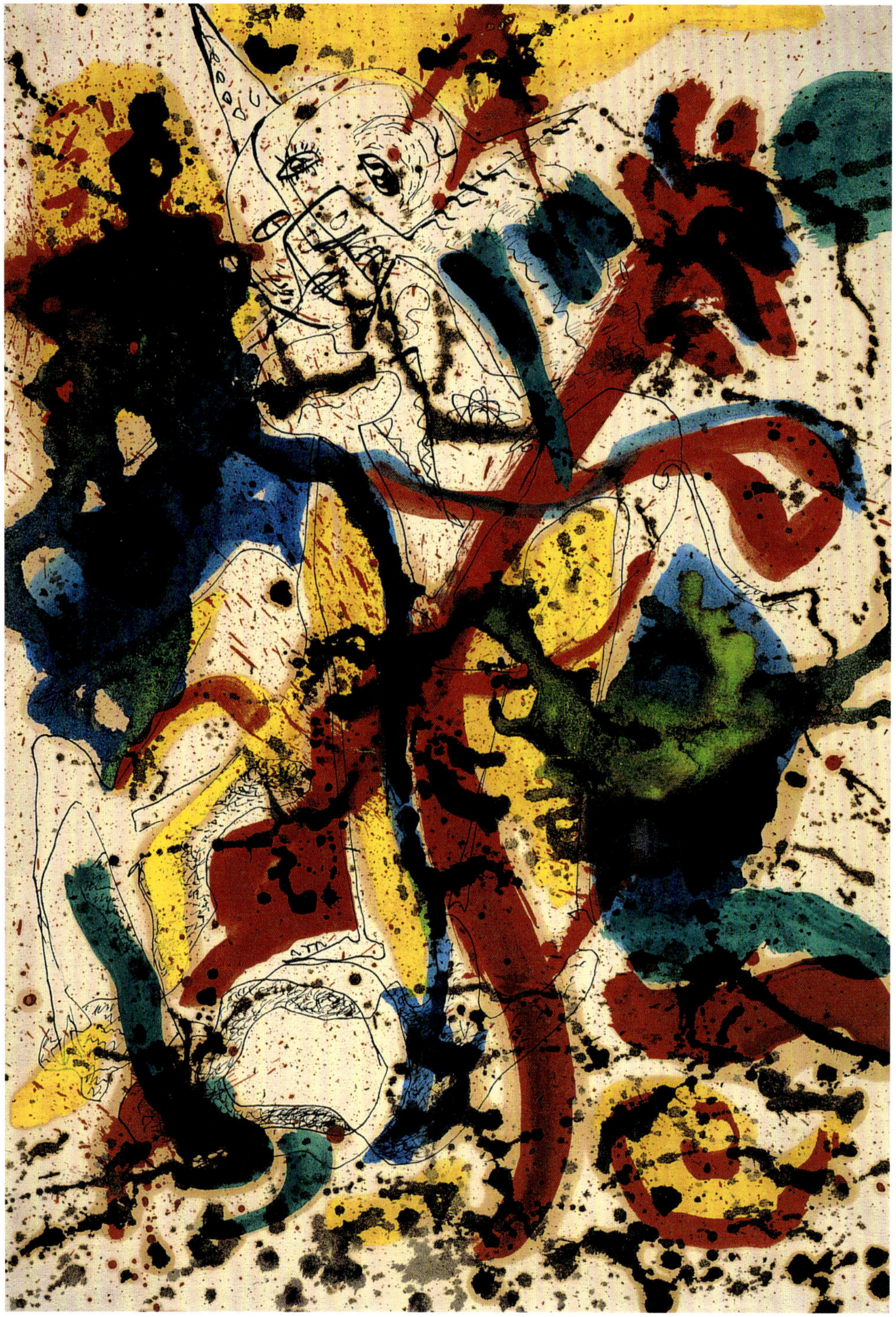

31
Untitled, ca. 1942–44
Oil, brush, spatter, and pen and ink on paper
$20^{1}/_{8}$ x $13^{1}/_{4}$ inches (51.1 x 33.7 cm)
Scottish National Gallery of Modern Art, Edinburgh (GMA 849)
JPCR 4:1005

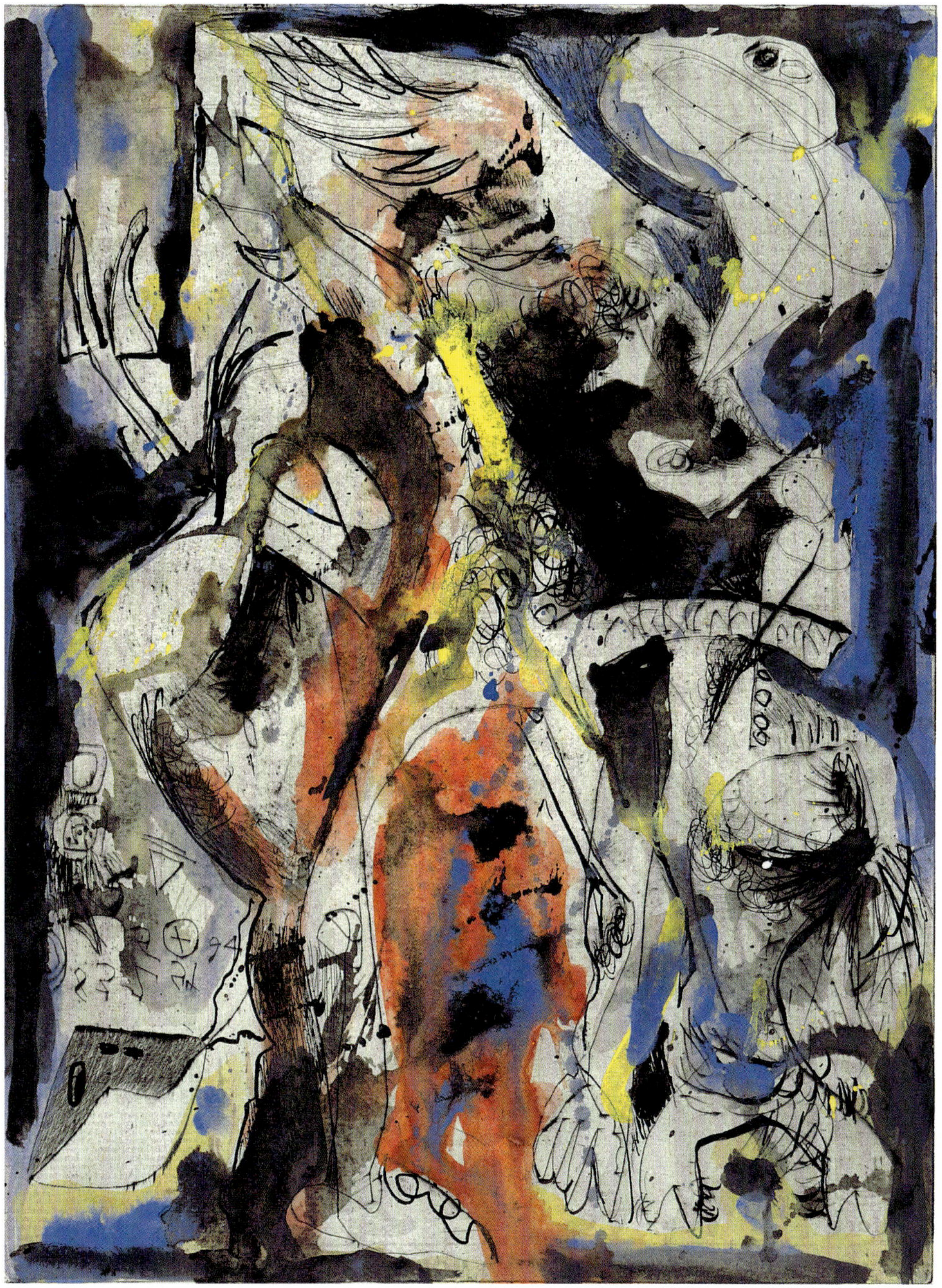

32
Untitled, ca. 1945
Watercolor and gouache over drypoint engraving
$11\frac{7}{8}$ x $8\frac{7}{8}$ inches (30.2 x 22.6 cm) image;
$15\frac{1}{2}$ x 11 inches (39.5 x 27.9 cm) sheet
Allen Memorial Art Museum, Oberlin College, Oberlin, Ohio. R. T. Miller Jr. Fund, 1958 (58.48)
JPCR 4:988

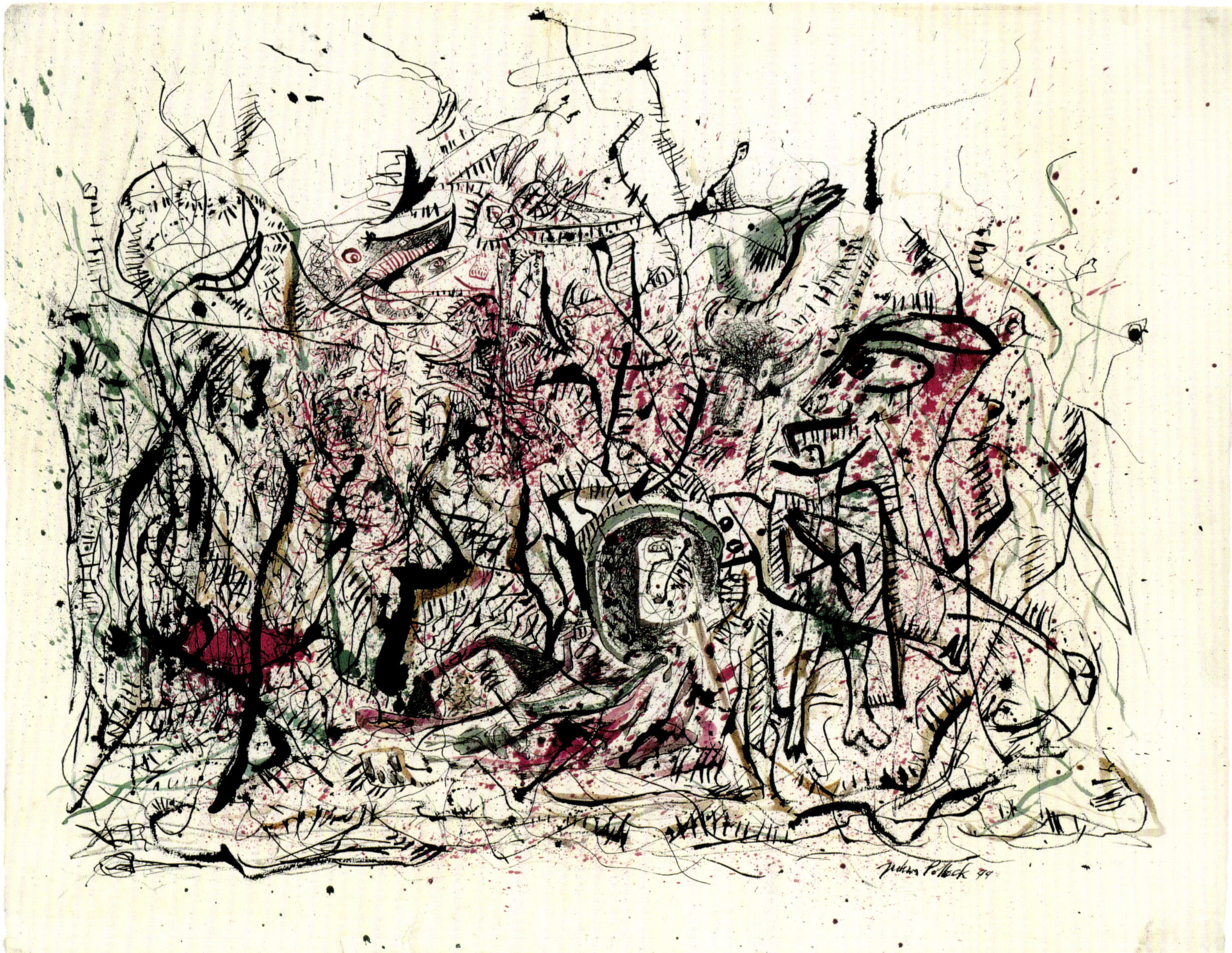

33
Untitled, 1944
Black and colored inks on paper
18 7/8 x 24 7/8 inches (48 x 63.2 cm)
The Art Institute of Chicago. Ada Turnbull Hertle Fund and gifts of Mrs. Leigh B. Block, Margaret Fischer, William H. Hartmann, and Joseph R. Shapiro
JPCR 3:724

34
Untitled, 1945
Gouache, pastel, brush, spatter, pen and black and colored inks, and sgraffito on paper
22 1/2 x 15 1/4 inches (57.2 x 38.7 cm)
The Israel Museum, Jerusalem, Bequest of Kay Merrill Hillman, New York to American Friends of the Israel Museum
JPCR 4:992

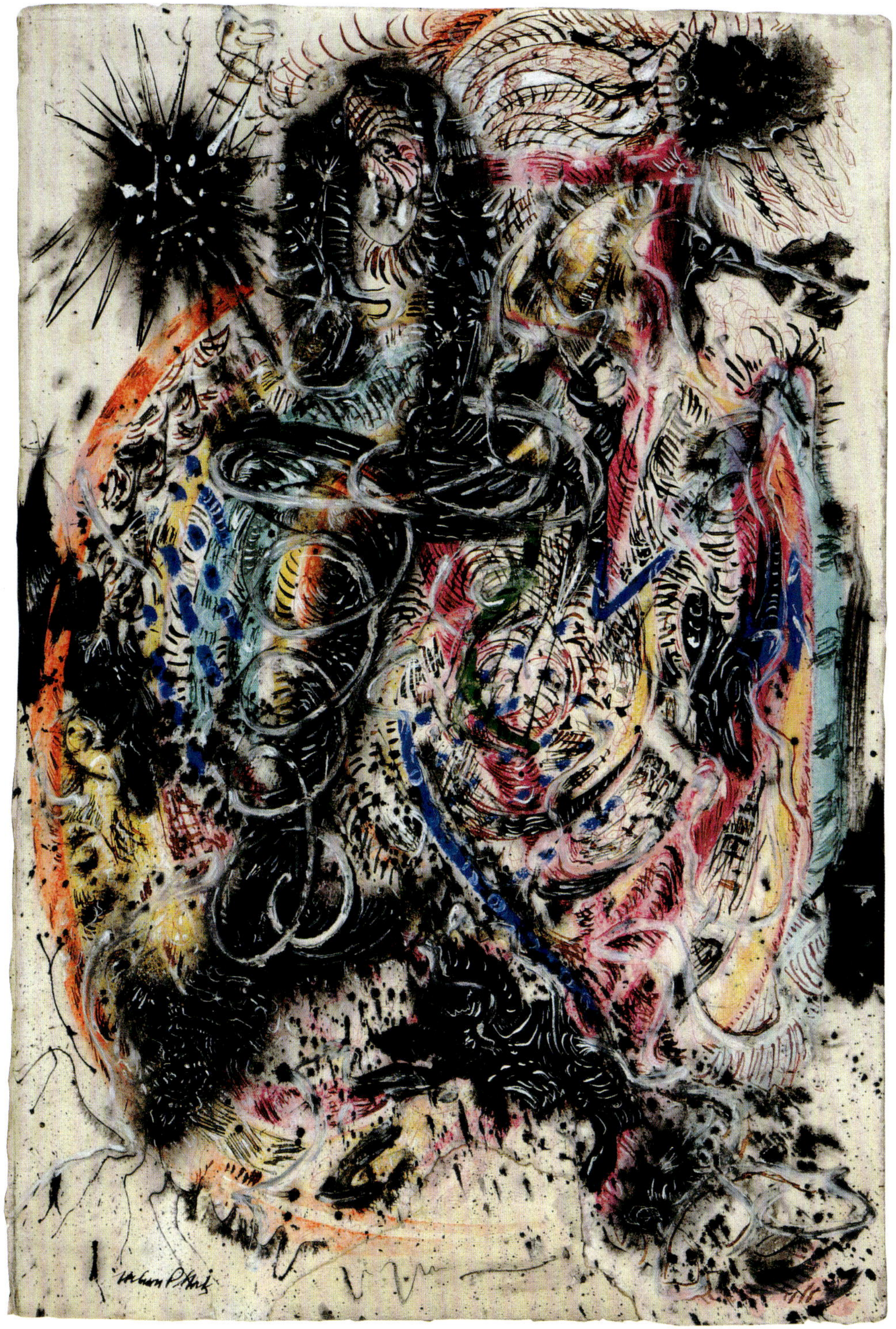

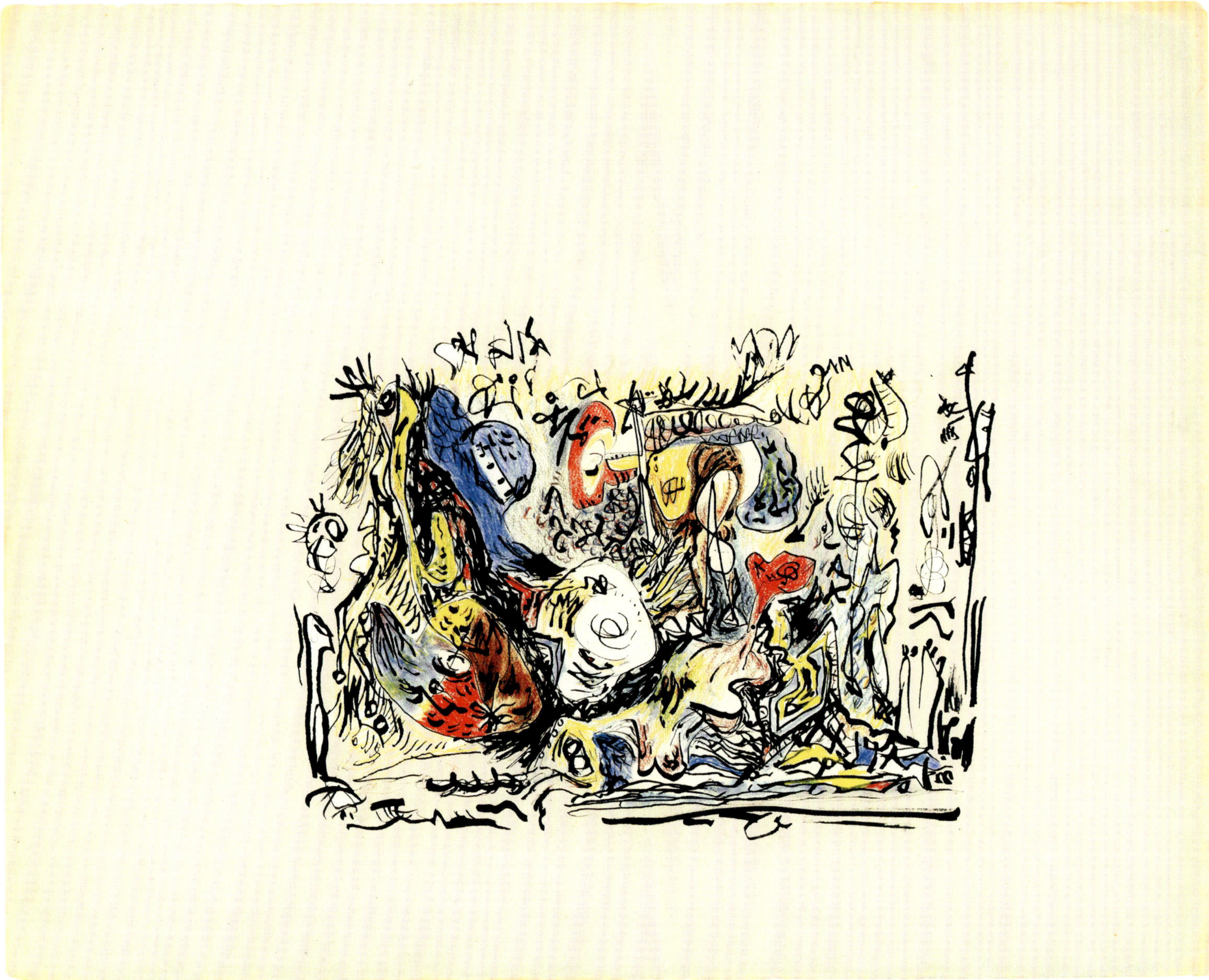

35
Untitled, ca. 1945
Crayon, colored pencil, brush, pen and ink, and watercolor on paper
20 1/4 x 25 inches (51.4 x 63.5 cm)
The Museum of Modern Art, New York. Gift of Philip Johnson, Abby Aldrich Rockefeller, Curt Valentin, and Edward M. Warburg (by exchange)
JPCR 3:742

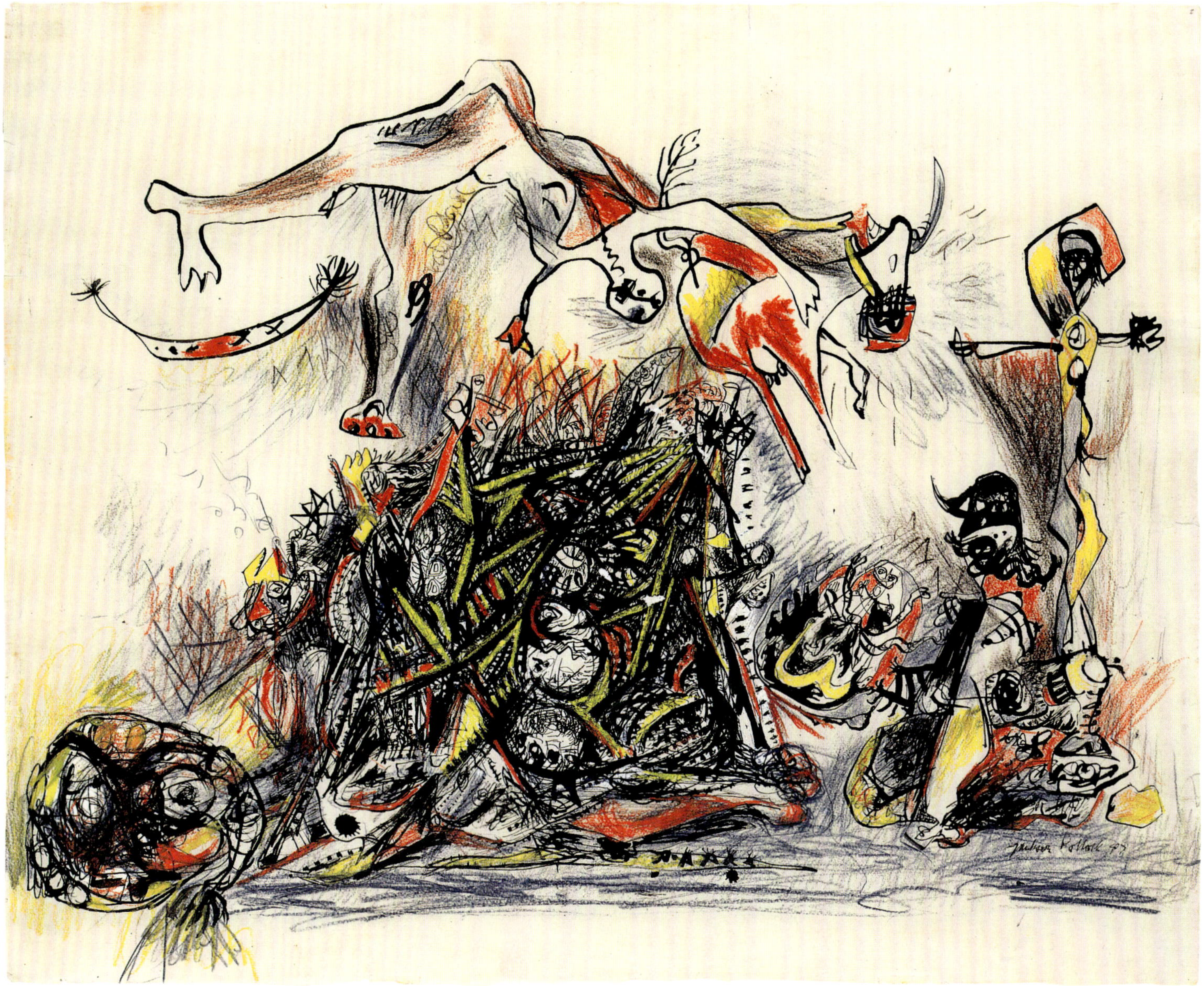

36
War, ca. 1944–46
Ink and colored pencils on paper
20 5/8 x 26 inches (52.4 x 66 cm)
The Metropolitan Museum of Art, New York. Gift of Lee Krasner Pollock in memory of Jackson Pollock, 1982 (1982.147.25)
JPCR 3:765

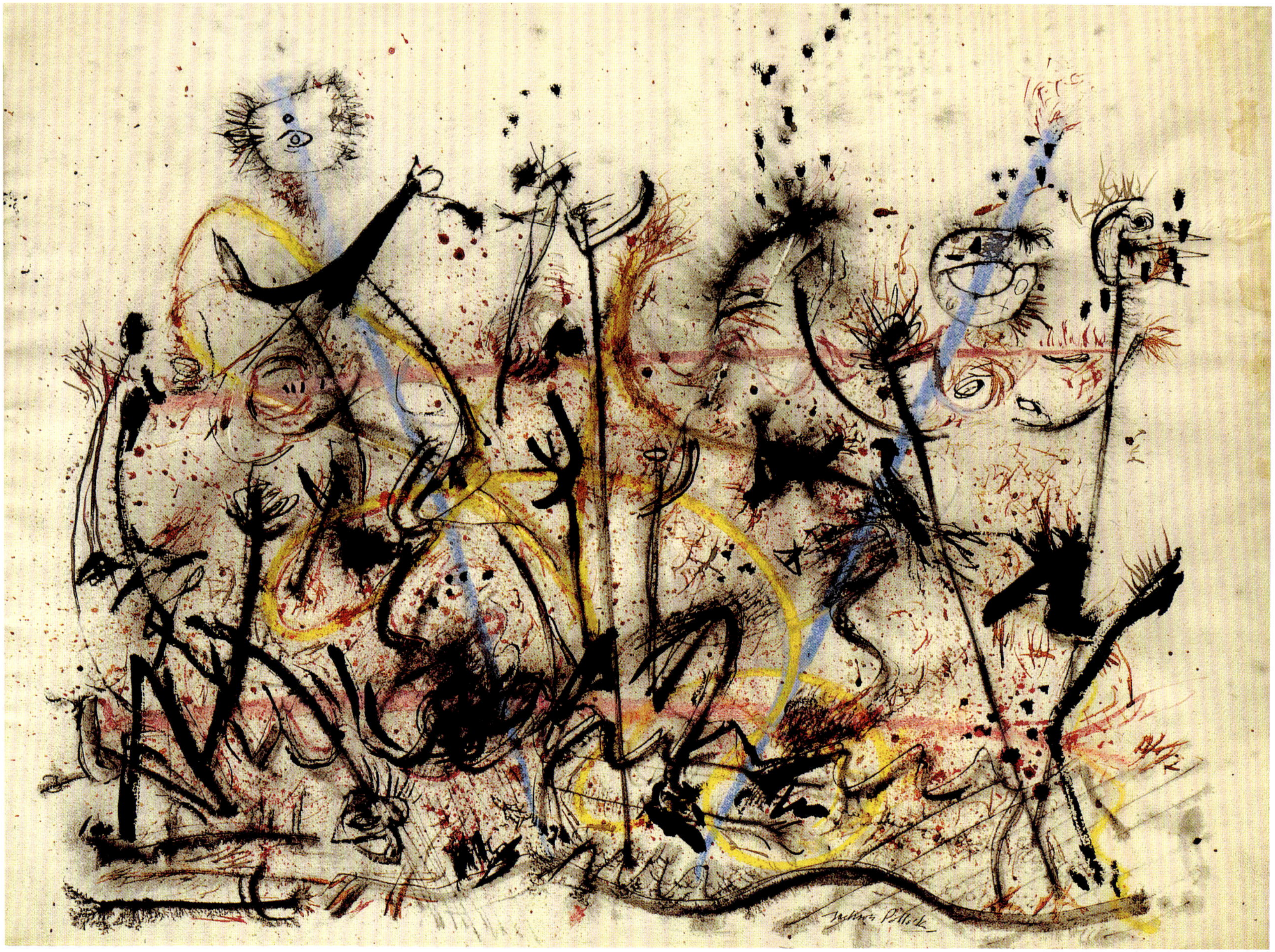

37
Untitled, ca. 1946
Ink, pastel, gouache, and spatter on paper
19 x 26 inches (48.3 x 66 cm)
Collection of Denise and Andrew Saul
JPCR 4:1014

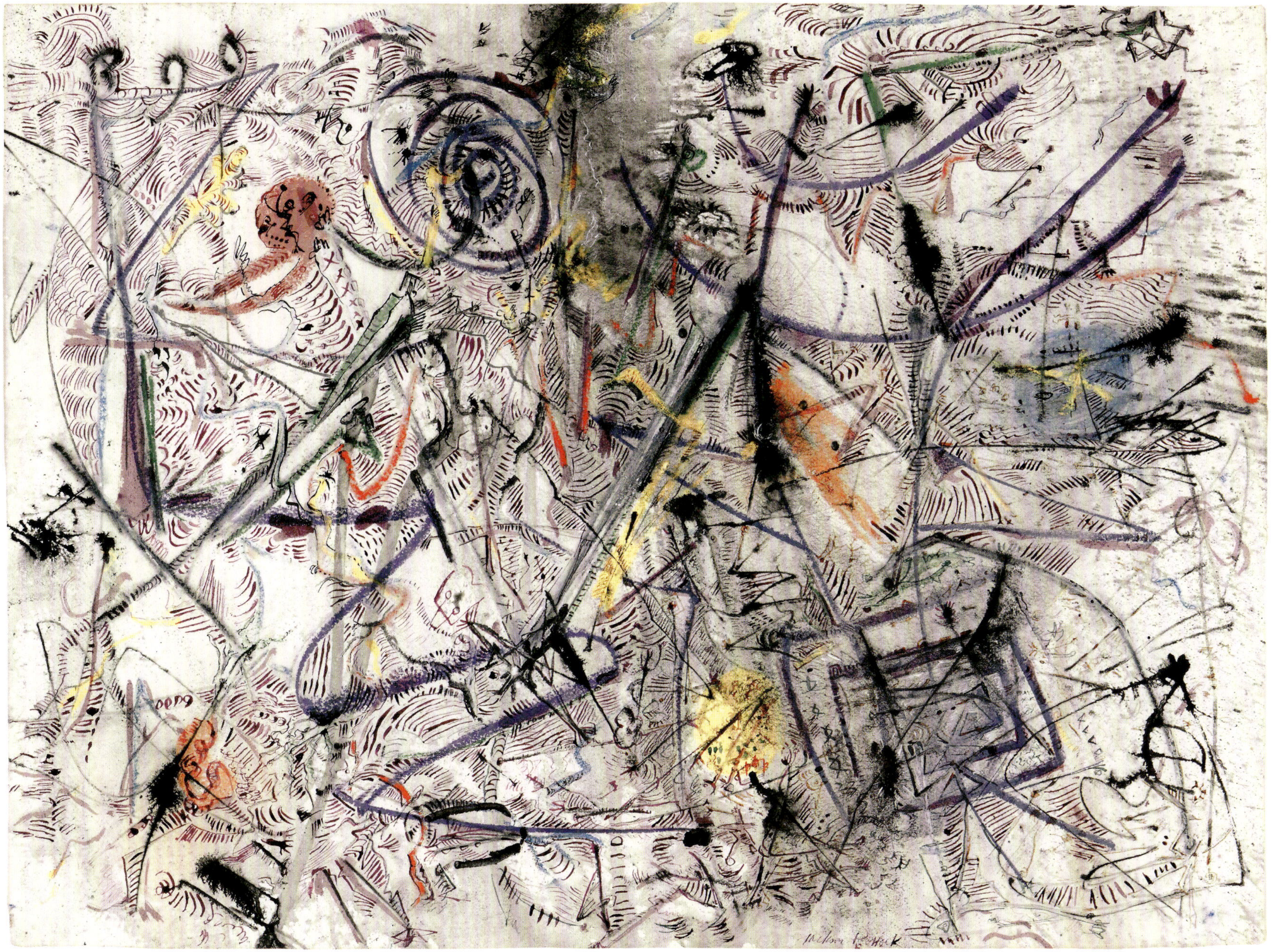

38
Untitled, ca. 1946
Brush, spatter, black and colored inks, pastel, gouache, and wash on paper
22 1/2 x 31 inches (57.2 x 78.7 cm)
Collection of Mr. and Mrs. Bertram L. Wolstein
JPCR Supplement 20

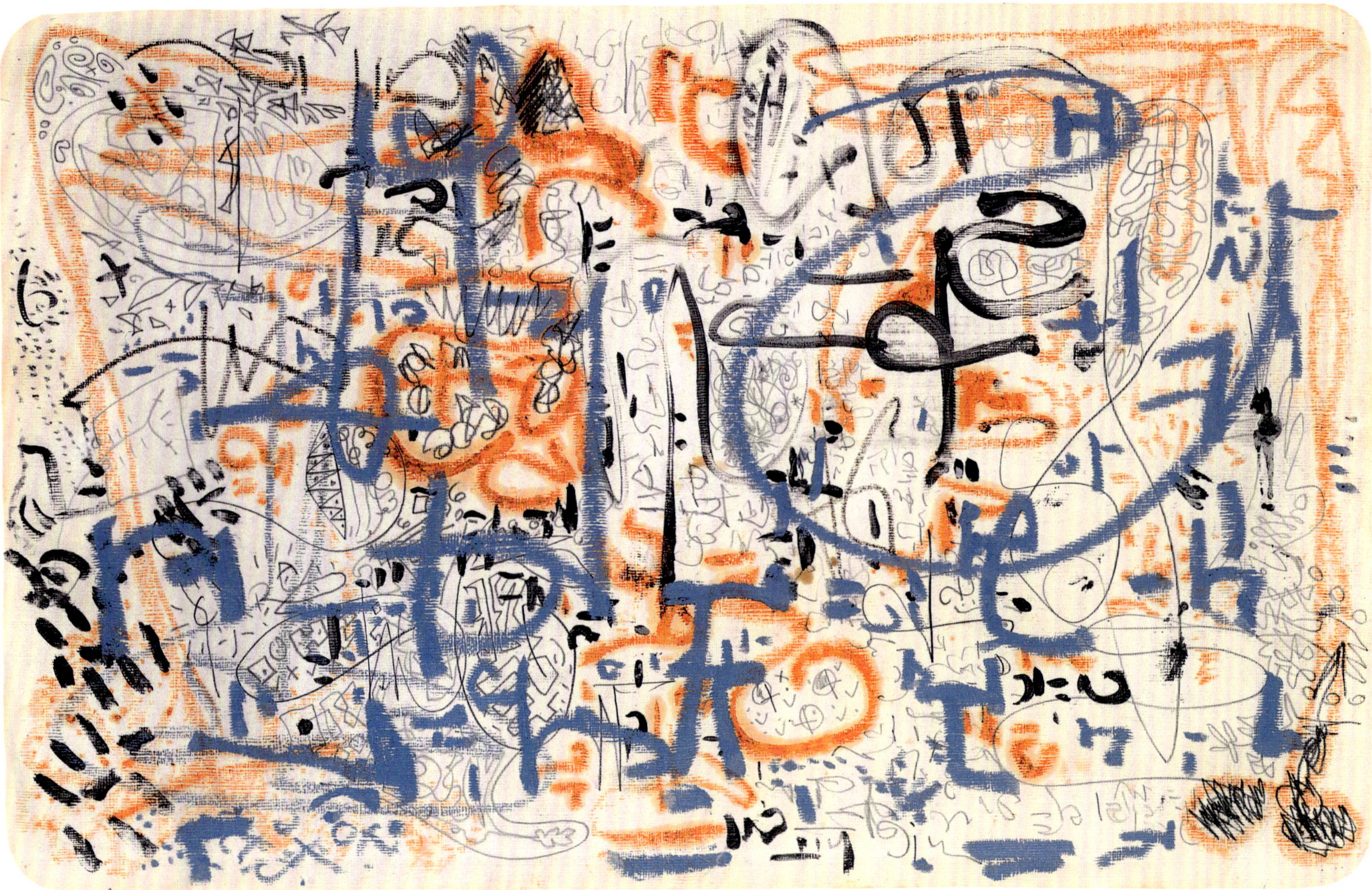

39
[Place Mat], ca. 1946–47
Pencil, crayon, and grease pencil on paper
$9\,^7/_8$ x $16\,^3/_4$ inches (25.1 x 42.5 cm)
Courtesy Joan T. Washburn Gallery, New York,
and The Pollock-Krasner Foundation, Inc.
JPCR Supplement 14

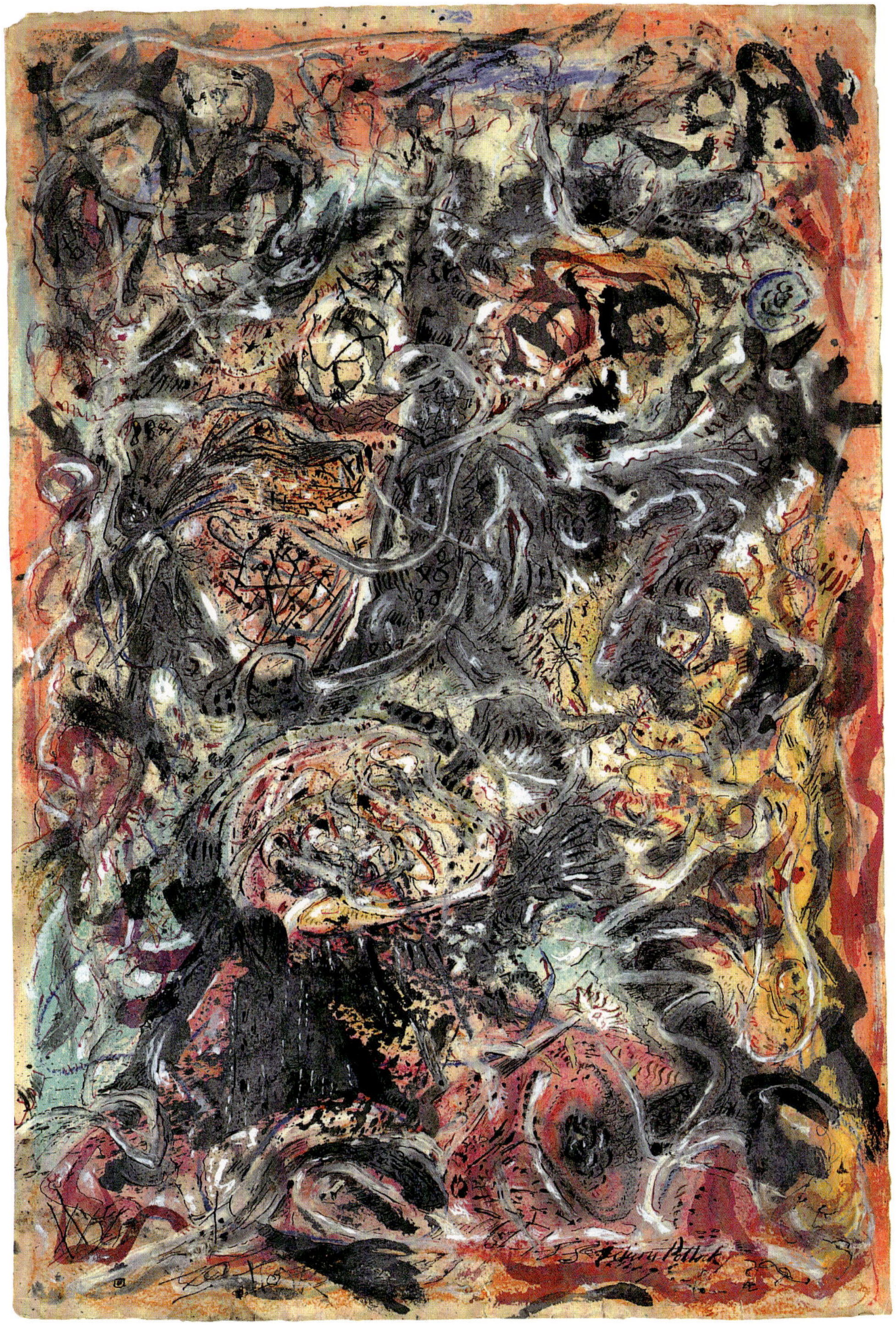

40
Untitled (*Pattern*), ca. 1945
Watercolor, ink, and gouache on paper
22 1/2 x 15 1/2 inches (57.2 x 39.4 cm)
Hirshhorn Museum and Sculpture Garden, Smithsonian Institution, Washington, D.C. Gift of Joseph H. Hirshhorn Foundation, 1966 (66.4086)
JPCR 4:993

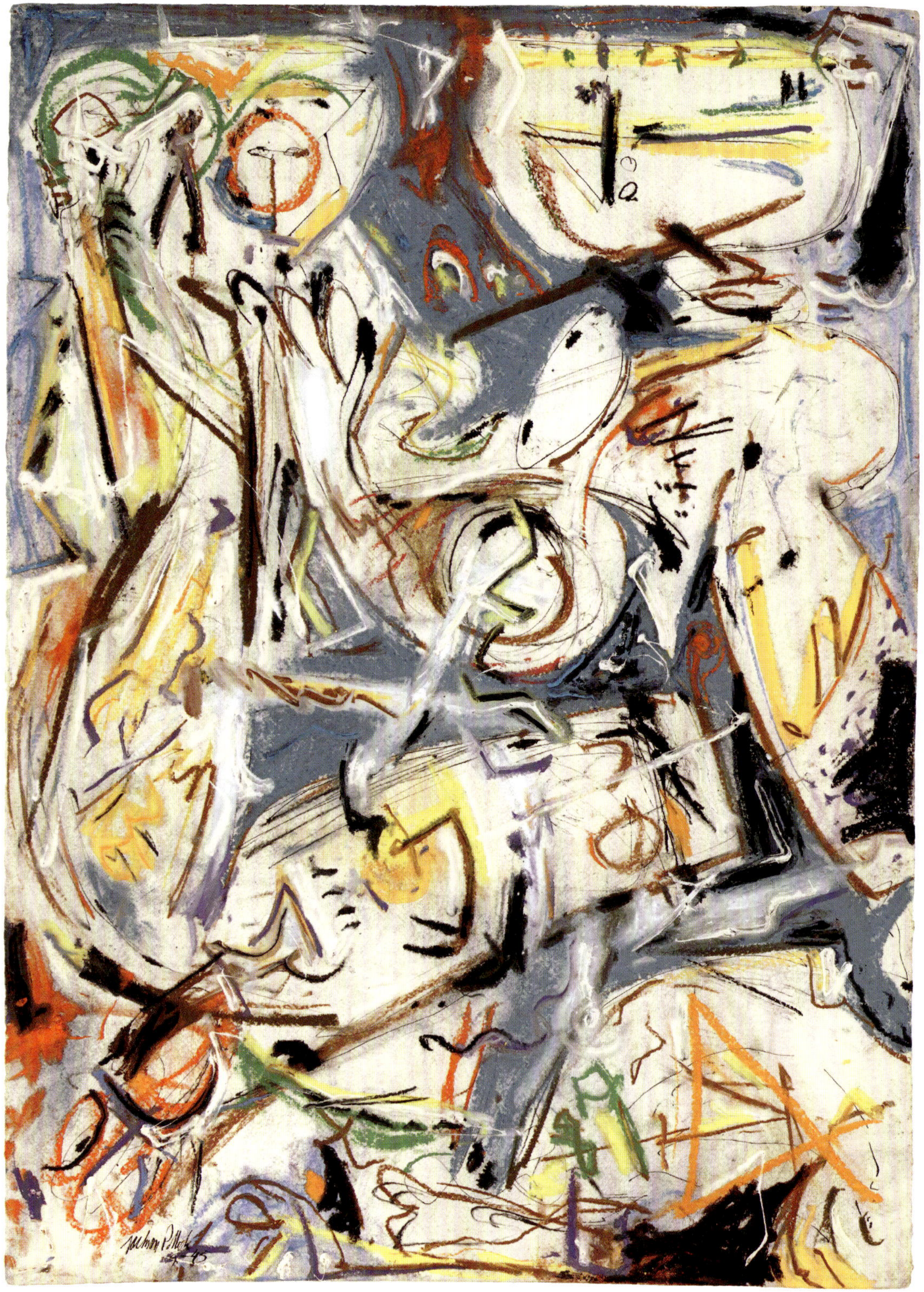

41
Untitled, 1945
Pastel, gouache, and ink on paper
$30\frac{5}{8}$ x $22\frac{3}{8}$ inches (77.8 x 56.7 cm)
The Museum of Modern Art, New York.
Blanchette Rockefeller Fund
JPCR 4:991

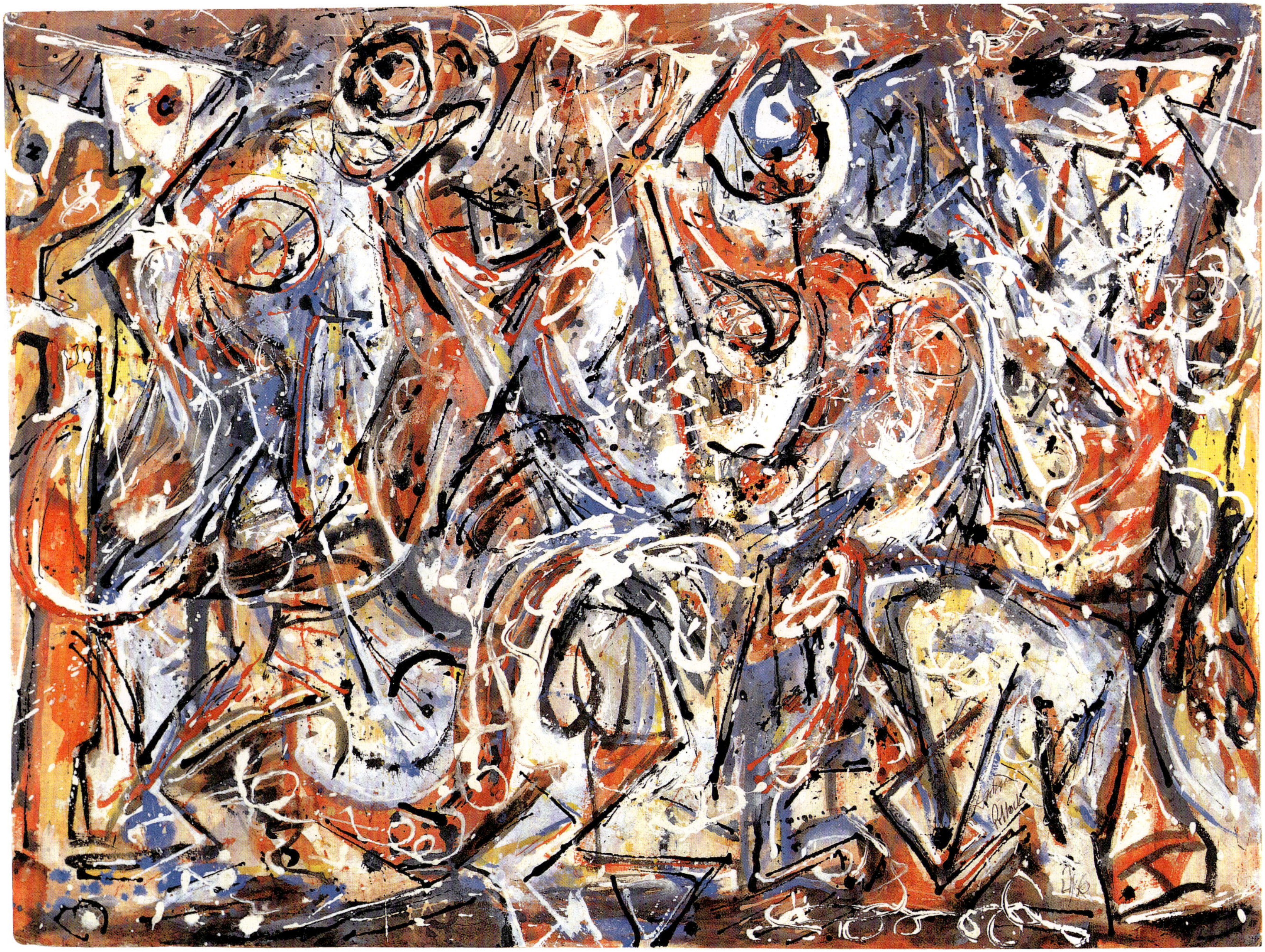

42
Untitled, 1946
Gouache on paper
$22\frac{1}{4}$ x $32\frac{1}{2}$ inches (56.5 x 82.6 cm)
Thyssen-Bornemisza Collections
JPCR 4:1010

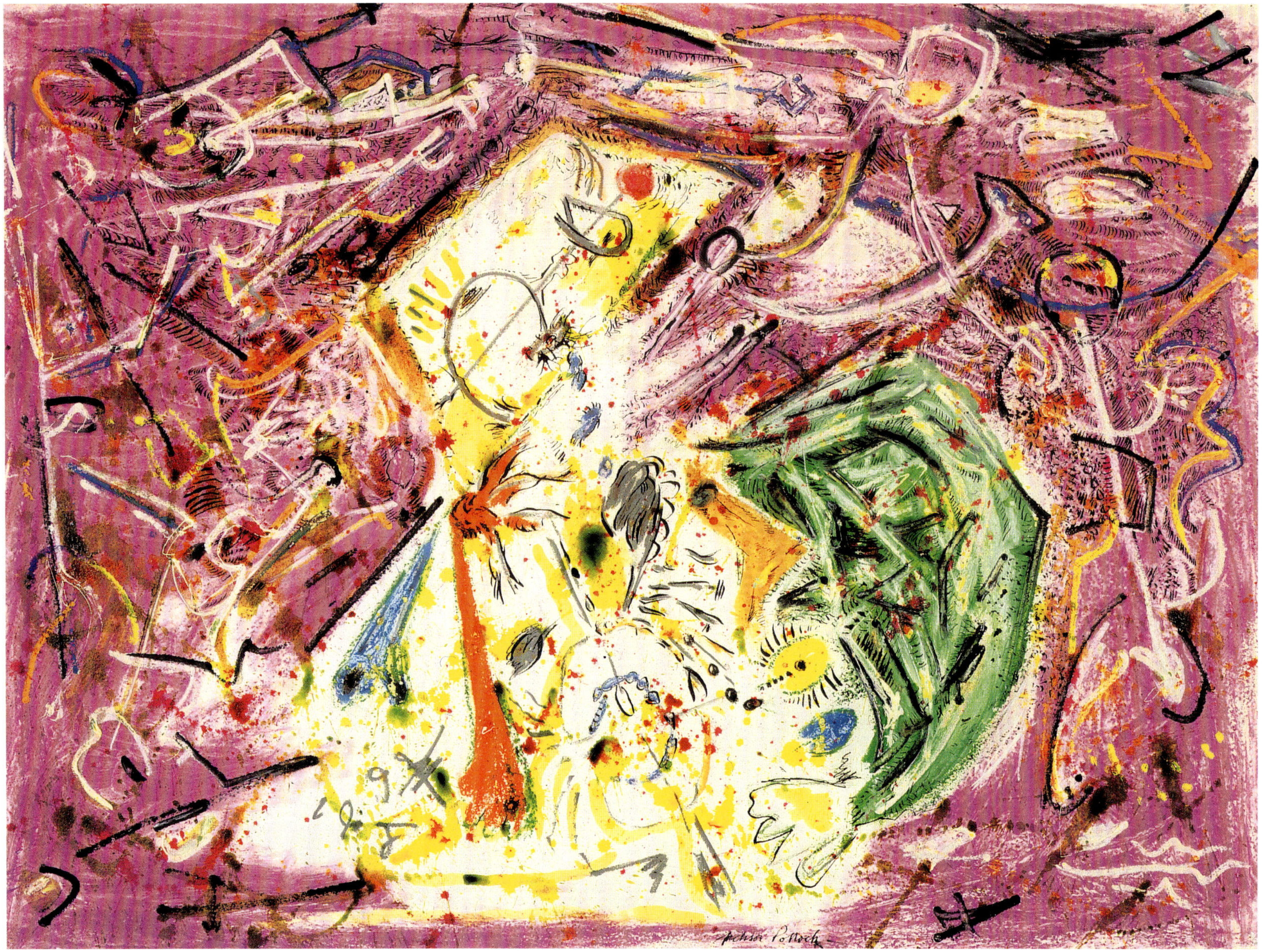

43
Untitled, ca. 1944 or 1946
Gouache, ink, and pastel on paper
$22^{5}/_{8}$ x $30^{5}/_{8}$ inches (57.5 x 77.8 cm)
Private collection, courtesy Jason McCoy, Inc., New York
Not in JPCR

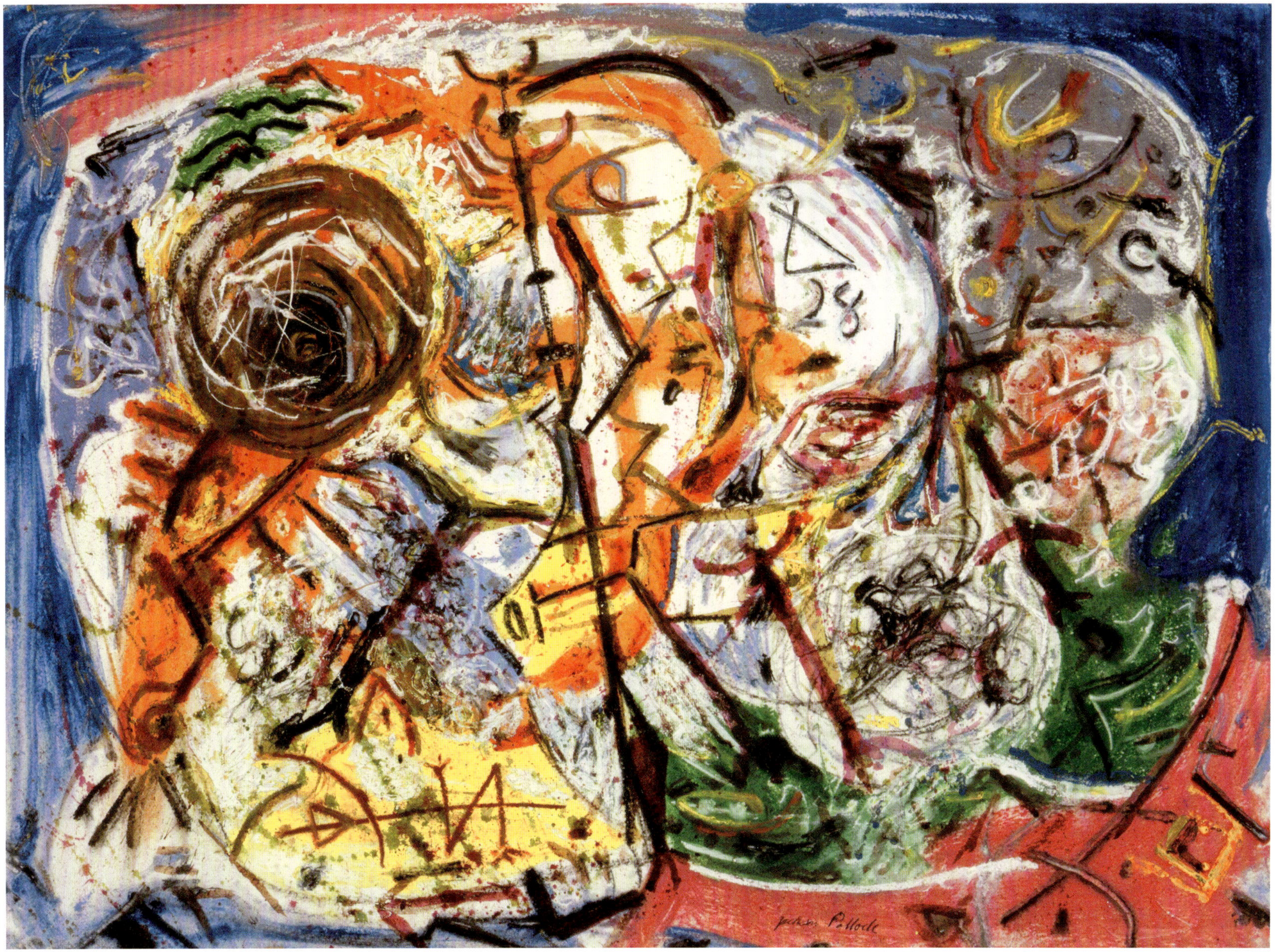

44
Untitled, ca. 1946
Gouache and pastel on paper
22 1/2 x 30 3/4 inches (57.2 x 78.1 cm)
Peggy Guggenheim Collection, Venice
JPCR 4:1008

45
Untitled, 1946
Spatter, pen and black and colored inks, gouache, wash, and sgraffito on paper
$22\,{}^{3}/_{8}$ x $30\,{}^{3}/_{8}$ inches (56.7 x 77 cm)
Art Gallery of Ontario, Toronto. Gift from the Volunteer Committee Fund, 1976
JPCR 4:1011

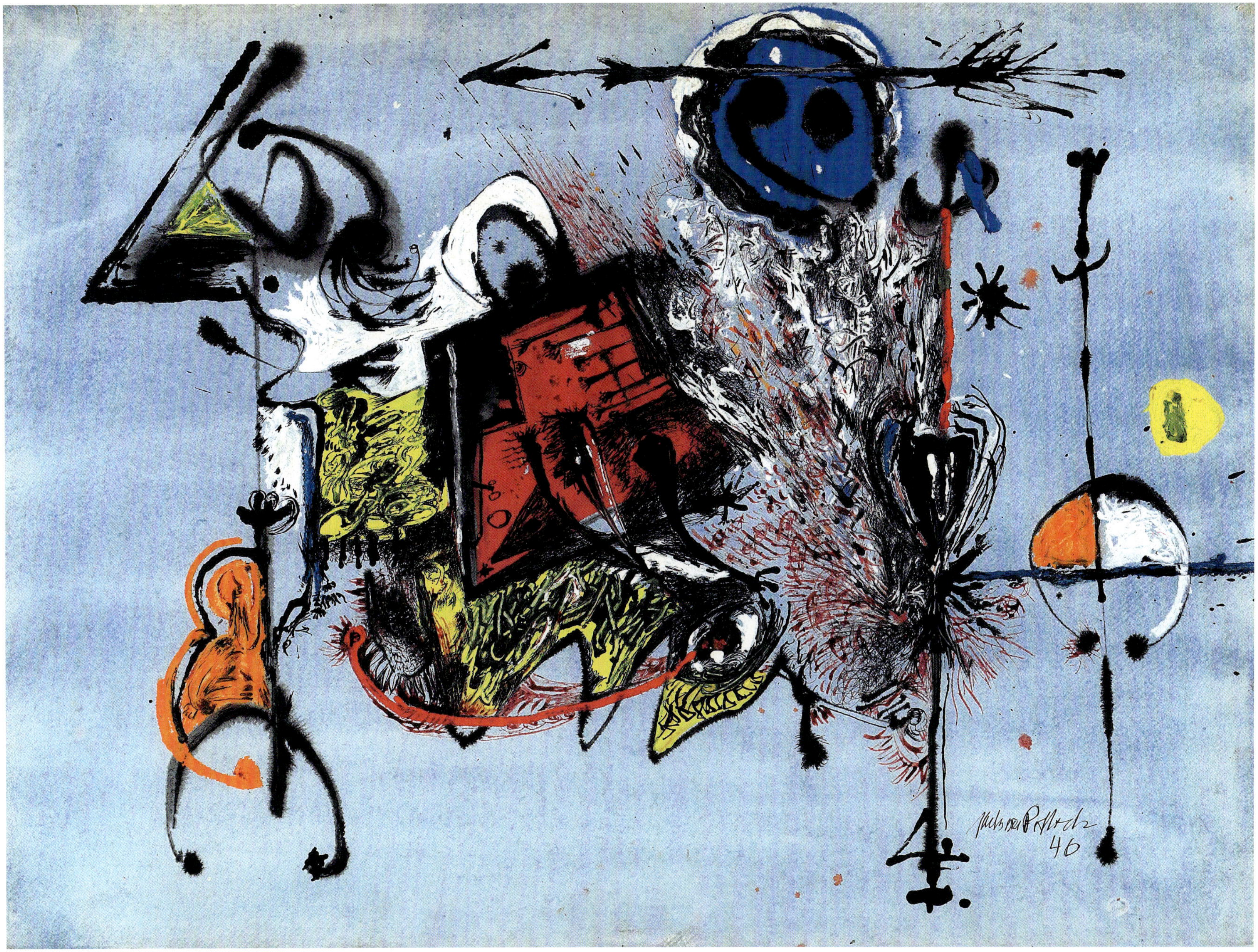

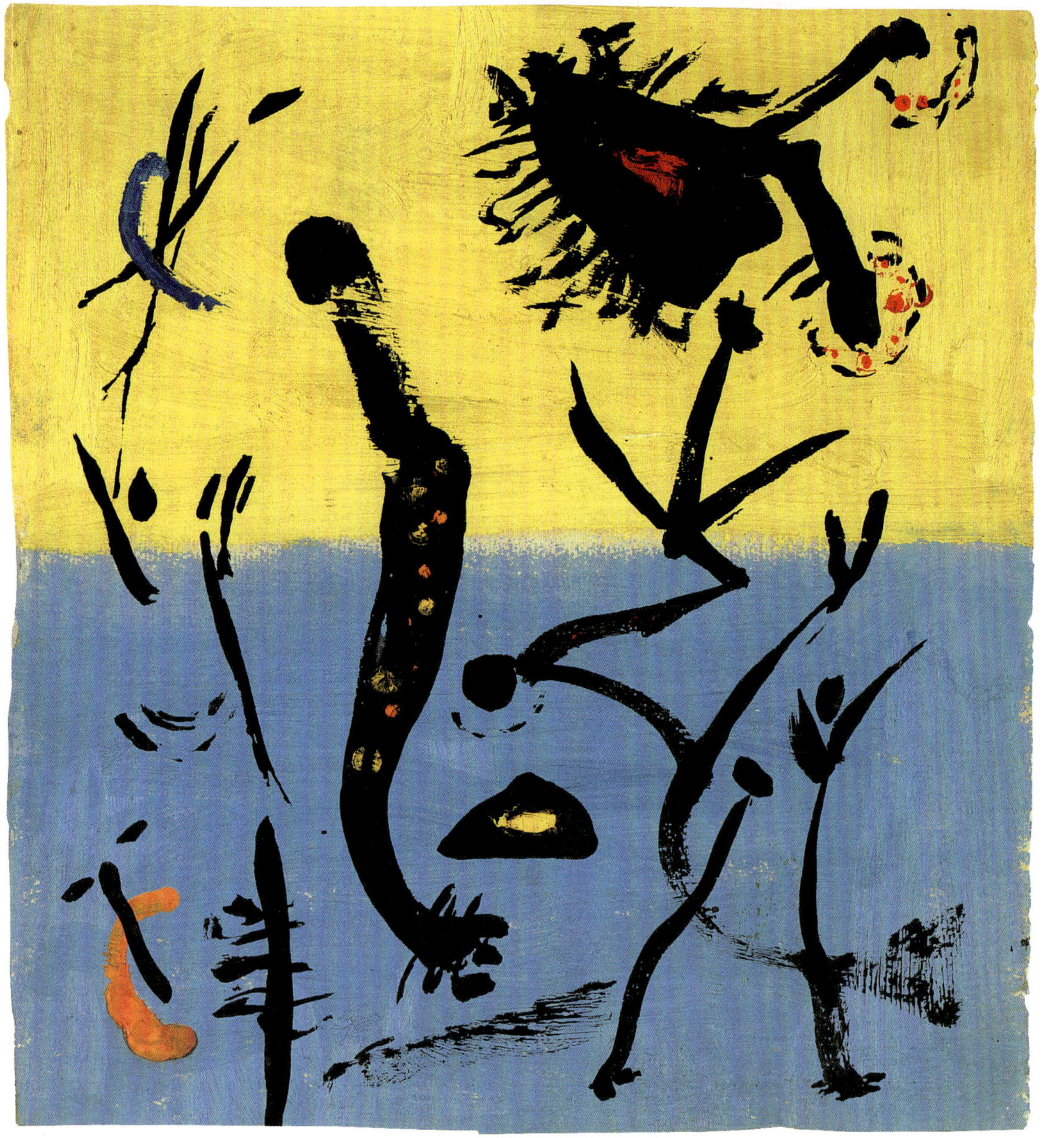

46
Untitled, ca. 1945
Oil and gouache on paper
10 1/4 x 9 1/2 inches (26 x 24 cm)
Private collection
JPCR 4:1002

47
Icarus, 1946
Gouache on cardboard
23 5/8 x 18 7/8 inches (60 x 48 cm)
Collection of Ulla and Heiner Pietzsch, Berlin
JPCR 4:996

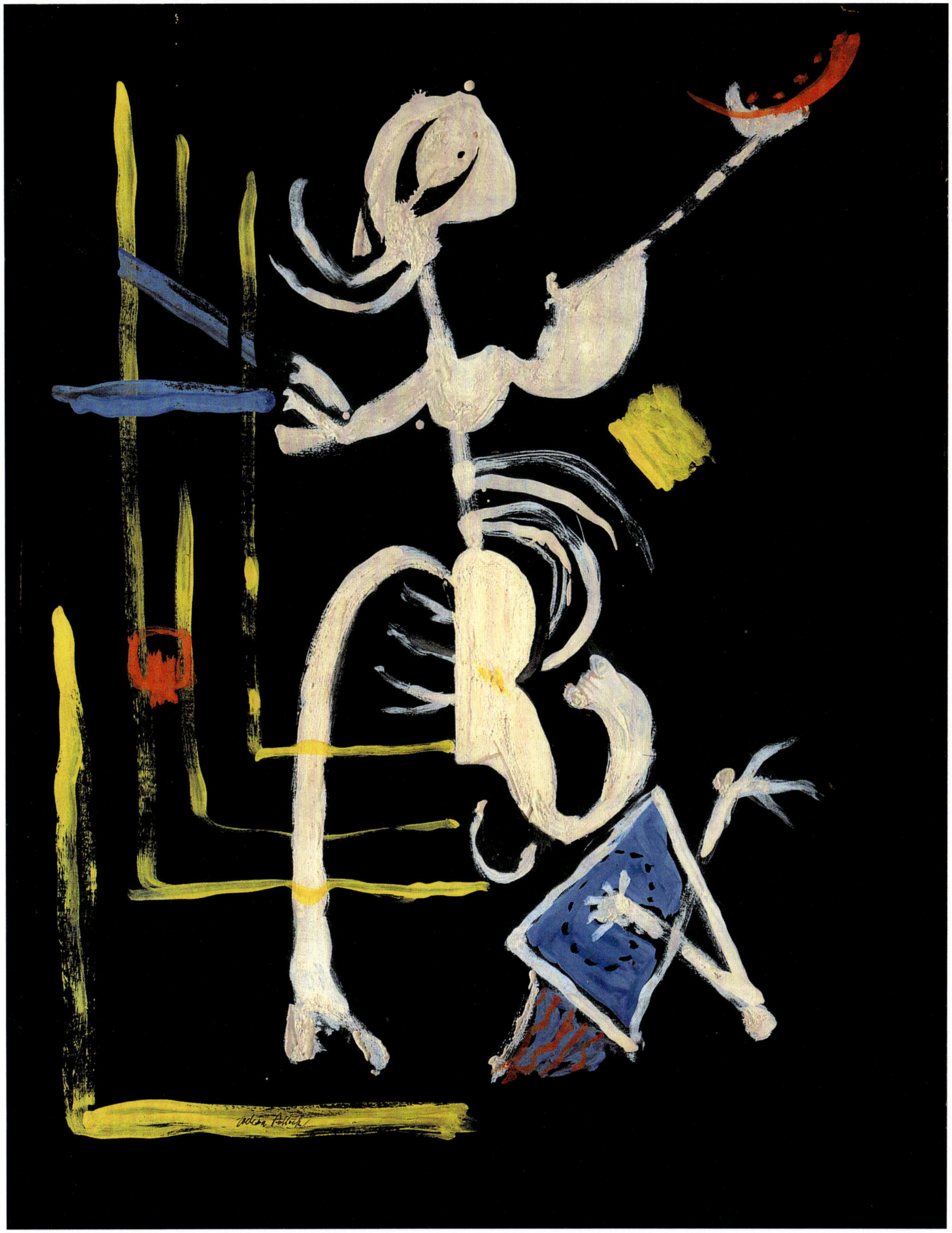

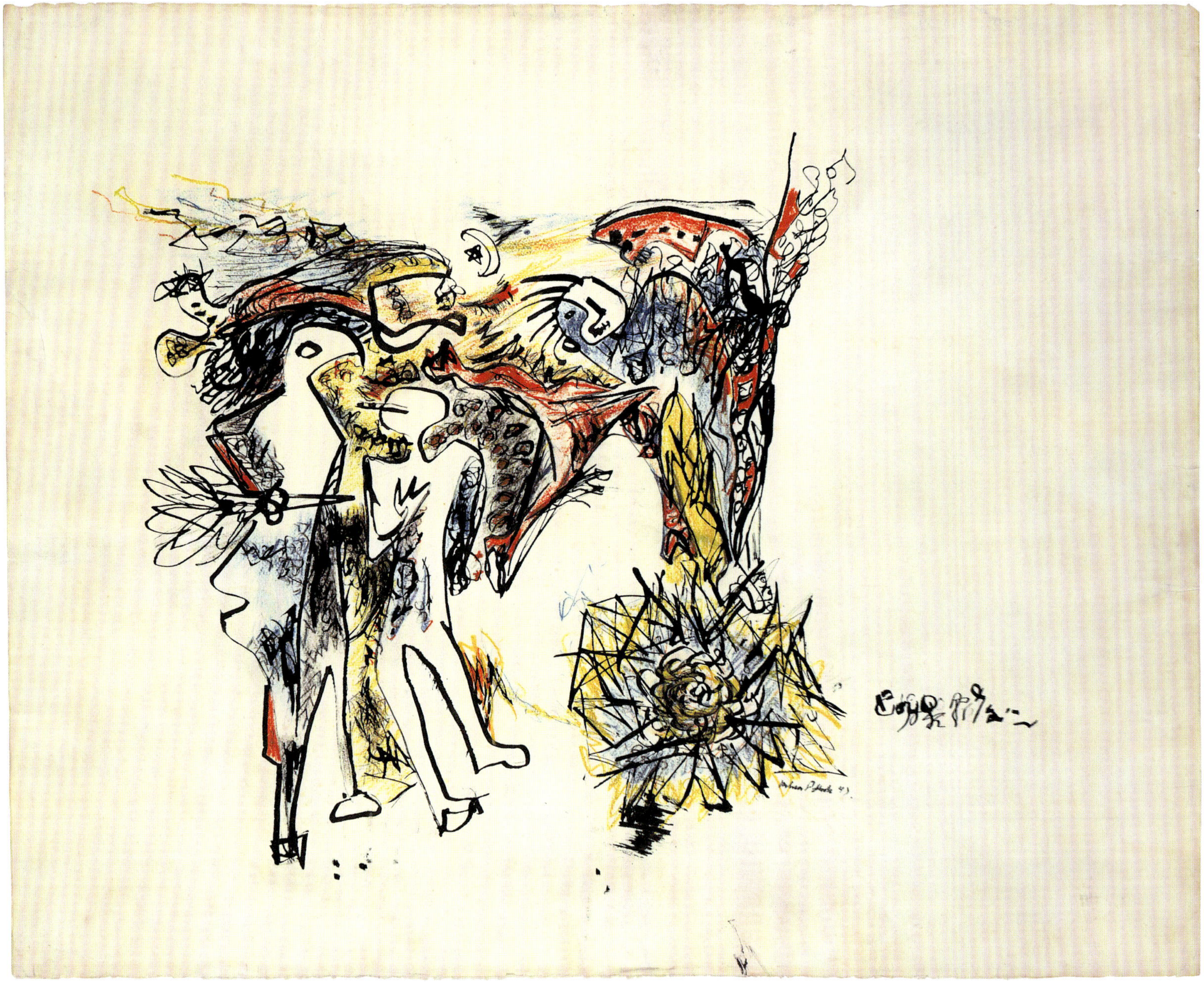

48
Untitled, 1947
Pen and ink and colored pencils on paper
$20^{5/8}$ x $26^{1/2}$ inches (52.4 x 66.6 cm)
The Metropolitan Museum of Art, New York. Gift of Lee Krasner Pollock, 1982 (1982.147.23)
JPCR 3:741

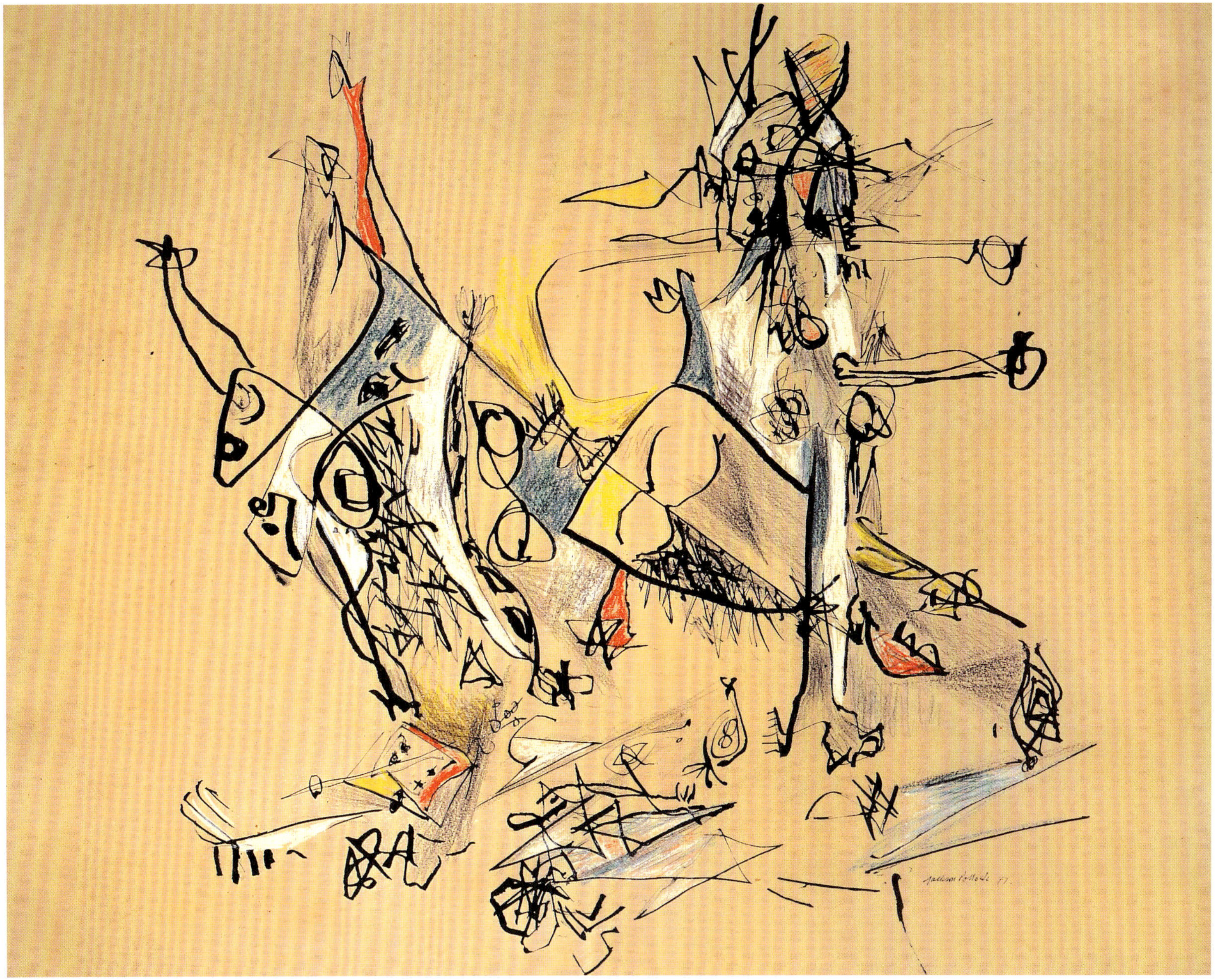

49
[Drawing on Brown Paper], 1947
Ink and crayon on paper
20 1/2 x 26 inches (52.1 x 66 cm)
Courtesy Herbert Palmer Gallery, Los Angeles
JPCR Supplement 13

50
Number 4, 1948: Gray and Red, 1948
Enamel on paper
22 5/8 x 30 7/8 inches (57.5 x 78.4 cm)
Frederick R. Weisman Foundation, Los Angeles
JPCR 2:202

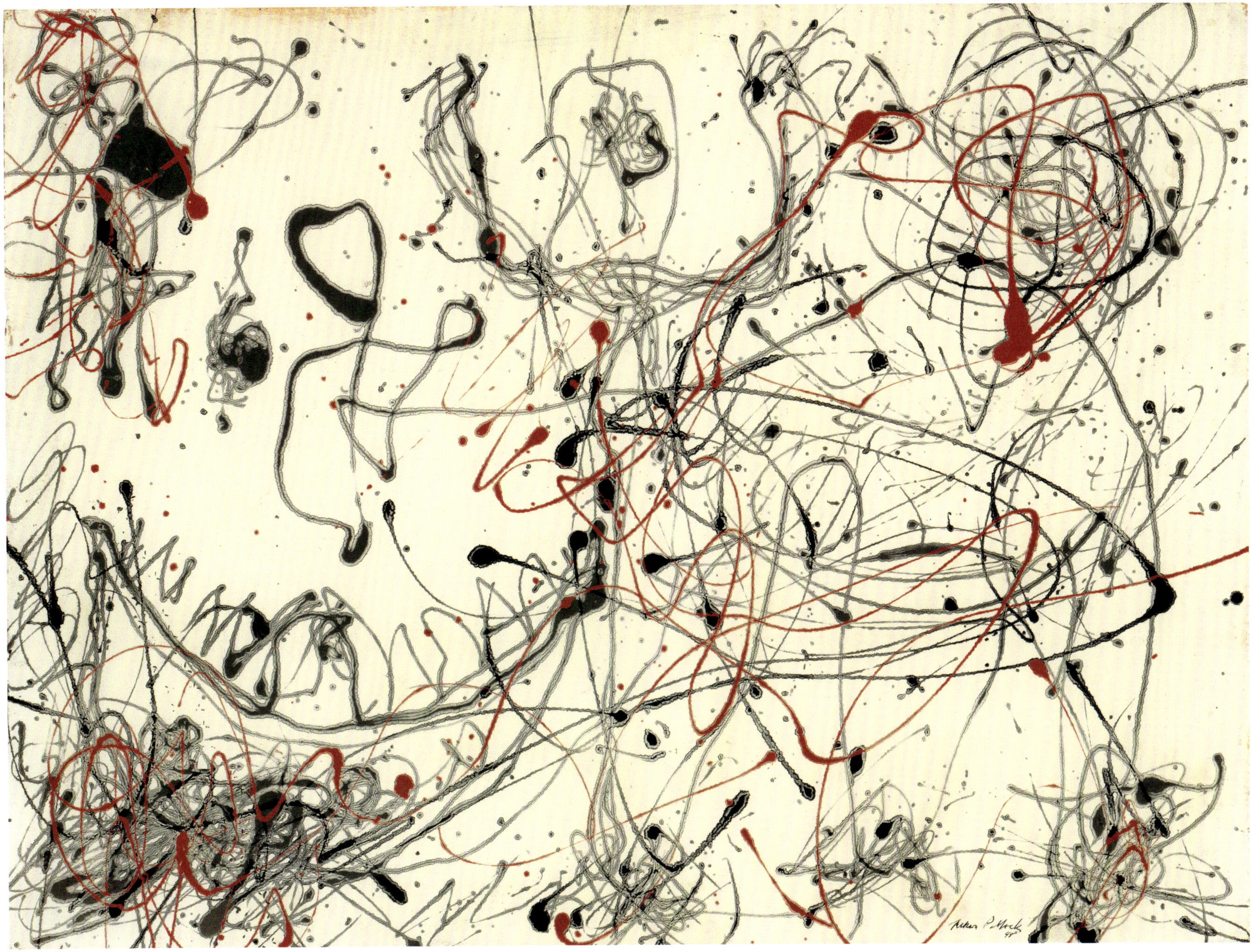

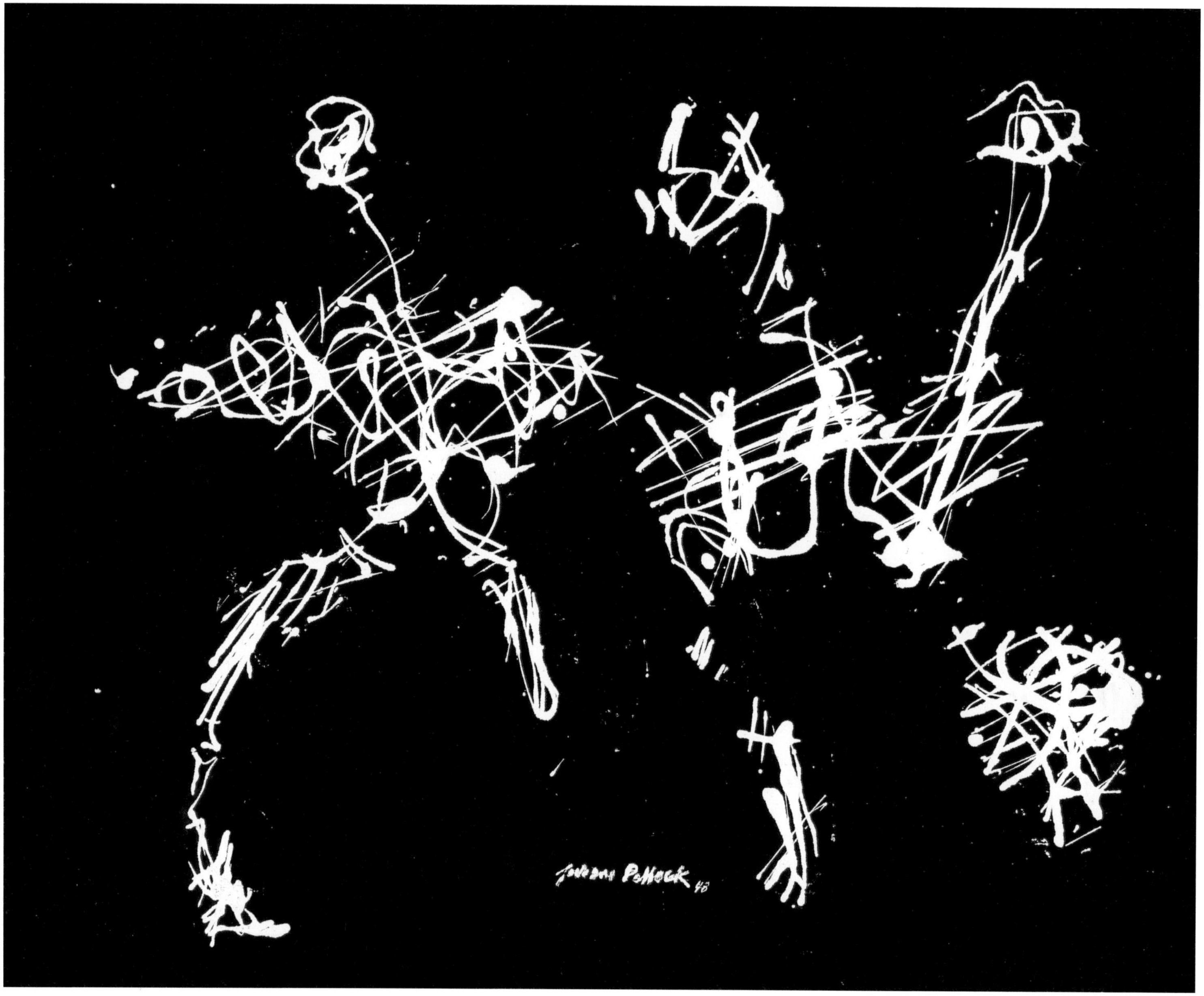

51
Triad, 1948
Oil and enamel on paper mounted on composition board
20 1/2 x 25 3/4 inches (52.1 x 65.4 cm)
Collection of Art Enterprises Ltd., Chicago
JPCR 2:198

52
Number 22A, 1948, 1948
Enamel on paper mounted on composition board
22 1/2 x 30 5/8 inches (57.2 x 77.8 cm)
The Museum of Fine Arts, Houston; Museum purchase with funds provided by the Brown Foundation Accessions Endowment Fund
JPCR 2:201

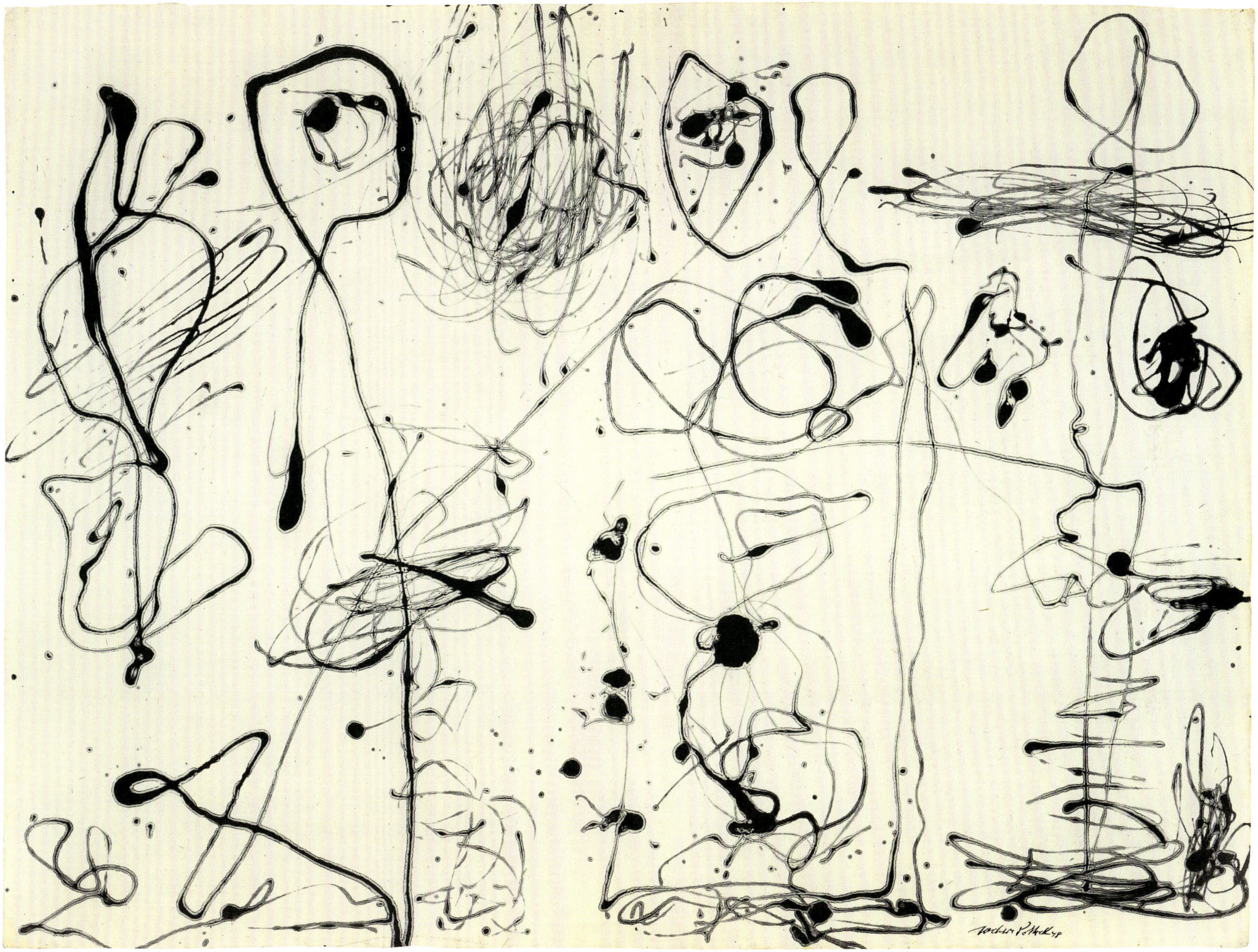

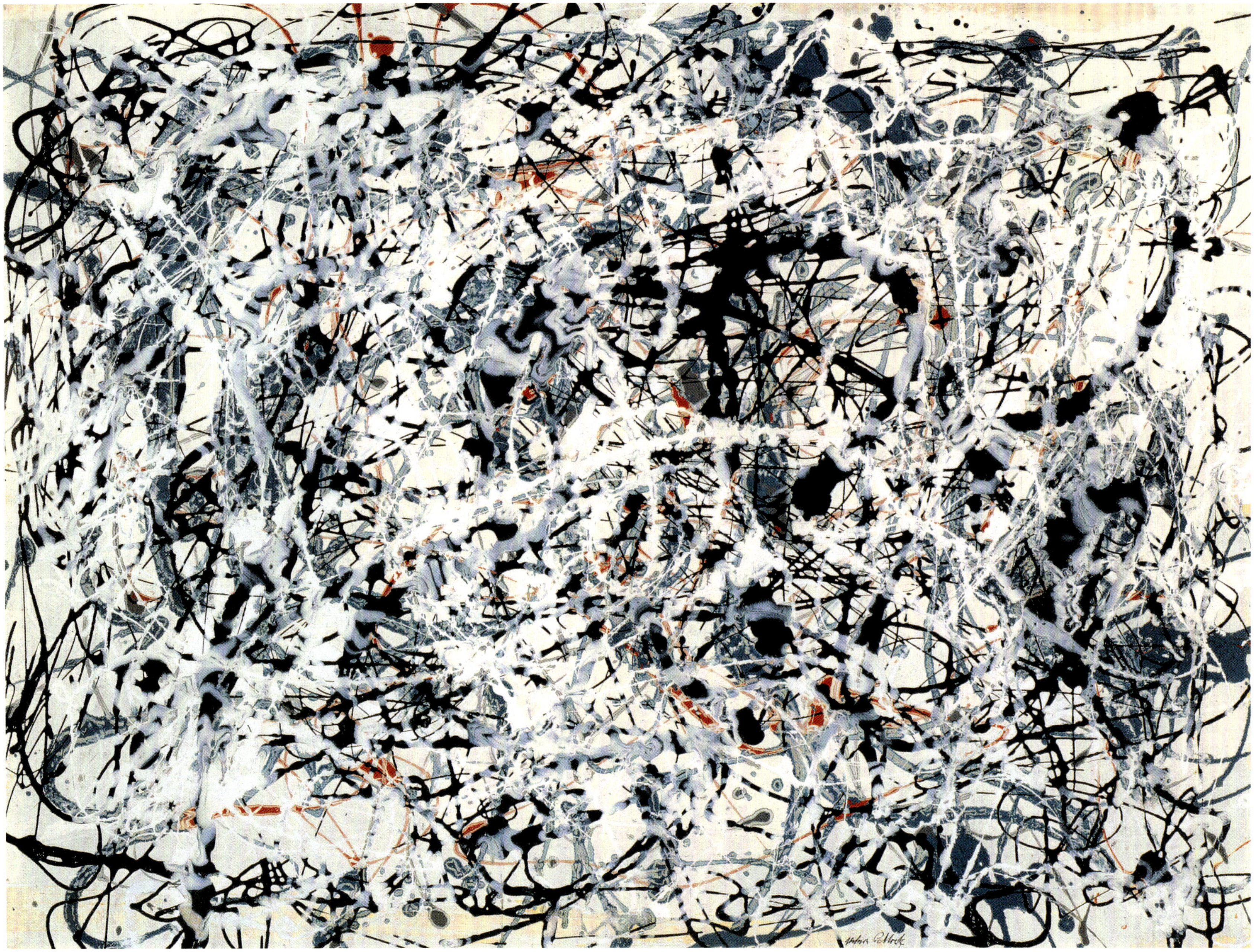

53
Composition (White, Black, Blue, and Red on White), 1948
Enamel on paper mounted on composition board
22 5/8 x 30 1/2 inches (57.5 x 77.5 cm)
New Orleans Museum of Art. Bequest of Victor K. Kiam (77.300)
JPCR 2:189

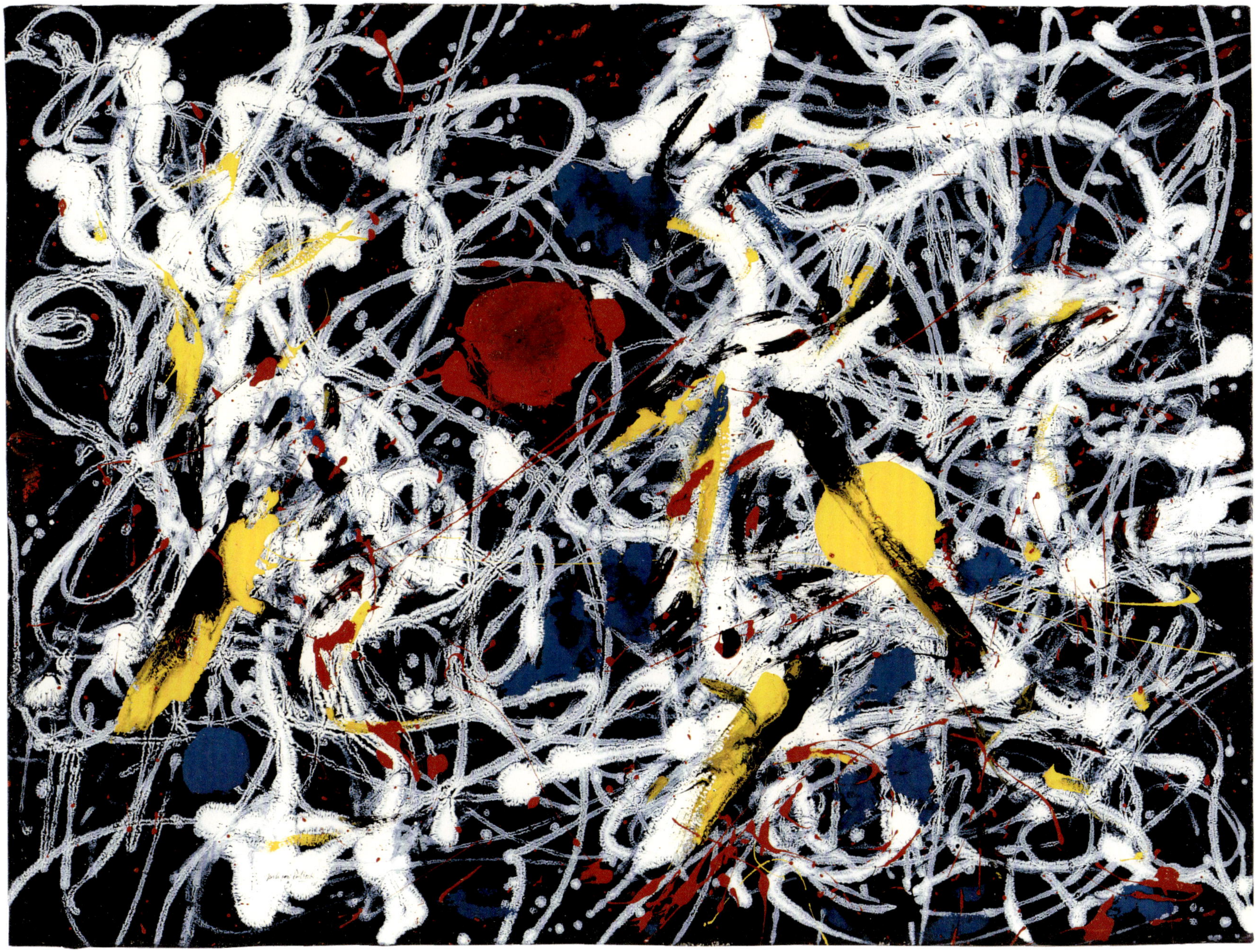

54
Number 15, 1948: Red, Gray, White, Yellow, 1948
Enamel on paper
$22^{1}/_{4}$ x $30^{1}/_{2}$ inches (56.5 x 77.5 cm)
Virginia Museum of Fine Arts, Richmond. Gift of Mr. Arthur S. Brinkley Jr.
JPCR 2:196

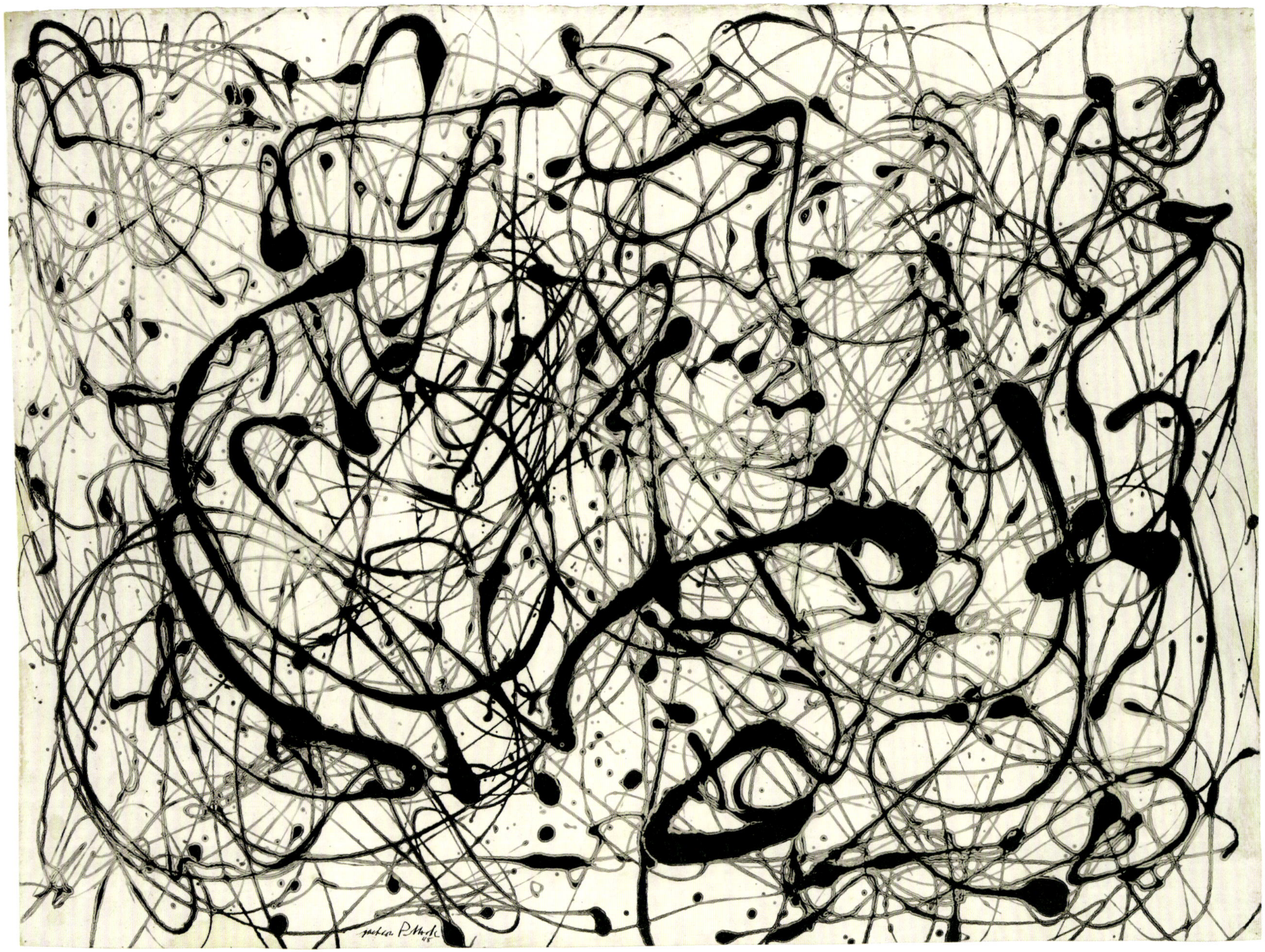

55
Number 14, 1948, 1948
Enamel on paper
22 3/4 x 31 inches (57.8 x 78.7 cm)
Yale University Art Gallery, New Haven, Connecticut.
The Katherine Ordway Collection (1980.13.74)
JPCR 2:204

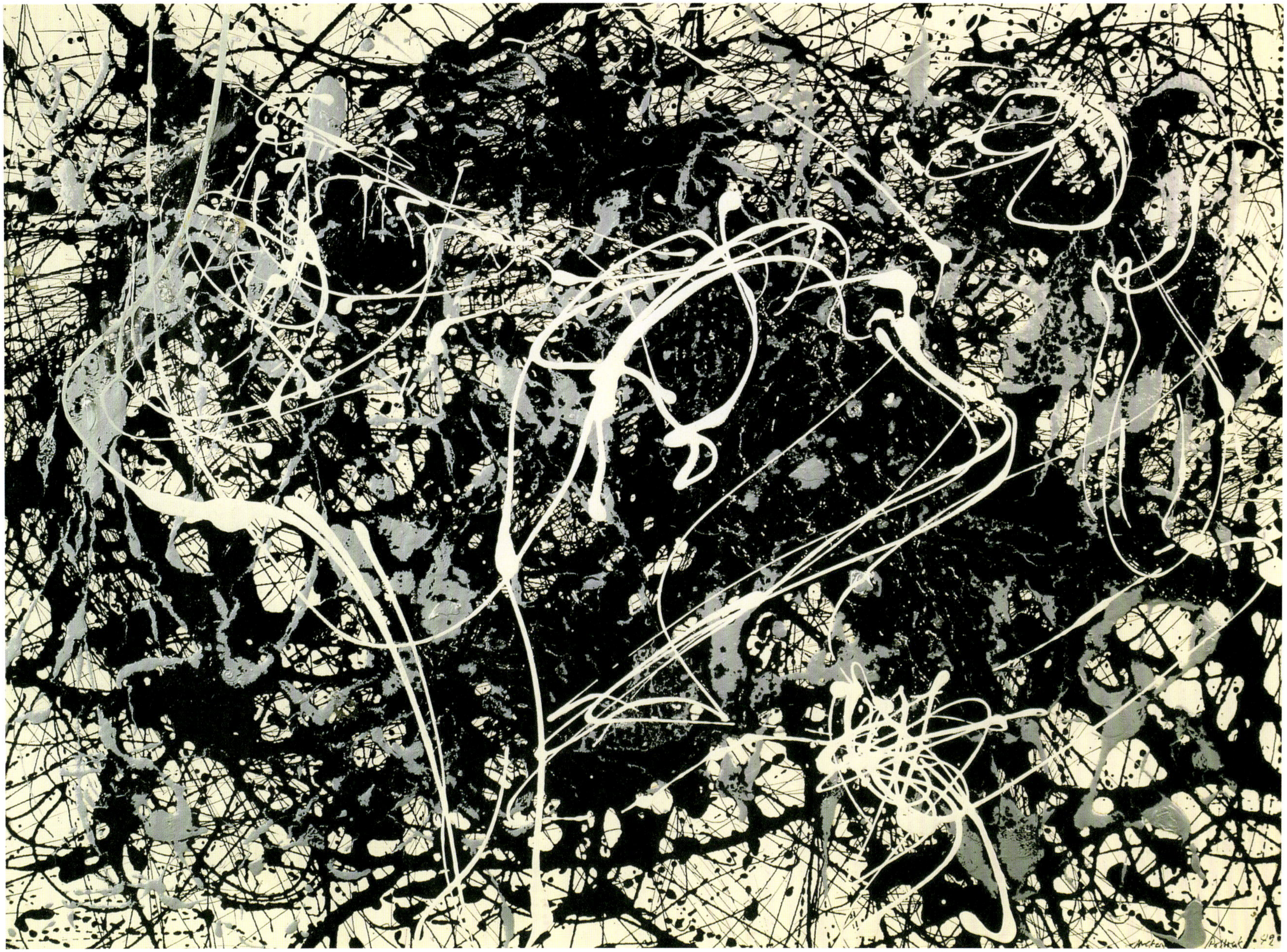

56
Number 33, 1949, 1949
Enamel and aluminum paint on paper mounted on composition board
$22^1/_2$ x 31 inches (57.2 x 78.7 cm)
Private collection
JPCR 2:234

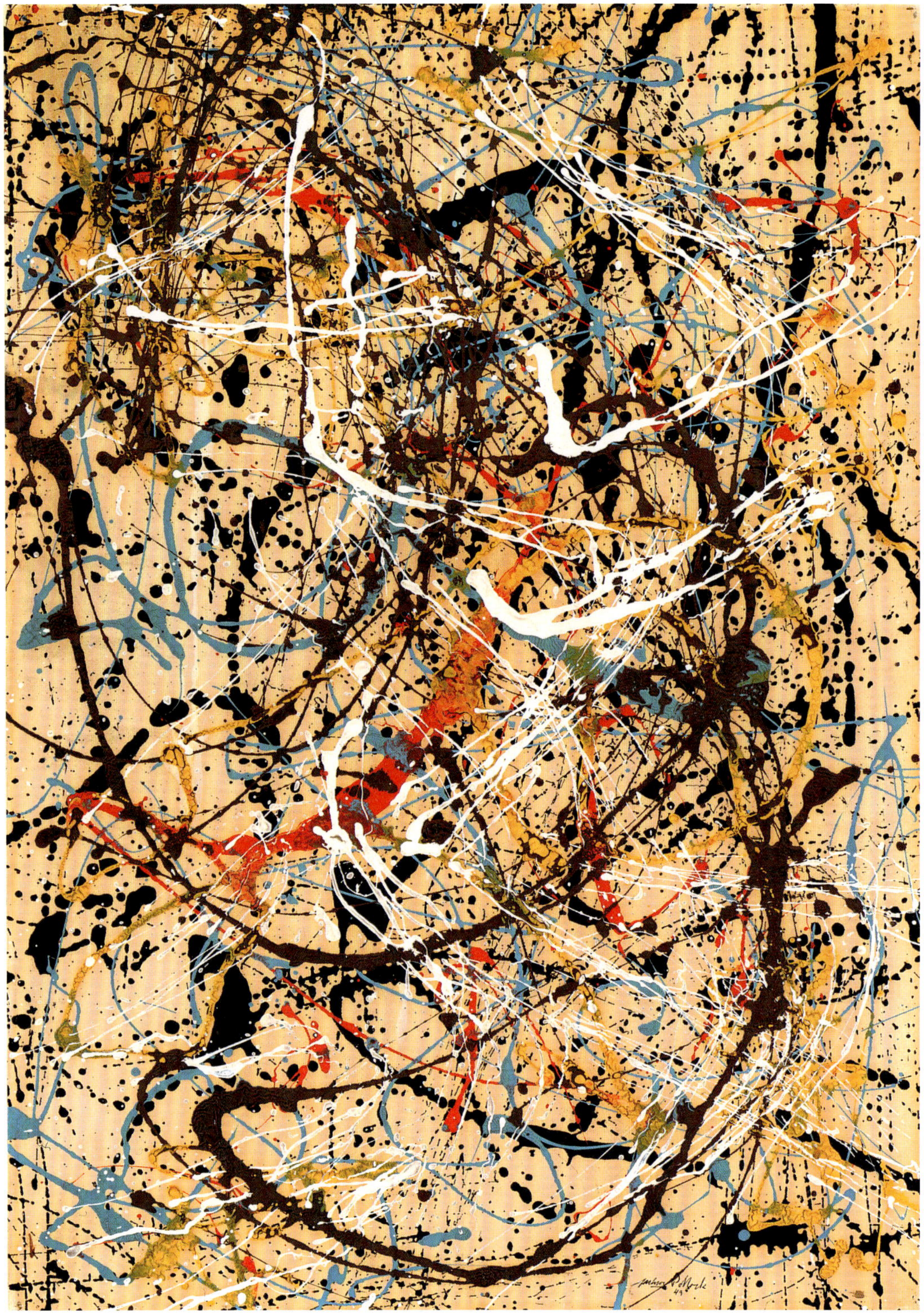

57
Number 20, 1949, 1949
Enamel on paper mounted on composition board
28 x 20 inches (71.1 x 50.8 cm)
Mr. and Mrs. Jon Shirley, Seattle. Partial and promised gift to Seattle Art Museum
JPCR 2:230

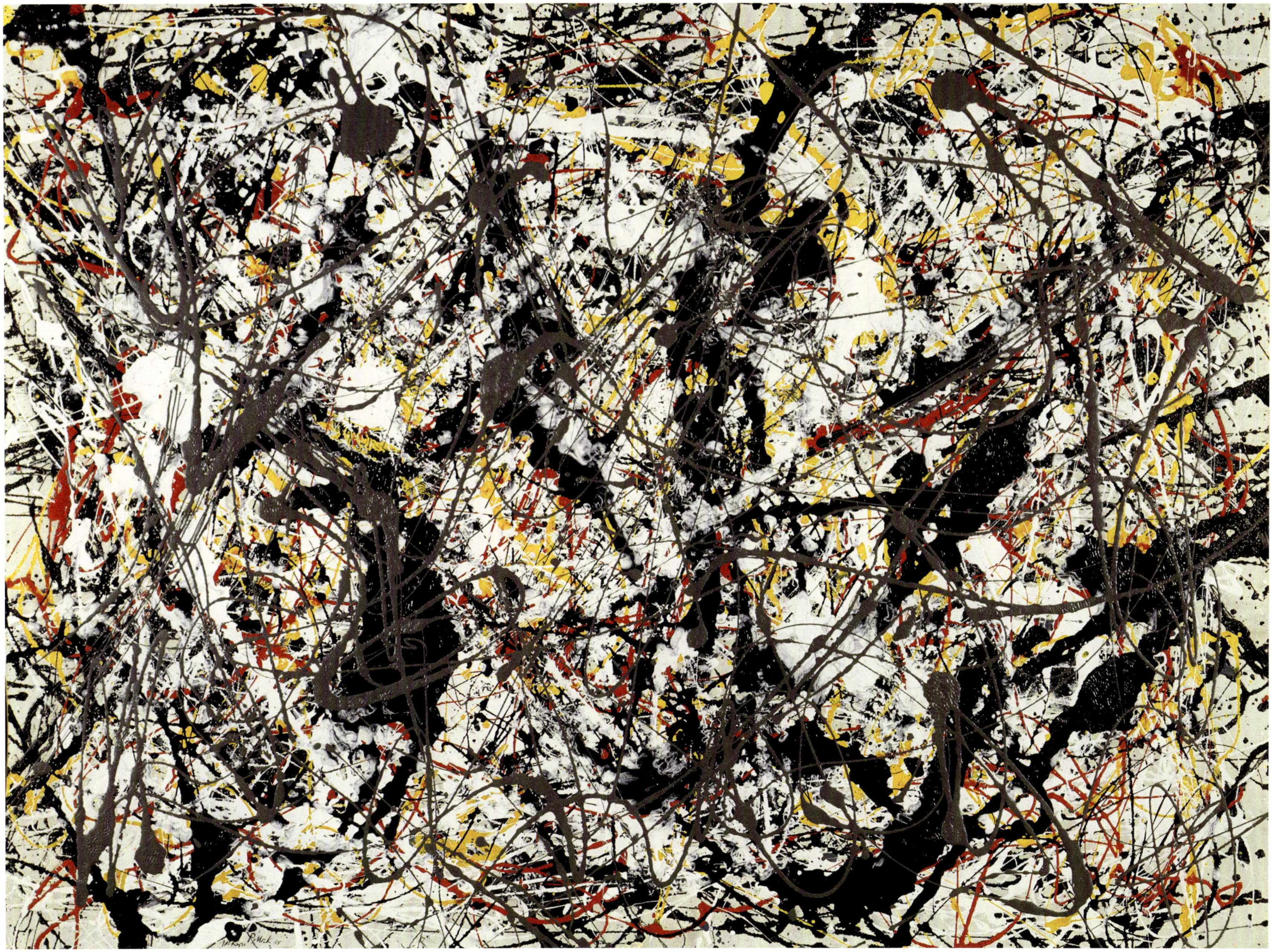

58
[Silver over Black, White, Yellow, and Red], 1948
Enamel on paper mounted on canvas
21 x 31 1/2 inches (61 x 80 cm)
Musée national d'art moderne, Centre Georges Pompidou, Paris
JPCR 2:192

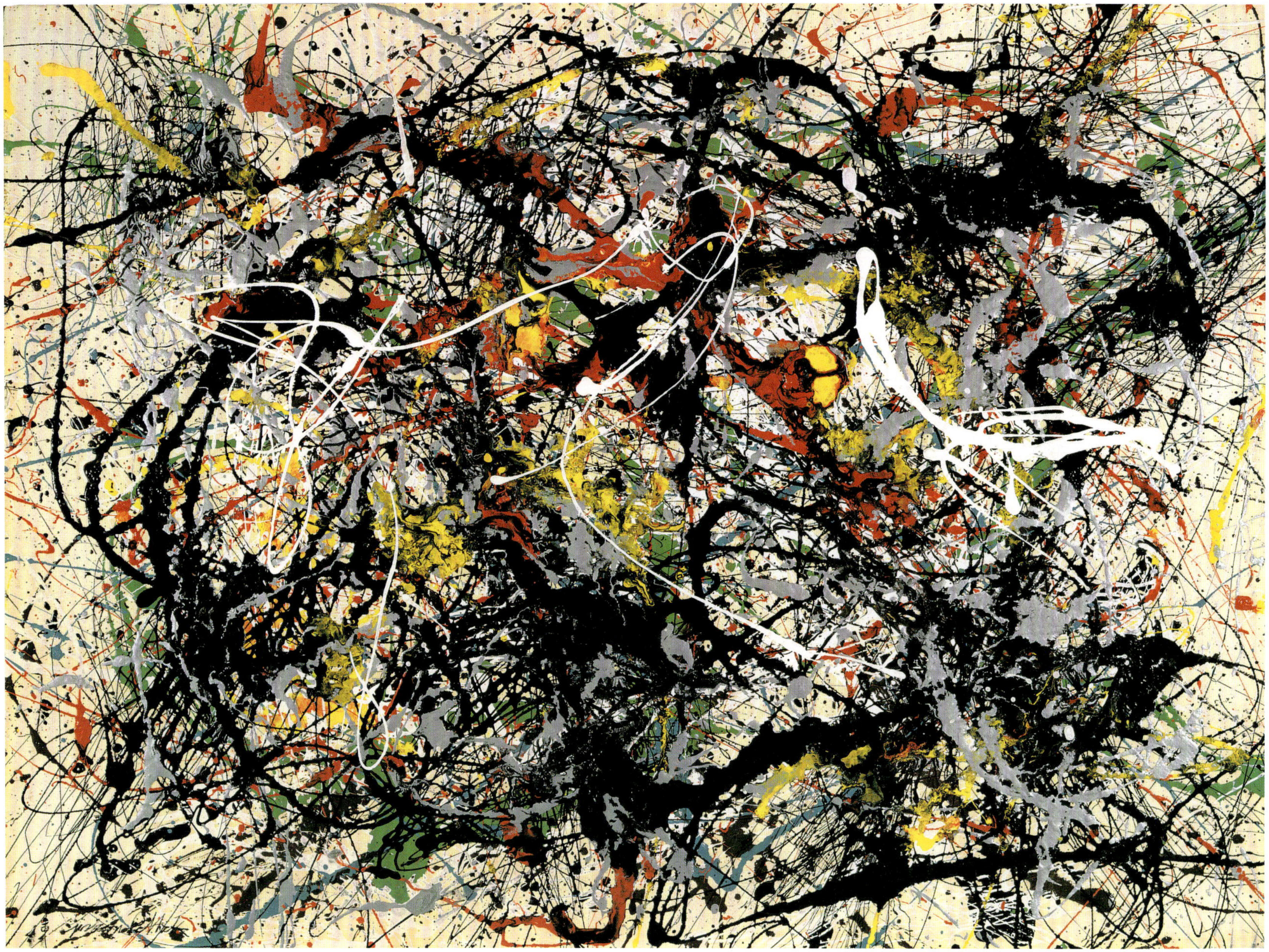

59
Number 34, 1949, 1949
Enamel on paper mounted on composition board
22 x 30½ inches (55.9 x 77.5 cm)
Munson-Williams-Proctor Arts Institute, Utica, New York.
Edward W. Root Bequest, 1961 (57.206)
JPCR 2:235

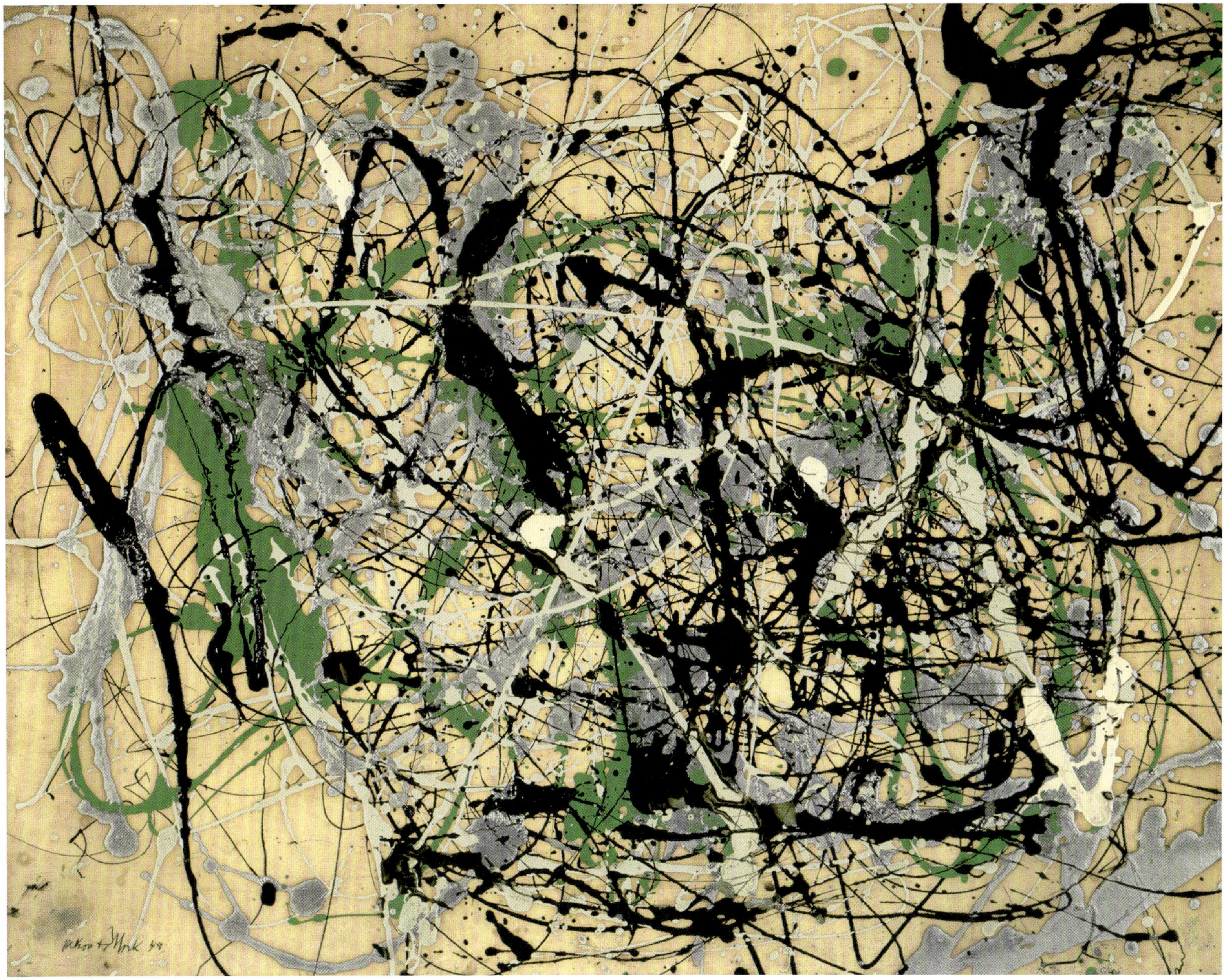

60
Number 17, 1949, 1949
Enamel and aluminum paint on paper mounted on composition board
22 1/2 x 28 1/2 inches (57.2 x 72.4 cm)
Private collection
JPCR 2:243

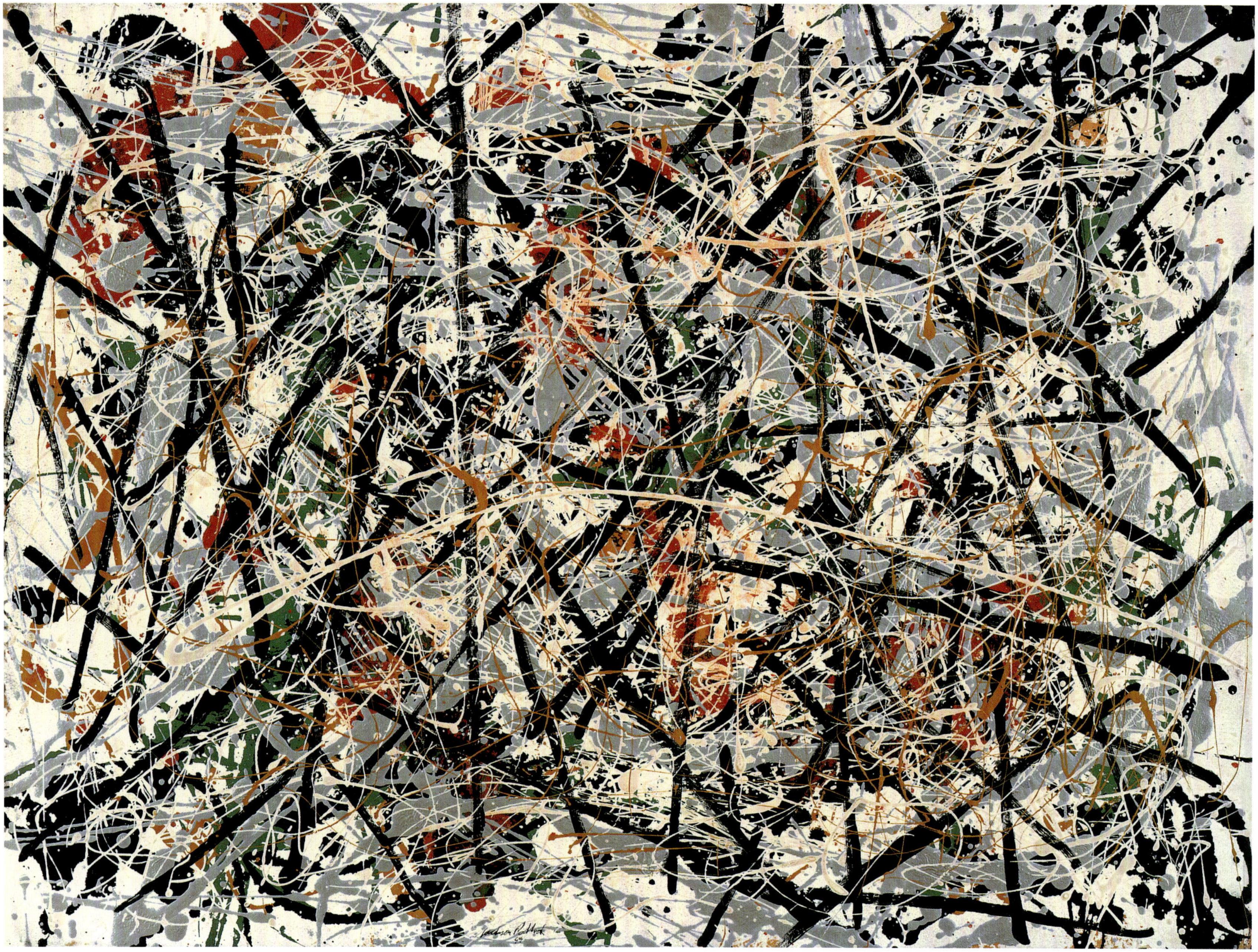

61
Number 13, 1949, 1949
Oil, enamel, and aluminum paint on paper mounted on composition board
22 3/4 x 30 7/8 inches (57.8 x 78.4 cm)
Collection of Samuel and Ronnie Heyman, New York
JPCR 2:231

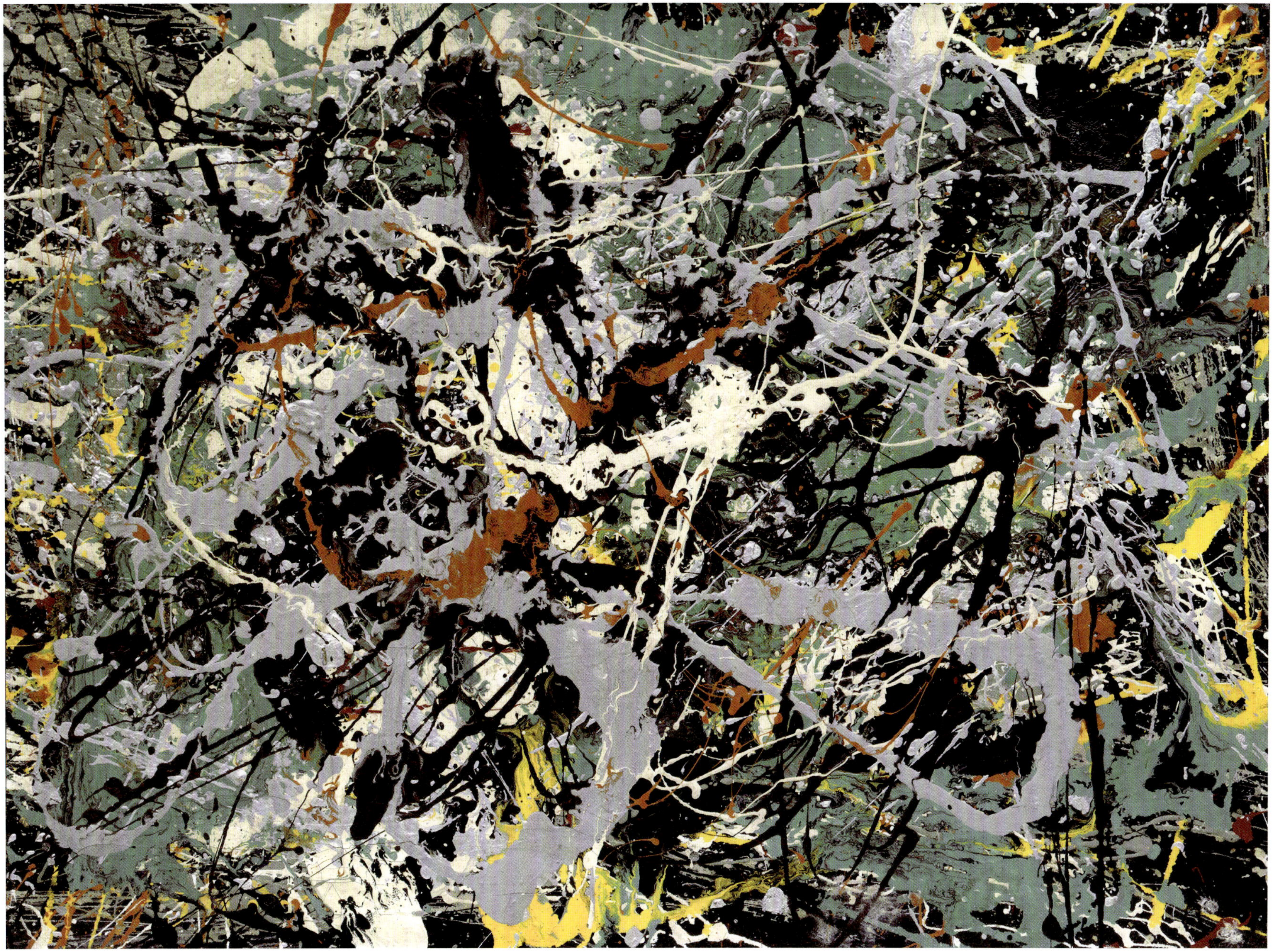

62
Untitled *(Green Silver)*, ca. 1949
Enamel and aluminum paint on paper mounted on canvas
22 3/4 x 30 3/4 inches (57.8 x 78.1 cm)
Solomon R. Guggenheim Museum, New York. Bequest of Barbara Slifka (2004.63)
JPCR 2:238

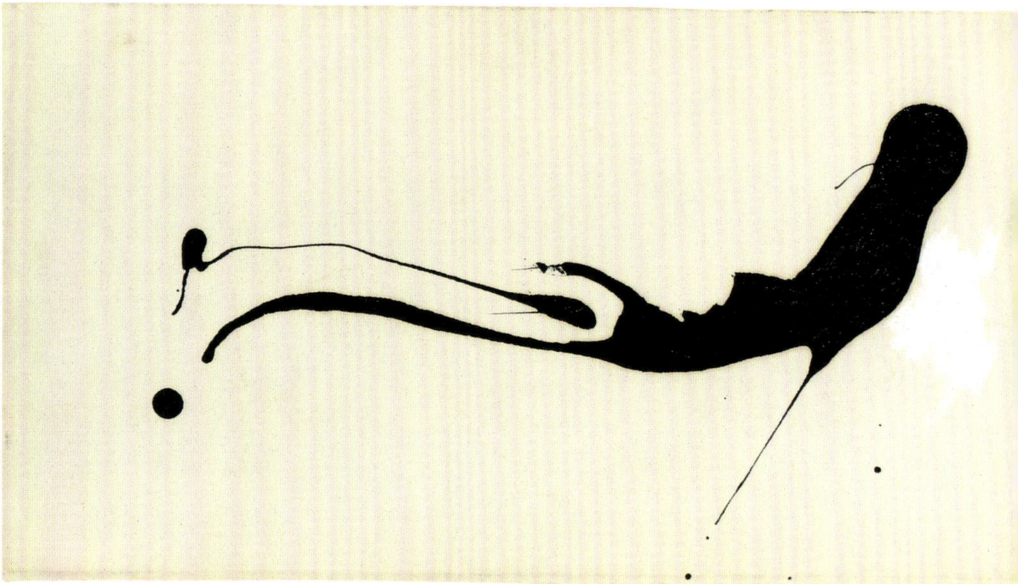

63
Untitled, ca. 1950
Enamel on paper
$11^{1}/_{8}$ x $59^{1}/_{8}$ inches (28.3 x 150.3 cm)
Staatsgalerie Stuttgart
JPCR 3:797

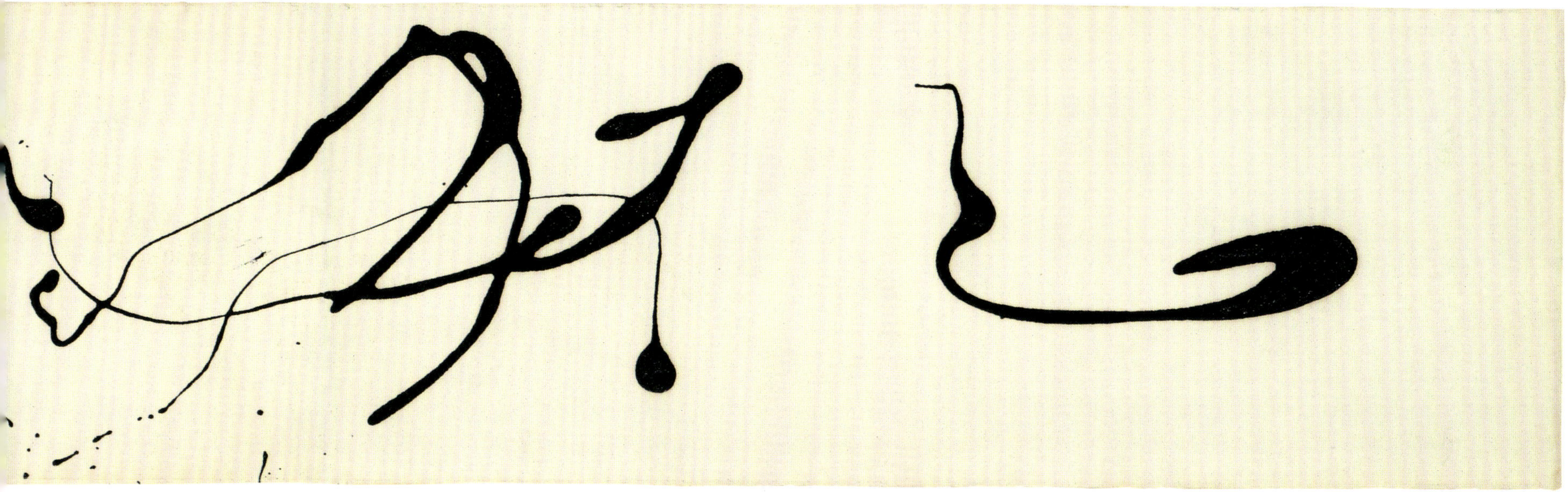

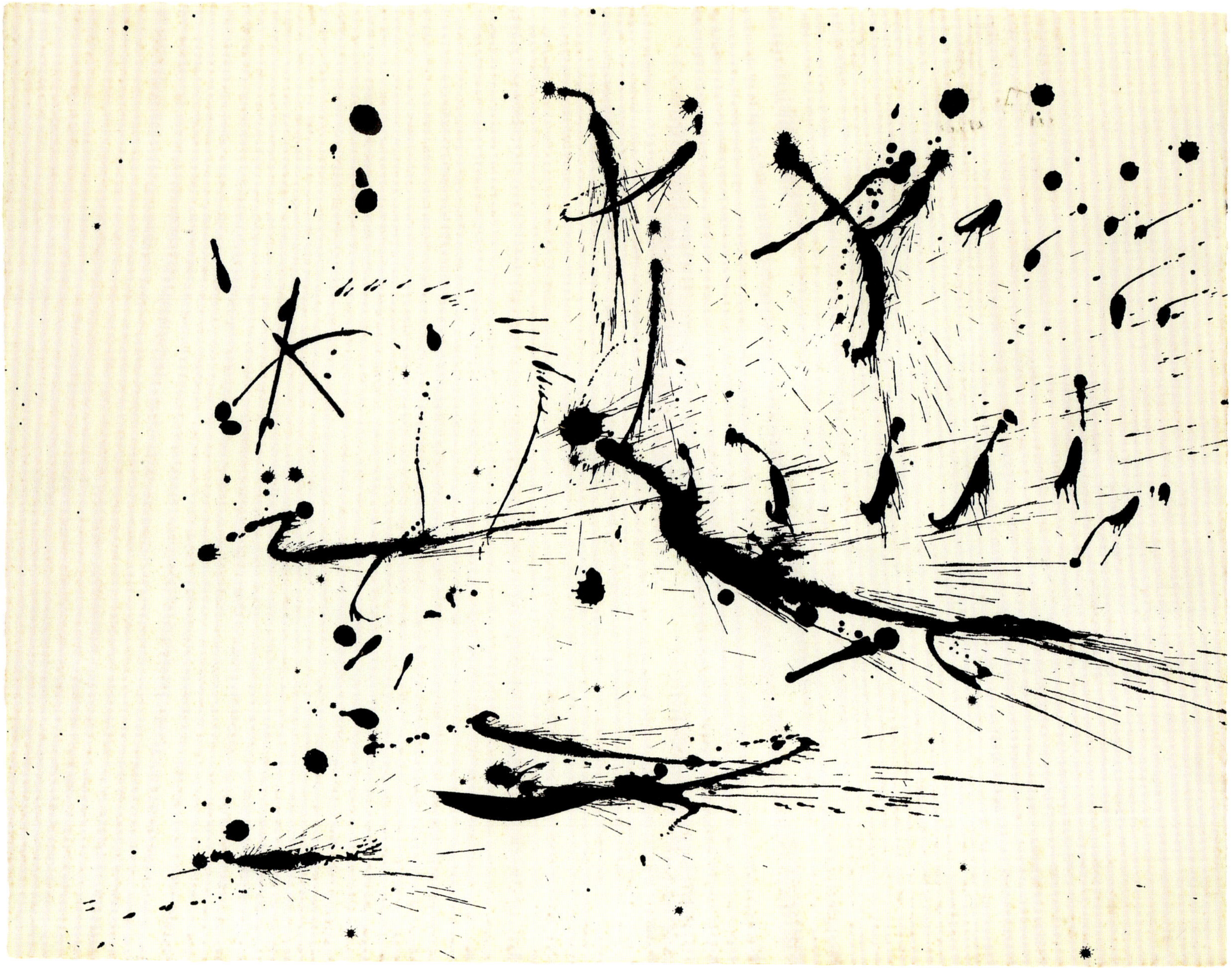

64
Untitled, ca. 1950
Ink on paper
$18^7/_8$ x $24^3/_4$ inches (47.9 x 62.9 cm)
The Metropolitan Museum of Modern Art, New York.
Gift of Lee Krasner Pollock, 1982 (1982.147.28)
JPCR 3:792

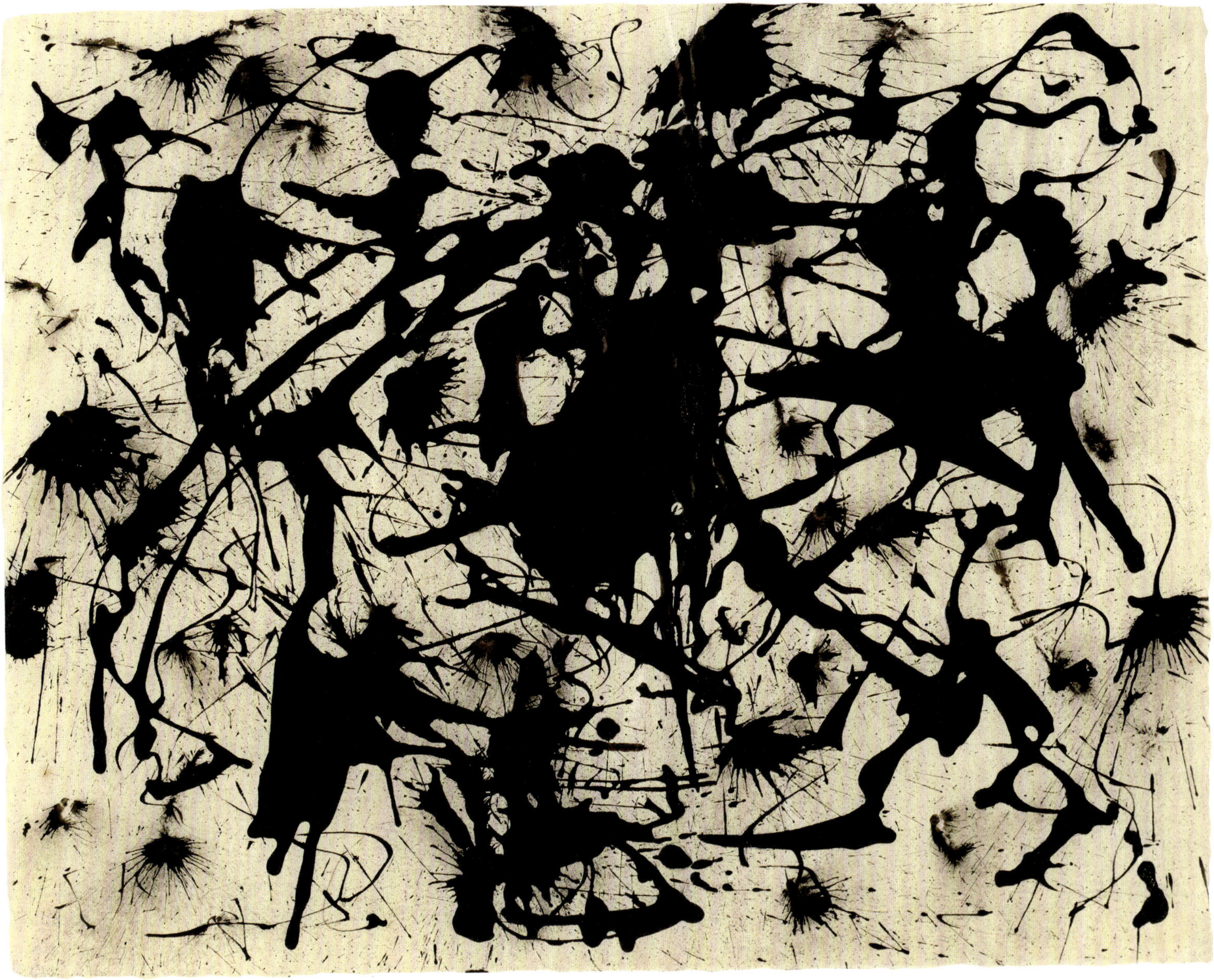

65
Untitled, ca. 1950
Ink on paper
17 3/8 x 22 1/4 inches (44 x 56.5 cm)
The Museum of Modern Art, New York. Gift of Mr. and Mrs. Ronald Lauder in honor of Eliza Parkinson Cobb (448.1982)
JPCR 3:801

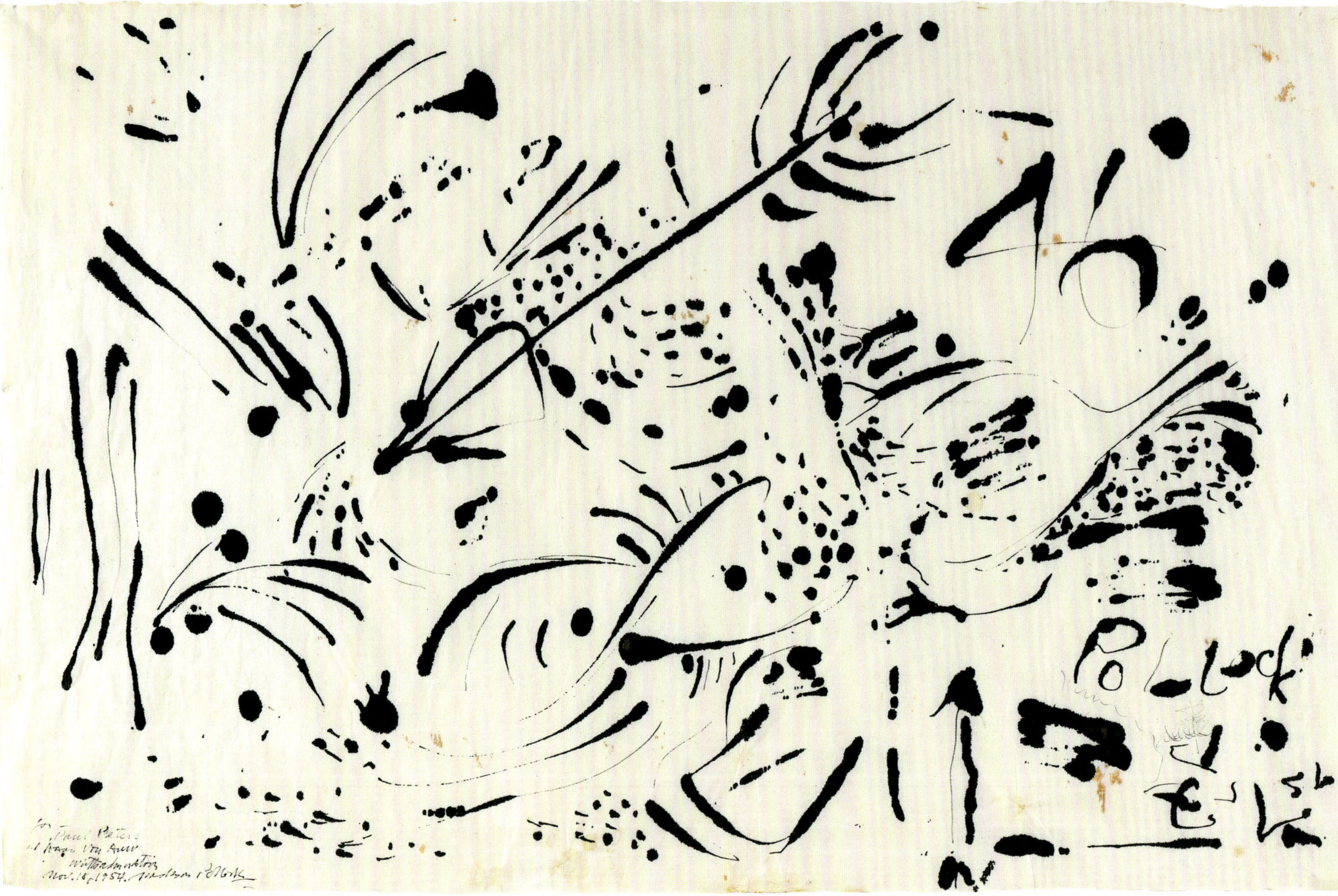

66
Untitled, ca. 1951
Ink and watercolor on Japanese paper
25 x 30 1/4 inches (63.5 x 76.8 cm)
The Menil Collection, Houston
JPCR 3:812

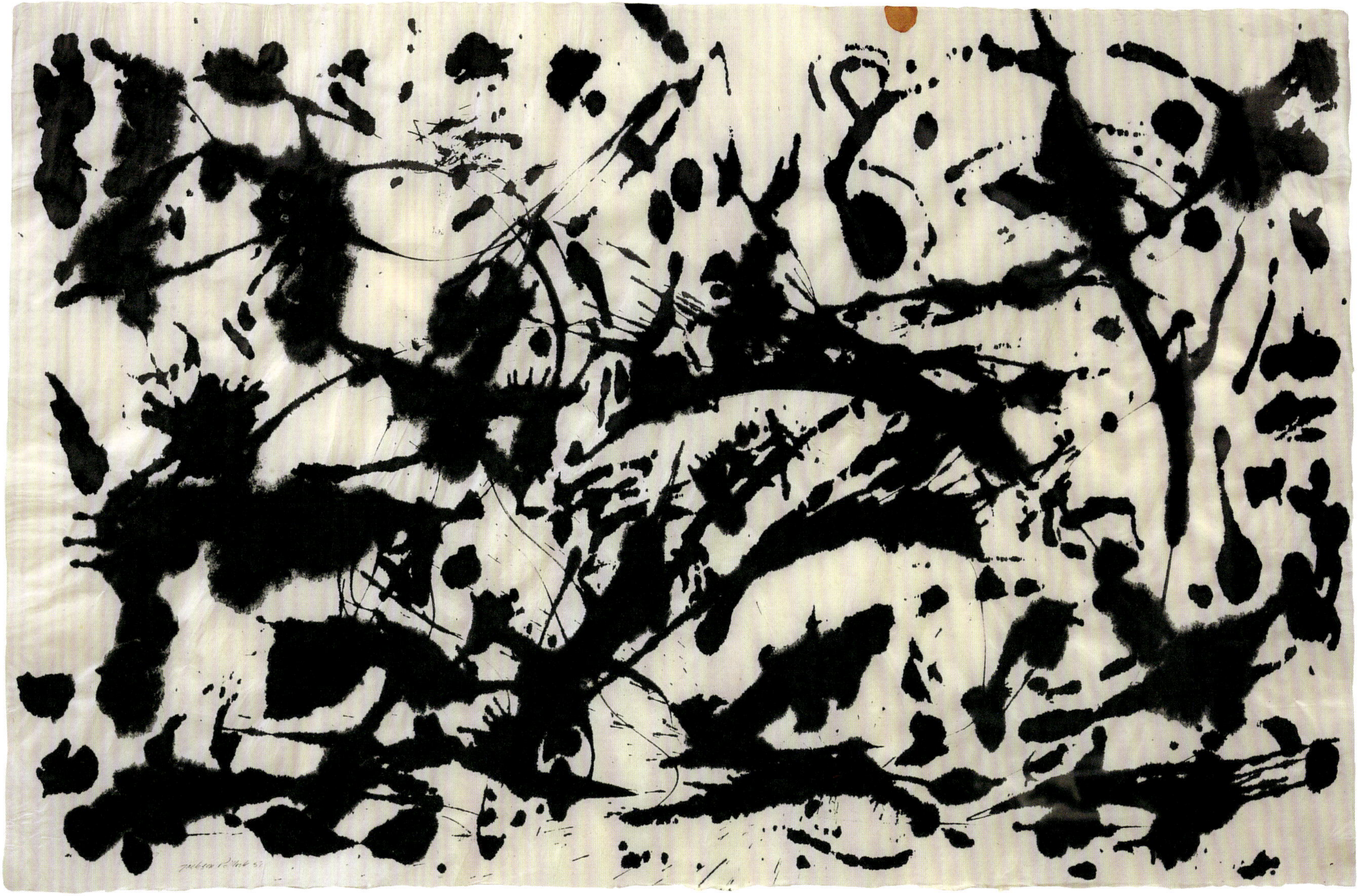

67
Number 3, 1951, 1951
Ink on Japanese paper
24 1/2 x 38 3/4 inches (62.2 x 98.4 cm)

Washington Art Consortium: Henry Art Gallery, University of Washington, Seattle; Museum of Art, Washington State University, Pullman; Northwest Museum of Arts and Culture, Spokane; Seattle Art Museum; Tacoma Art Museum; Western Gallery, Western Washington University, Bellingham; Whatcom Museum of History and Art, Bellingham
JPCR 3:818

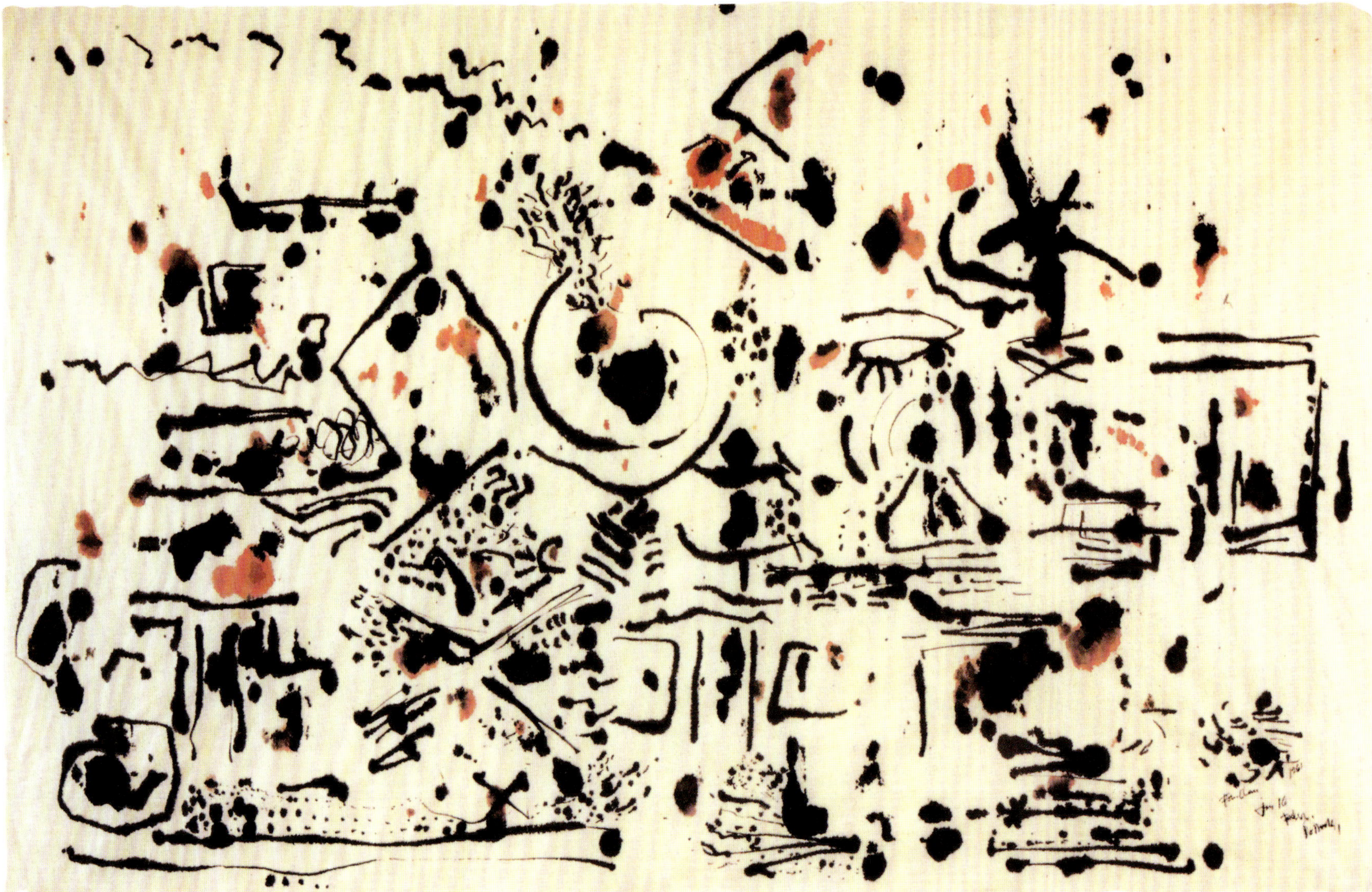

68
Untitled, 1951
Black and colored inks on Japanese paper
24¾ x 39 inches (62.9 x 99.1 cm)
Collection of Jane Lang Davis, Medina, Washington
JPCR 3:813

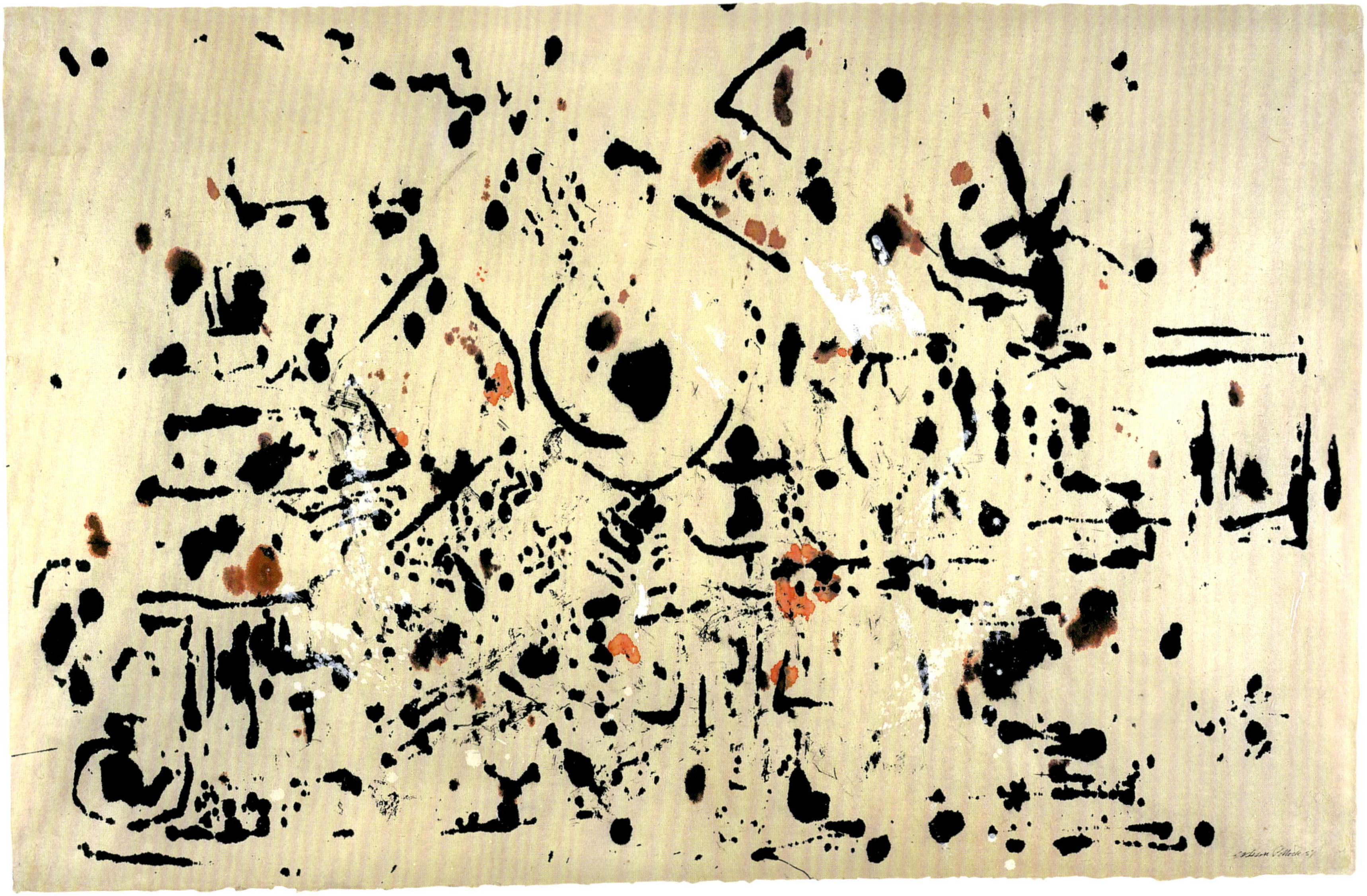

69
Untitled, 1951
Colored inks and gouache on Japanese paper
$24^{3}/_{4}$ x 39 inches (62.9 x 99.1 cm)
Scottish National Gallery of Modern Art, Edinburgh
JPCR 3:814

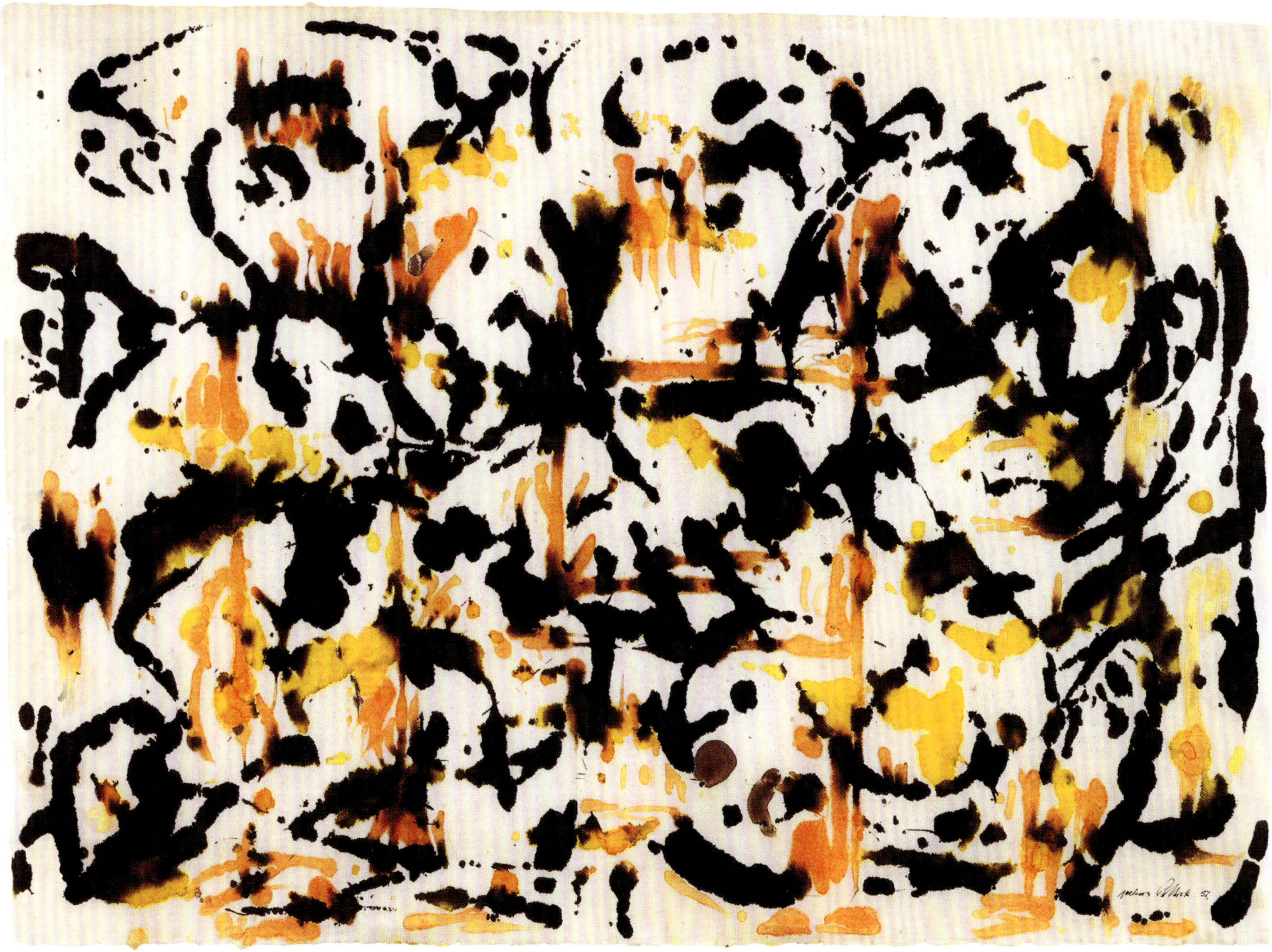

70
Untitled, 1951
Colored inks on Japanese paper
24 1/4 x 34 inches (61.5 x 86.4 cm)
Collection of Barbaralee Diamondstein and Carl Spielvogel, New York
JPCR 3:825

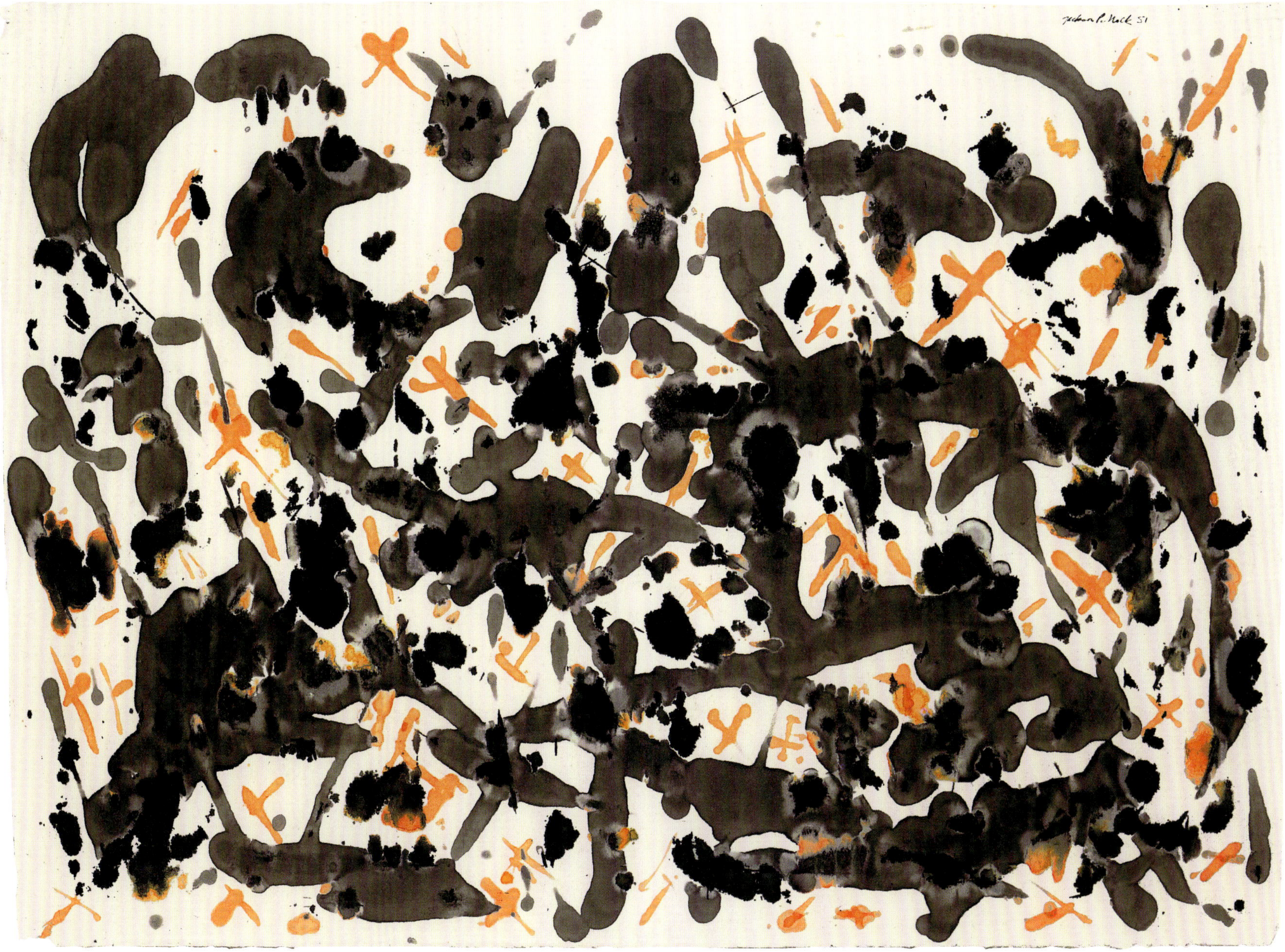

71
Untitled, 1951
Ink and watercolor on Japanese paper
24 1/2 x 34 inches (62.2 x 86.4 cm)
Solomon R. Guggenheim Museum, New York. Fractional gift, Barbara and Donald Jonas, New York (92.3984)
JPCR 3:824

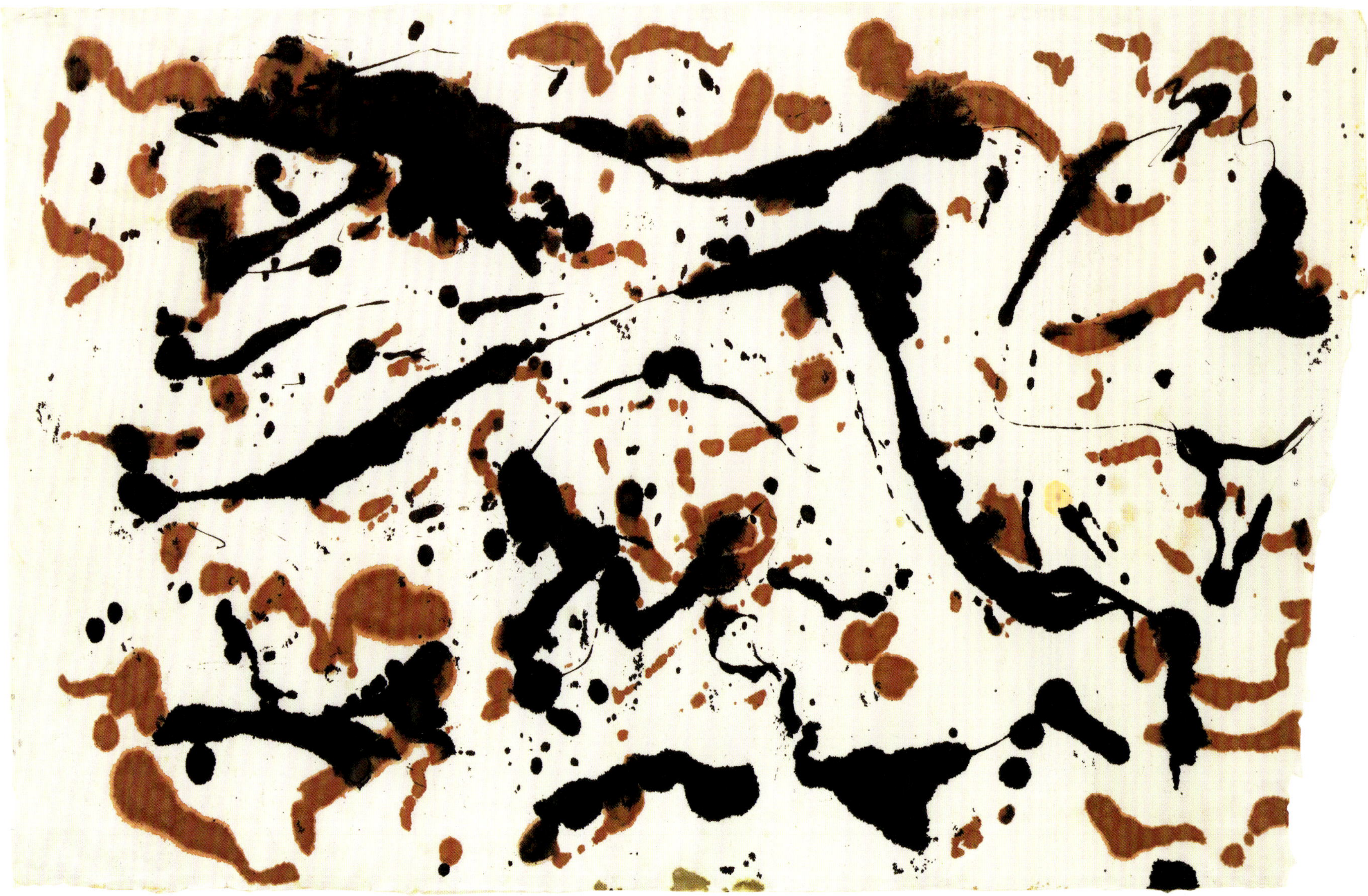

72
Untitled, 1951
Black and colored ink on Japanese paper
25 x 38 3/4 inches (63.5 x 99.4 cm)
The Museum of Modern Art, New York. Gift of
Lee Krasner in memory of Jackson Pollock (666.1983)
JPCR 3:820

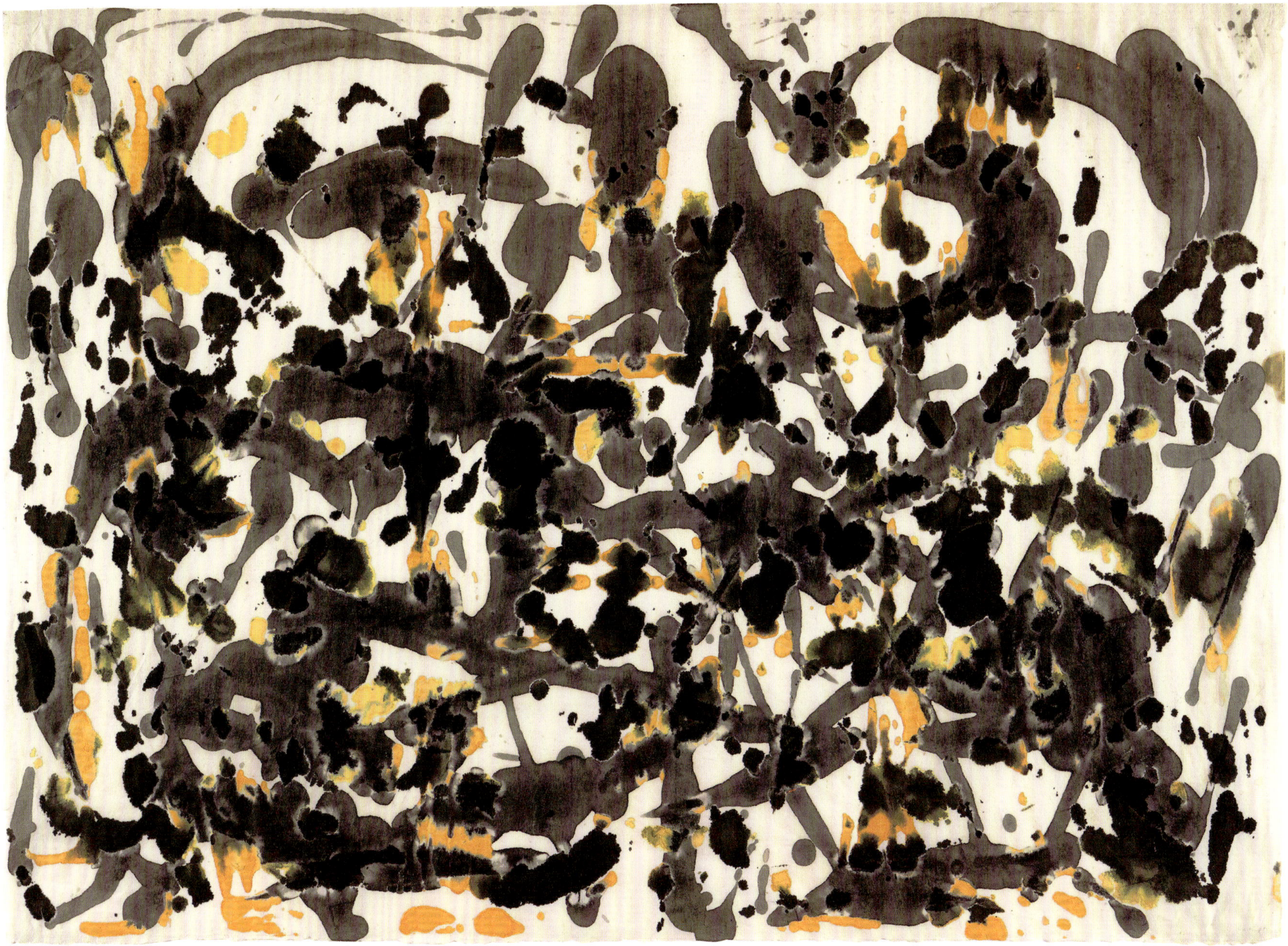

73
Untitled, 1951
Black and colored inks on Japanese paper
24 3/8 x 34 3/8 inches (61.9 x 97.2 cm)
The Museum of Modern Art, New York.
The Joan and Lester Avnet Collection (153.1978)
JPCR 3:823

74
Number 15, 1951, 1951
Colored inks on Howell paper
17 5/8 x 22 inches (44.8 x 55.9 cm)
The Museum of Contemporary Art, Los Angeles.
Gift of The American Art Foundation
JPCR 3:837

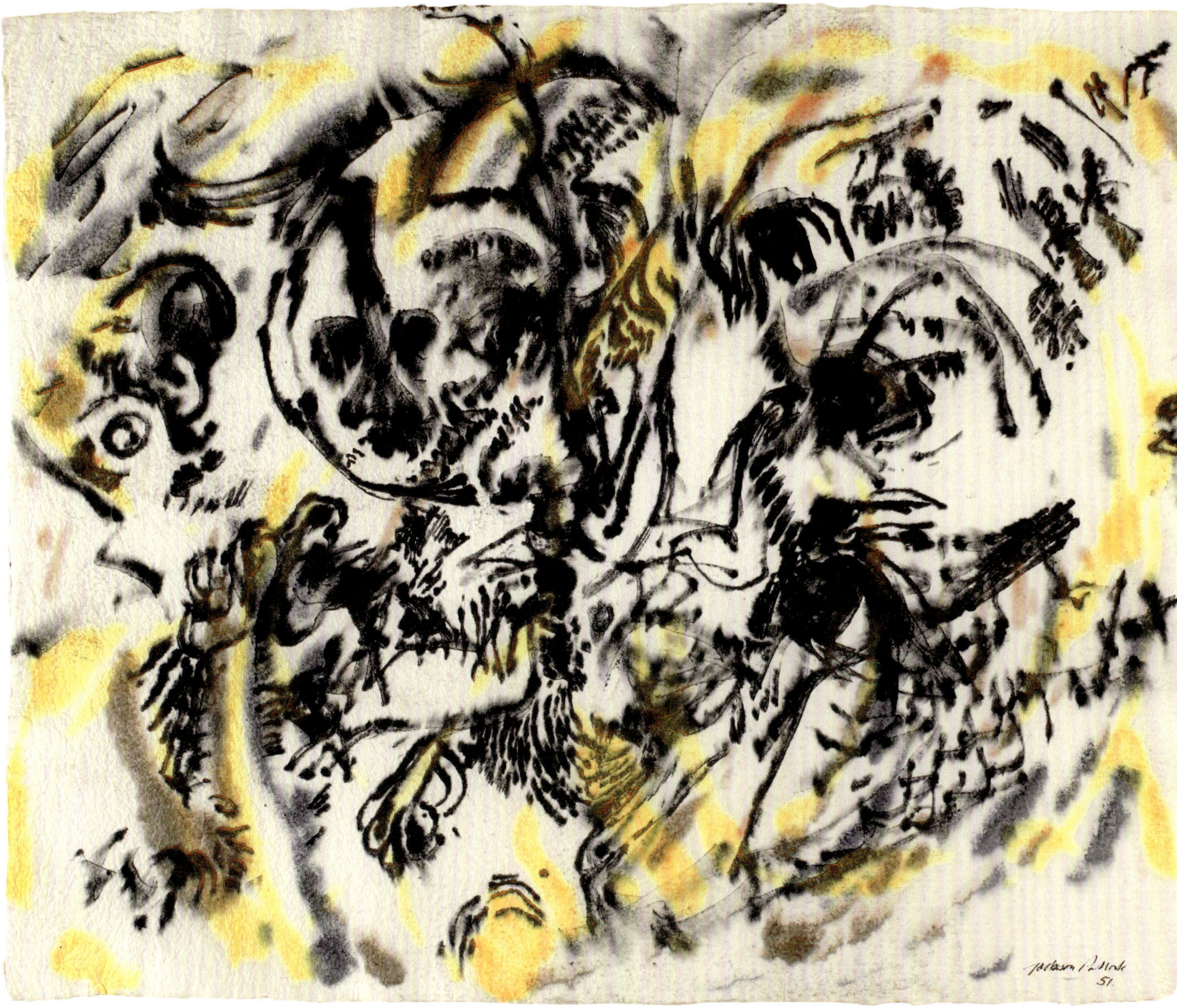

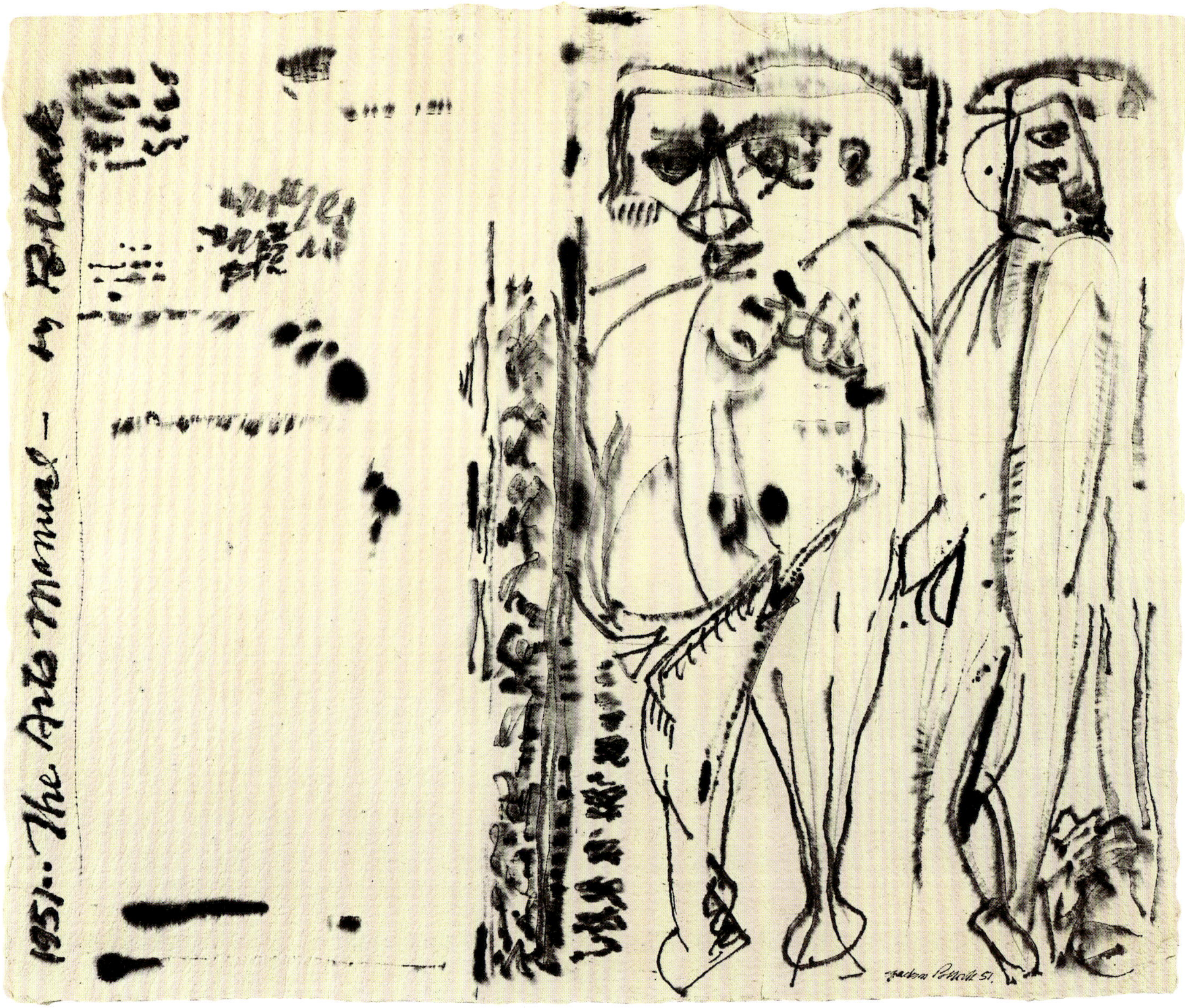

75
[Design for the Arts Manual], 1951
Ink on Howell paper
$17\frac{3}{4}$ x $21\frac{1}{2}$ inches (45.1 x 54.6 cm)
Courtesy Jason McCoy, Inc., New York
JPCR Supplement 22a

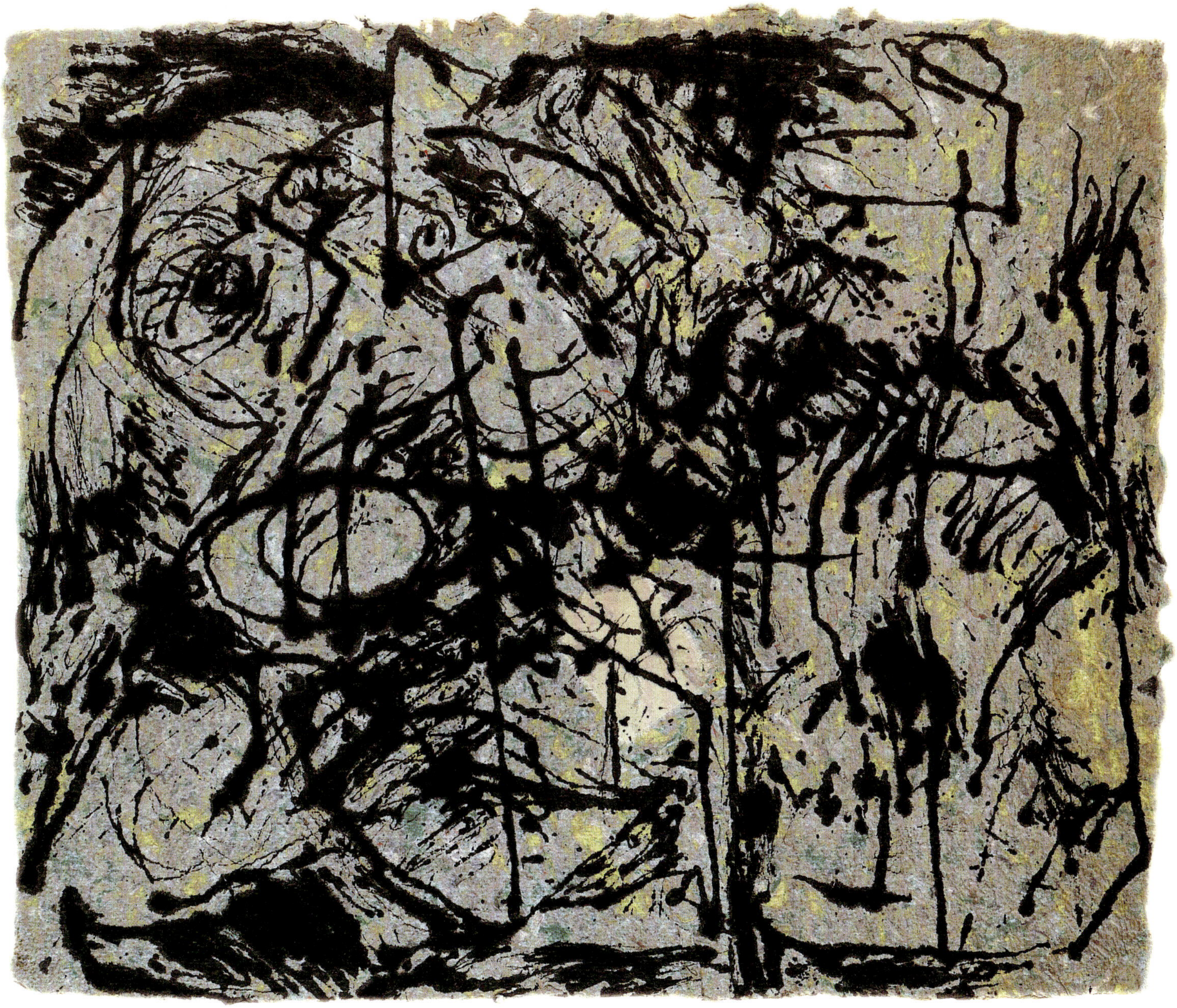

76
Untitled, ca. 1952–56
Ink on Howell paper
$18\frac{1}{8}$ x $21\frac{7}{8}$ inches (46 x 55.6 cm)
The Metropolitan Museum of Art, New York.
Gift of Lee Krasner Pollock, 1982 (1982.147.30)
JPCR 3:854

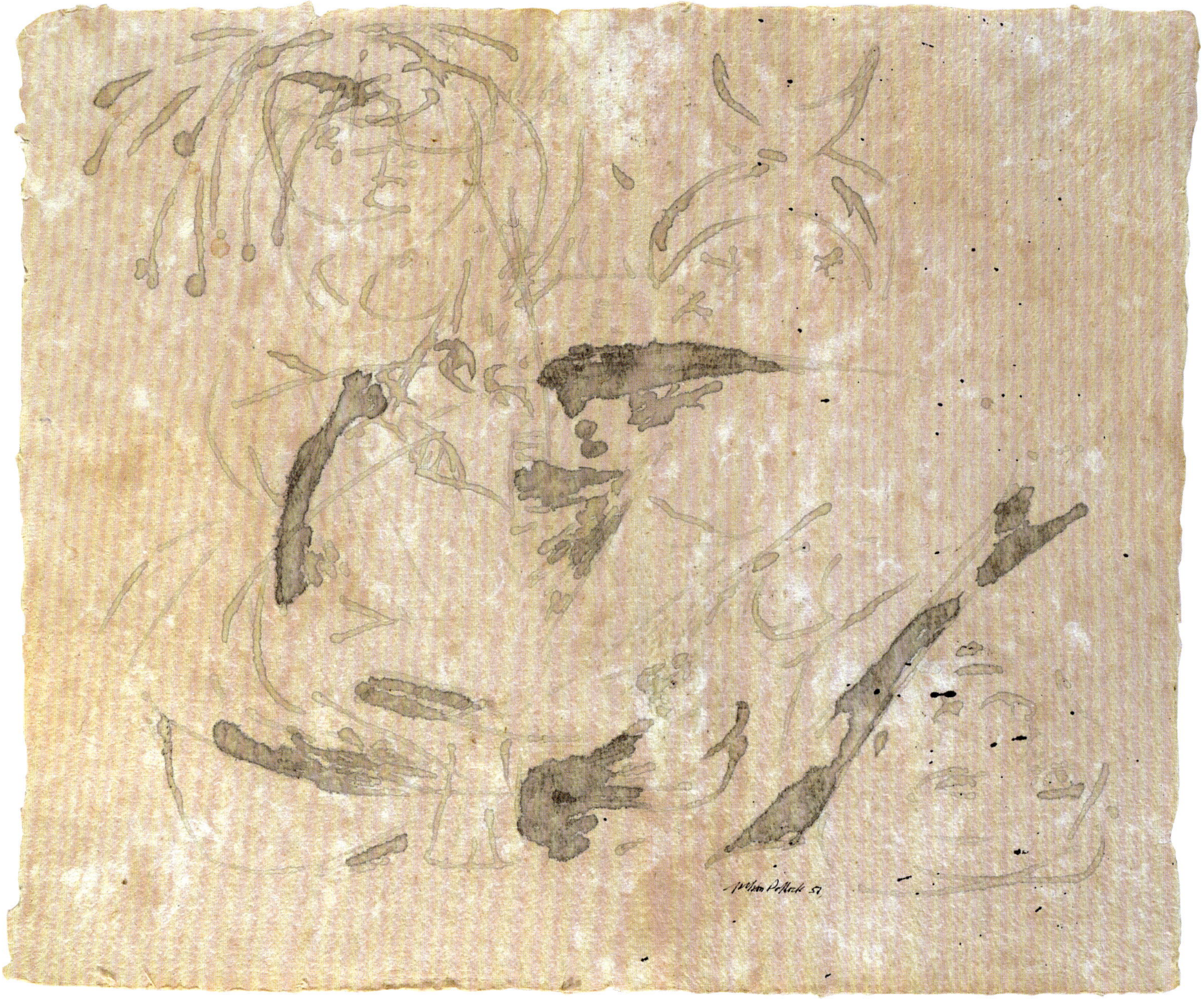

77
Untitled, 1951
Ink on Howell paper
18 x 22 inches (45.7 x 55.9)
Collection of Mr. and Mrs. Howard Karshan, London
JPCR 3:838

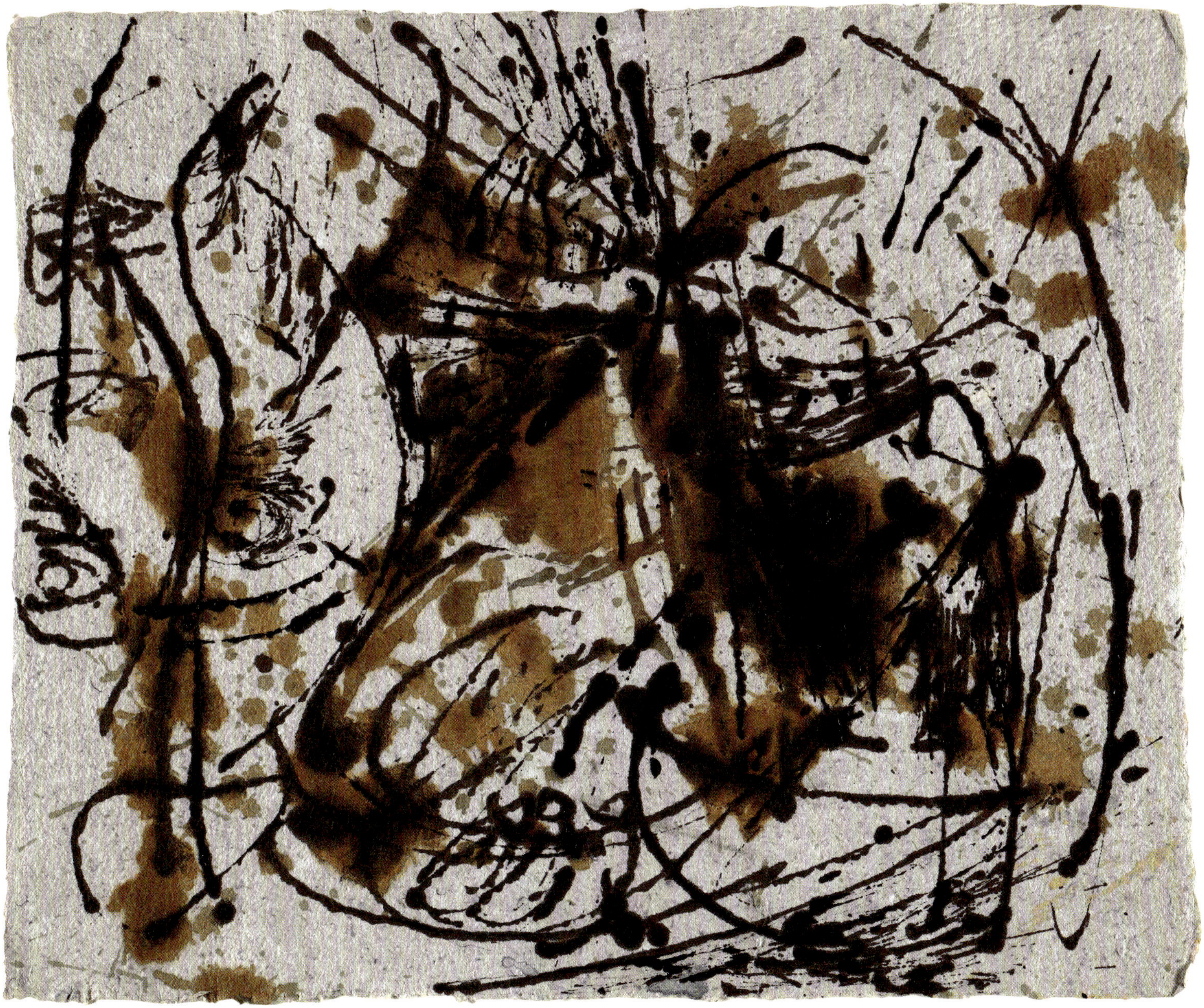

78
Untitled, ca. 1952
Ink and gouache on Howell paper
17 7/8 x 22 inches (45.4 x 55.9 cm)
The Museum of Modern Art, New York. Gift of Lee Krasner
in memory of Jackson Pollock (667.1983)
JPCR 3:855

Materials, Tools, and "Technics": Works on Paper by Jackson Pollock

Margaret Holben Ellis

IN A HANDWRITTEN STATEMENT that has since been widely quoted, Jackson Pollock declared that he considered drawing as a distinct act and not as a preparatory step in the process of making a painting: "I approach painting the same way I approach drawing, that is direct—with no prelimary [sic] studies."[1] The artist viewed his iconoclastic approach as simply "a means of arriving at a statement."[2] One might assume, therefore, that the materials and techniques he used in his works on paper are distinct from those he used in his paintings. However, a second sentence, not often included in the Pollock literature, follows the first: "The drawings I do are relative to my painting but not for it."[3] This qualifier suggests that the materials and techniques of his works on paper are in some other way related to those of his paintings.

Indeed, a close examination of Pollock's mature works on paper shows that he pushed to the very limits the substance and action of drawing concurrently or even before achieving similar sought-after effects in his paintings.[4] The materials with which he experimented include absorbent Japanese papers, large-format sheets, and solvent-based inks that dry quickly and penetrate papers more deeply than other inks.[5] His experiments were not confined to his materials, however. New "technics," he wrote, were needed in the age of "the airplane, the atom bomb, the radio,"[6] and in this arena he dragged and spurted black and vibrant dye-based inks from droppers akin to mini turkey basters, misted them from mouth atomizers (fig. 24), and spontaneously interrupted dry drawn lines with bright washes by activating copying and indelible pencils with water.[7] In a time of rapid technological advances, Pollock eagerly embraced the first felt-tipped markers and ballpoint pens as new tools. Like the carefully controlled pouring of paint, these implements effortlessly produced Pollock's acclaimed "continuous unbroken line" and disassociated the artist from his tools.[8]

Despite a hard-won ability to harness the "stuff" of art, Pollock's range of drawing materials was limited and unremarkable. External factors no doubt contributed to his habitual use of modest drawing papers and mediums, most notably the constraints imposed on artists' materials during the Depression and World War II. In 1931, for example, 95 percent of the graphite pencils purchased in the United States were domestically produced, despite the finer clay and smoother graphite of imported brands.[9] During World War II, American manufacturers were forced to resort to using inferior grades of graphite found in Mexico, Canada, and the Ticonderoga mine in New York State.[10] Most of Pollock's dry drawing mediums made in Germany and Czechoslovakia were probably acquired before the war. Similar economic restrictions also resulted in Pollock's infrequent use of papers made in Europe. Peter Busa described the impact of wartime shortages as follows: "We would spend the afternoon doing these automatic things. Jackson used a tube of paint because he couldn't get brushes then, squeezing the tube almost like frosting. . . . I sensed a breakdown with the war. We were isolated without materials."[11]

Shortages of merchandise were reported in the 1942 catalogue of Art Brown: "As this catalogue goes to press the future supply of many of the imported items listed is very uncertain. All stock of foreign material we have on hand is subject to prior sale."[12] MBM Ingres d'Arches paper, identified in several of Pollock's drawings, and Wolff's Carbon Drawing Pencil, found in his studio after his death, were among the imported items listed. Even after the war ended, shortages of imported art supplies continued for several years. One reason for the sudden appearance of large sheets of Japanese paper in Pollock's oeuvre in 1951 may be that they simply were not exported from the war-torn country until then.

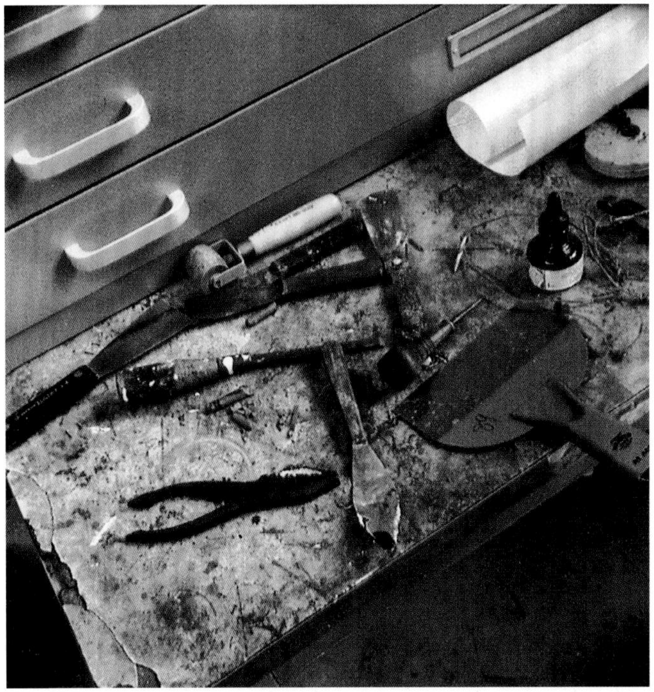

PAPERS

Pollock's selection of papers mirrored the precarious state of his personal finances as well as the nation's turbulent political and economic times. Although at first glance they appear to have been randomly selected, Pollock's papers constitute several predictable and, later in his career, carefully chosen types.

From 1930 to 1943, while he studied at the Art Students League and worked for the Works Progress Administration, Pollock had access to "standard issue" art supplies, such as brown paper, Manila paper, business stationery, and whatever else could be scavenged.[13] Axel Horn's description of students "busily scratching out a drawing with a grocer's pencil on brown wrapping paper" in a typical Thomas Hart Benton class at the Art Students League, for which Pollock served as monitor, conveys a stark image of the utilitarian and nondescript materials that were distributed.[14]

Groups of drawings on identical papers would suddenly appear in Pollock's oeuvre as he hungrily consumed newfound

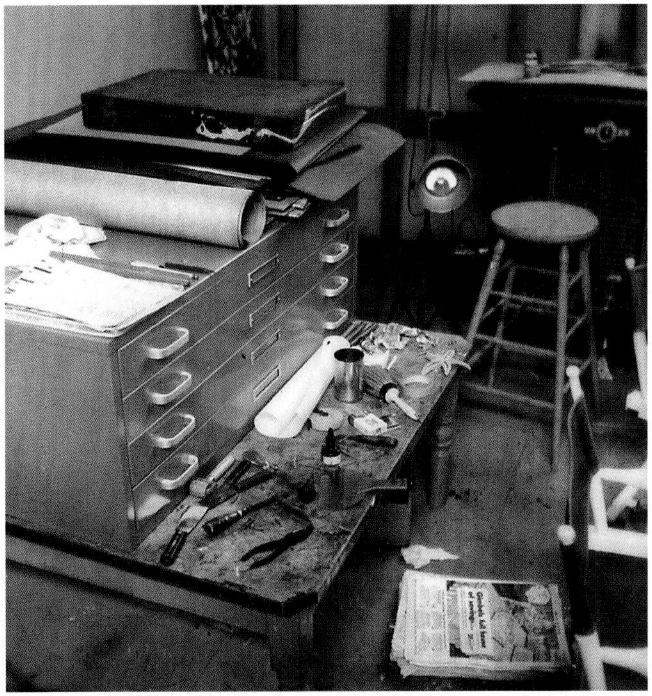

FIGS. 22 & 23
Drawing materials and tools in Jackson Pollock's studio, The Springs, Long Island, New York, late August or early September 1956 (soon after the artist's death). Photograph by Maurice Berezov

stashes of paper. Around 1934–38, for example, Pollock produced a handful of drawings that appear to be on stipple paper, an embossed hard-surfaced paper intended for the direct transposition of waxy crayon marks into the dot and squiggle patterns required for photo-engraving, zinc etching, and transfer lithography (such as pl. 1). It is conceivable that the WPA used these papers for its printing projects or that they were given free samples from vendors anxious to secure orders from an ever-shrinking customer base. Pollock routinely cannibalized complimentary paper-sample books for his drawings as well.[15] These provided him with scores of colored and textured papers, imported and domestic, handmade and machine-made. Three paper-sample books, pirated and disassembled by Pollock between 1939 and 1940, have been ingeniously reconstructed by Francis V. O'Connor, who was able to put into chronological order 28 sheets of gradually increasing lengths.[16] Plates 10 and 16, on rust and blue papers, respectively, are from one of these sample books. The existence of an off-set drawing on the verso of plate 16 suggests that Pollock used the sample books like sketchbooks—that is, while they were still intact.[17]

The purchase of artists' sketchbooks and pads of drawing paper likewise catalyzed torrents of intense exploratory studies. Pollock likely picked up these supplies in the vicinity of his work and home. The address of one art-supply store—Robert Rosenthal, Inc., at 11 East Eighth Street—is stamped on the backboard of a spiral-bound Grumbacher "Leonardo" sketchbook that supplied the paper for three drawings made between 1938 and 1941: plates 5–7. Pollock lived at 46 East Eighth Street at this time, but even after he left the city in 1945 he continued to patronize stores in his old neighborhood, including Philip Rosenthal at 47 East Ninth Street, Joseph Mayer Co., Inc. at 5–9 Union Square West, and the Cooper Union Supply Store.[18] A spiral-bound sketchbook was also the source for plate 3, which issued forth from a Parallex pad advertised by Art Brown as being "fine quality rag content paper suitable for any medium from pencil to watercolor."[19] Spiral-wire bindings, which allow the book's cover and pages to open completely and stay flat, had only recently been incorporated into artists' sketchbooks.[20]

Around 1943 to 1944, Pollock acquired a supply of American-made, 100% rag Strathmore two- or three-ply drawing "boards," easily recognizable by their embossed thistle trademark and available only in sheets measuring 23 x 29 inches.[21] Plate 24 was made on a full-sized sheet,[22] but Pollock would often divide this heavy and more expensive paper into quarters (for example, pl. 27).[23] Fine papers, too, did not always appear in quantity, resulting in the sporadic appearance of single sheets thriftily halved or quartered, alongside works on cardboard or foraged or recycled papers.[24]

Gradually, Pollock moved on to a better-quality and versatile unmarked watercolor paper measuring 20 5/8 x 26 inches, but he still continued to cut it down into quarters, as evidenced by several drawings with two irregularly cut edges. Identification of this paper is only possible by close examination of drawings measuring roughly 10 1/4 x 13 inches. Eight works have been confirmed as being on quarter sheets of this paper,[25] and at least one work is confirmed as being on a full sheet (pl. 48).

Pollock was well acquainted with finer-quality papers, and not only through paper-sample books. French papers, such as RIVES BKF and MBM Ingres d'Arches, were routinely used in printmaking, including his own prints (for example, pls. 32 and 33).[26] Most of Pollock's drawings done on MBM Ingres d'Arches measure the full "Royal" sheet size of approximately 18 3/4 x 24 3/4 inches.[27] Pollock commented to William Wright in late 1950 that he had come to prefer working in a larger format,[28] and although he was referring to his paintings on canvas, he could also have been recalling his paintings on sturdy wove paper from the previous four years, all measuring approximately 22 x 30 1/2 inches, the standard "Imperial" size for watercolor and drawing papers. Many of these works, such as *Number 22A, 1948* (1948; pl. 52), *Composition (White, Black, Blue, and Red on White)* (1948; pl. 53), *Number 33, 1949* (1949; pl. 56), *Number 13, 1949* (1949; pl. 61), and Untitled (*Green Silver*) (ca. 1949; pl. 62), have been mounted to composition board or canvas, making paper identification difficult.

The appearance of large sheets of Japanese paper in Pollock's oeuvre in 1951 proves that he was at last ready and able to deliberately purchase a supply of paper for a specific purpose at this time. No fewer than sixteen drawings, including plates 68, 69, and 72, appear in the large *kikuban* format, 25 x 39 inches, the dimensions of the papermaking mold in which the sheets were formed.[29] An additional four sheets have been preserved to serve as documents of Pollock's stain technique, whereby black and colored inks were allowed to penetrate several layers of paper and thereby presage the design of the drawing immediately following.[30] The soft and compliant Japanese papers confirm Pollock's predilection for larger and more porous painting surfaces. The delicacy of the absorbed ink and long-fibered paper produced an effect similar to his dripped enamel paint on unprimed canvas.[31]

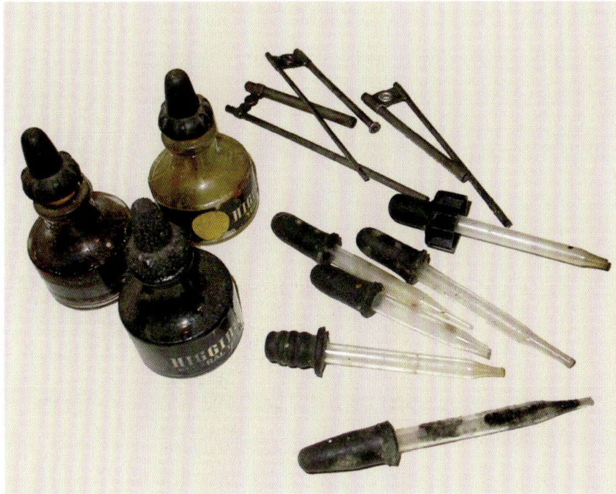

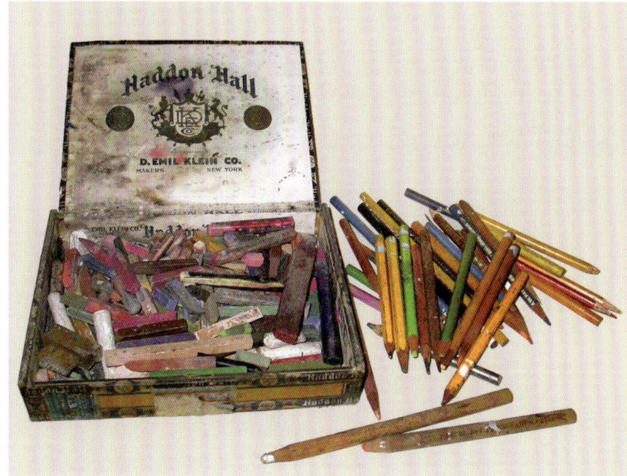

Also in 1951, Pollock met Douglass Morse Howell, whose handmade papers Pollock used in plates 74–78. These works serve as poignant testimony that Pollock had finally succumbed to the charms of paper in and of itself and used it as a resplendent and absorbent surface perfectly suited to his never-ending calligraphy.[32] Sadly, Pollock was never seduced again by the purity of paper or, it seems, of mark making.

DRAWING MATERIALS

Like his papers, Pollock's drawing mediums were accumulated in a piecemeal fashion throughout his career and offer few surprises when considered in the context of his employment and social environment. His drawing mediums share some general characteristics: all could be directly applied, lacked a formalized program of proper usage, and required little in the way of precise manual control (it should be remembered that Pollock was missing the tip of his right index finger). Pollock did not seem interested in mastering the nuances of traditional watercolor, pastel, or tonal charcoal drawing, nor was he comfortable with the "madeness" that resulted from deliberate execution.[33]

In his early career, Pollock seemed to ignore entirely the intended working properties of his drawing mediums. For example, the smooth, satiny colored pencils that could be turned into watercolor washes by applying water were used in combination with standard colored pencils in his representational works of 1939–42; applied in heavy layers, the waxy pencils smeared and smudged from the heat and pressure of his hand (see, for example, pl. 9).[34] Years later, Pollock would exploit their solubility by causing their dry lines to explode unexpectedly into transparent washes of brilliant color, suggesting a fully realized familiarity with them. Because Pollock often disregarded the working properties of his mediums or combined them in unusual ways, it is often impossible to arrive at accurate medium identification for his works on paper. Part of the problem is that different materials have remarkably similar appearances, as is the case with black colored pencil versus soft graphite pencil, black gouache versus black India ink, watercolor pencil applied wet versus colored dye-based inks, and water-activated color pencils applied dry versus standard colored pencils. The identification of Pollock's drawing mediums and the ability to differentiate between them was aided enormously by the prescient segregation and subsequent accounting of more than sixty-six drawing implements, colored and graphite pencils, pastels, and crayons shortly after Pollock's death in 1956. Thanks to the "reference set" provided by the studio inventory, it has been possible to identify mediums that would be difficult to confirm by visual examination alone. A list of the artist's mediums, compiled by comparing this studio inventory with illustrations and descriptions found in art-supply

FIG. 24
Higgins Ink, mouth atomizers, and spare droppers from Jackson Pollock's studio, The Springs, Long Island, New York. Collection of Pollock-Krasner House and Study Center. Photograph 2004

FIG. 25
Cigar box with chalks and pencils from Jackson Pollock's studio, The Springs, Long Island, New York. Collection of Pollock-Krasner House and Study Center. Photograph 2004

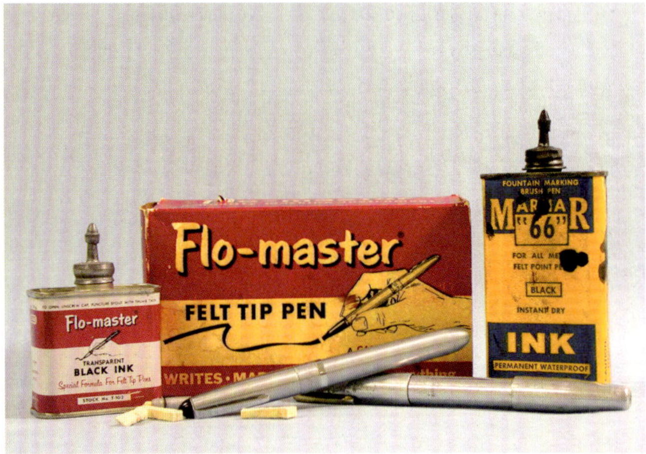

catalogues dating from pre-1900 to 1953 as well as advertisements in popular artists' magazines such as *American Artist*, appears on pages 132–34 of this volume.[35]

In addition to the materials found in the artist's studio, several substances have been identified in the works themselves or identified in photographs taken of Pollock's studio during his lifetime. Like others of his generation, Pollock seemed to be attracted to the compliant and direct character of simple Crayola crayons. A section of a broken Crayola crayon is identifiable by its wrapper in a photo of the studio interior taken by Maurice Berezov in late August or early September 1956 (fig. 22). Pollock often combined these crayons with colored pencils, which contain a smaller percentage of wax. Lines drawn by wax crayons can be differentiated from those drawn with colored pencils by their more sticky, greasy appearance and blunt ends; additionally, they have a tendency to "sink" as their dye components and wax are absorbent by the paper.[36]

Pollock's gouache or "show card" colors were popular and inexpensive commercial paints typically employed in posters and signage, silkscreen mock-ups, and other commercial applications. Pollock resorted to a limited range of these matte water-based paints without apparent enthusiasm, probably due to their unresponsiveness and opaqueness.

Two drawing tools that appealed to Pollock in his search for an expressive but expedient line were introduced in the mid-twentieth century: the felt-tipped pen and the ballpoint pen. Available in the American marketplace as early as 1940, the felt-tipped pen (variously described in advertisements as a "fountain-brush" or "brush-pen") was marketed specifically as an artists' tool.[37] Its selling points were its interchangeable felt nibs and brilliant, transparent, quick-drying inks; artists' testimonials raved, "Different textural effects can be obtained with a single stroke . . . on any surface without a single dipping of the brush" and "It makes the artist independent of his implement," claims that surely fell on Pollock's receptive ears.[38] The pen's inks and nibs provided Pollock with an efficient and versatile means of mark making. It is likely that he purchased at least one of the more popular brands, the Marhar Fountain Brush Marking Pen, the Cado Flo-master (fig. 26), or the Dri-Ink Floquil Pen, as evidenced in a number of supersaturated and penetrating marks found in his works from 1950 until his death (for example, JPCR 3:782). The qualities of the black ink, the only color he seems to have used, are plainly visible in his last sketchbook of 1956 (JPCR 3:879–915). Pollock also used a felt-tipped pen to sign and misleadingly date as 1938 several sketches from 1939–42 (JPCR 3:604 and 3:612, recto and verso).[39]

Around the same time, Pollock also obtained one of the first commercially successful ballpoint pens, probably the Reynold's Rocket, introduced with great fanfare at Gimbel's department store in 1946.[40] Pollock's use of a blue ballpoint pen seems to have been confined to post-1950, when the artist used it to make nervous hatches among black ink lines and washes. Inked lines produced by the early ballpoint pens tended to remain sticky on the paper and slowly "sink" into it over time due to their oil content.

As an adherent to the goal of the 1936 Siqueiros Experimental Workshop to "find the proper technical methods to correspond with the industrial life of the U.S.,"[41] Pollock embraced the use of cellulose nitrate and oil-modified alkyd "enamels," aluminum and silver paints, and house paints, and in 1952 even ventured to use a new acrylic resin paint, Magna, formulated by Leonard Bocour.[42] Pollock took advantage of these quick-drying paints in his works on paper, exploiting, as in his paintings, the evocative

FIG. 26
Flo-master and Marhar fountain brush pens, nibs, and ink. Private collection. Photograph 2004

patterns and textures that could be created by his acclaimed pouring technique, as in Untitled *(Green Silver)* and, humorously, in *The Debutante* (ca. 1946; pl. 22).[43] Along with the drawing materials and tools described on pages 132–34, Krasner also saved eighteen cans of paint, several of which have been analyzed and matched to the multilayered tracery of poured paint that remained undisturbed on Pollock's studio floor for almost thirty-five years.[44]

CONSERVATION PROBLEMS

The prevailing conservation problems of Pollock's works on paper are not so much a result of their so-called "inherent vice" as from the way they were managed and handled by the artist and subsequent owners.[45] Photographs and firsthand accounts detail the untidy state of Pollock's studio in The Springs; Selden Rodman, for example, noted the existence of a "table covered with dusty sketches" and a "stack of drawings going back to the thirties."[46] The drawings themselves bear witness to long-term neglect. Several are creased, smudged, or stained by water, which in some cases has caused the water-soluble colored pencils to bleed. In suites of drawings done in rapid succession, specifically those created by pouring enamel directly onto paper, the uppermost drawing became adhered to the still-sticky enamel below. When separated, the versos of these drawings are often skinned and torn, while the enamel is fuzzy with embedded paper fibers (see, for example, pl. 63).[47] The paper in these drawings is severely darkened and embrittled in patterns corresponding to the swirls of the chemically unstable enamels on the paper that once lay below (long thought to be exclusively cellulose nitrate but recently identified as oil-modified alkyds as well). This kind of deterioration could only have occurred from years of undisturbed contact.

These works do have their own inherent problems, however: Enamel, by its nature, is brittle and hard, and when it is poured onto a flexible paper, which expands and contracts with humidity changes, cracking and flaking of the paint can occur. Insecurity of the paint layer also occurs in Pollock's gouache-on-paper works. Pollock's drawings have also been the victims of their own popularity. Works incorporating dye-based mediums, including ballpoint pen, are generally classified as "sensitive."[48] Even with light levels as low as 50 lux (5 footcandles), some dyes will fade noticeably in as little as a year.[49] Overexposure to light has significantly faded many of the brilliant and transparent dye-based colors that Pollock preferred. In some cases where the ink was applied as a stain penetrating through the paper, its true color is preserved only on the verso. Papers, too, have shifted in color, as described by a previous owner of Untitled (ca. 1943; pl. 19): "By the time we sold it, it was starting to fade and when we saw it in 1967 we realized we had had the best years of its life; it was sadly faded."[50]

Surprises abound when conservators are called in to treat damaged works on paper by Pollock. Since the majority of Pollock's colored pencils are soluble in water and copying pencils exceedingly so, any form of moisture can cause unexpected bleeding of their dye component. For this reason, all colors, including those that look like graphite, need to be carefully pre-tested.

CONCLUSION

The "puzzle" of Pollock's oeuvre has tantalized us for over fifty years, and attempts to decipher his artistic and technical message will no doubt continue. A better understanding of Pollock's materials, tools, and "technics" will unveil the mysteries of his works on paper, point the way to interpreting his paintings, and preserve the physical essence of both for others to ponder in the future.

DRAWING MEDIUMS INVENTORY

The following is an inventory of drawing mediums found in Pollock's studio after his death, with additional information gleaned from illustrations and descriptions found in art-supply catalogues dating from pre-1900 to 1953 as well as advertisements in popular artists' magazines such as *American Artist*. Imprints transcribed from the drawing mediums themselves appear in bold.

Naturally, one might question whether these materials were used by Pollock or by his wife, Lee Krasner; however, all materials in the inventory were set aside and identified by Krasner as Pollock's, and all can be reasonably identified in Pollock's works on paper. Many were spattered with his paints. Some items, such as a Blaisdale Charcoal Pencil, were eliminated because they could not be dated with certainty.

I. Graphite and Carbon Pencils

MADE IN ENGLAND BB – WOLFF'S CARBON DRAWING PENCIL
Manufactured by the Royal Sovereign Pencil Co. Ltd., London. "Best Quality Cedar Manufactured from 'Compressed Carbon,' possessing many qualities superior to ordinary Chalks, and produce an effect similar in tone and equal in delicacy of tint to the finest Lithograph, without the gloss so common to Black Lead Drawings. Made in Six Degrees." (M. M. Ross Co., *Catalog Artists' Materials and School Supplies* [Boston, n.d.], p. 87.)

. . . JET BLACK EXTRA SMOOTH EBERHARD FABER USA 6325
Full imprint: EBONY JET BLACK EXTRA SMOOTH EBERHARD FABER USA 6325. Manufactured by Eberhard Faber, New York. "Round, very black, smooth, soft and strong." (Art Brown [Arthur Brown and Bro.], *General Catalogue Artists' Materials Drafting Materials Screen Process Supplies* [New York, 1942], p. 103.)

VAN DYKE EBERHARD FABER USA – 4H/ MICROTOMIC GRAPHITE 4H (fig. 27)
Manufactured by Eberhard Faber, New York. "The all-new MICROTOMIC. For absolute control of pencil tones Style No. 736. You will never be annoyed by an off-grade hard or off-grade soft lead . . . when you use the All-New MICROTOMIC! Thanks to Eberhard Faber's newly developed quality controls, these pencils are absolutely uniform in every degree!" (Bert L. Daily Inc., *Sign Writers Supplies and Artists Materials Catalog Number 26* [Dayton, Ohio, 1953], p. 98.)

. . . HARD FABER MADE IN USA 547
Full imprint: EBERHARD FABER MADE IN USA 547. Manufactured by Eberhard Faber, New York. Probably an Eberhard Faber Mongol graphite drawing pencil.

. . . CASTELL" 2H GERMANY
Manufactured by A. W. Faber, Newark, New Jersey, and Stein, Germany.

. . . RAUGHTING Chemi-Sealed . . .
Full imprint: EAGLE DRAUGHTING Chemi-Sealed [followed by graphite hardness designation]. Manufactured by Eagle Pencil Company, New York. Eagle claimed that its patented Chemi-Sealed process, which firmly united lead and wood, reduced breakage of the lead by 34 percent. Chemi-Sealed pencils were available after 1933. (See Henry Petroski, *The Pencil* [New York: Alfred A. Knopf, 1990], p. 244.)

MADE IN USA DIXON'S ELDORADO 6B
THE MASTER DRAWING PENCIL (fig. 28)
MADE IN USA DIXON'S ELDORADO 2B
THE MASTER DRAWING PENCIL
MADE IN USA DIXON'S ELDORADO 2H
THE MASTER DRAWING PENCIL
. . . DIXON . . .
. . . DI . . .
Manufactured by Joseph Dixon Crucible Co., Jersey City, New Jersey. Dixon's Eldorado pencils were introduced in 1917 and were among the first American pencils to use the European hardness scale.

II. Colored Pencils and Copying/ Indelible Pencils

. . . HARD FABER MADE IN USA MONGOL 765 HARD BLUE
Full imprint: EBERHARD FABER MADE IN USA MONGOL 765 HARD BLUE. Manufactured by Eberhard Faber, New York. "A thin strong lead for fine detail work.

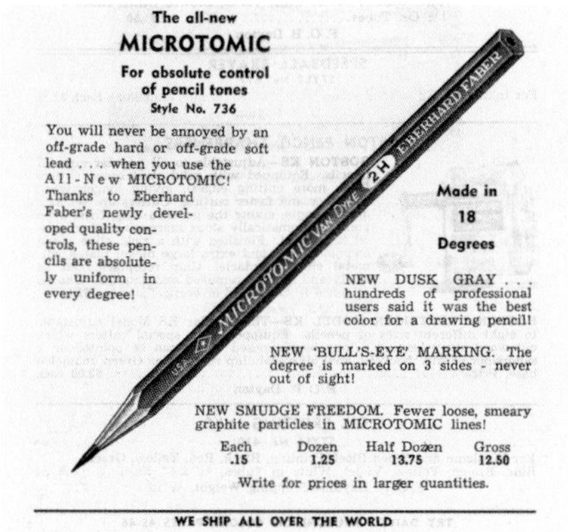

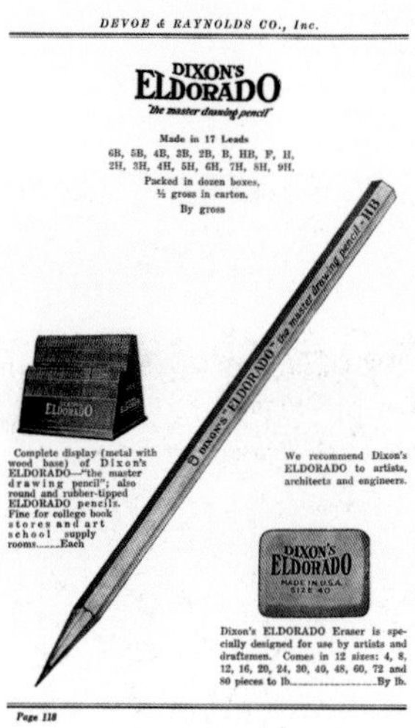

FIG. 27
Eberhard Faber's Microtomic, as it appears in Bert L. Daily Inc., *Sign Writers Supplies and Artists Materials Catalog Number 26* (Dayton, Ohio, 1953), p. 98. The product name as it appears on the pencil found in Pollock's studio varies slightly from the way it appears here but does match the wording in Charles Bruning Company, *General Catalog 13th Edition* (New York, 1939), p. 242

FIG. 28
Dixon's Eldorado Pencil, as it appears in Devoe & Raynold's Co., Inc., *Catalogue of Artists' Materials and Drawing Supplies*, 20th ed. (New York, 1928), p. 118

For wash effects simply use brush and water." (Art Brown, *General Catalogue Artists' Materials Drafting Materials Screen Process Supplies* [New York, 1942], p. 106.)

PARCEL Red A. W. Faber 2328 Made in Bavaria
PARCEL Yellow A. W. Faber 2332
Manufactured by A. W. Faber, Newark, New Jersey, and Stein, Germany.

MADE IN BAVARIA A. W. FABER "Castell" Polychromos :14 [lime green]
MADE IN BAVARIA A. W. FABER "Castell" Polychromos :15 [green]
MADE IN BAVARIA A. W. FABER "Castell" Polychromos :28 [blue]
MADE IN BAVARIA A. W. FABER "Castell" Polychromos :41 [yellow] (2)
MADE IN BAVARIA A. W. FABER "Castell" Polychromos :46 [brown] (2)
MADE IN BAVARIA A. W. FABER "Castell" Polychromos :47 [brown]
Manufactured by A. W. Faber, Newark, New Jersey, and Stein, Germany.

No. 281 B L & C Hardtmuth No. 50 [yellow]
No. 281 B L & C Hardtmuth No. 52 [orange]
Manufactured by L & C Hardtmuth Austria, Czechoslovakia/Czech Republic/USA. These are probably versions of the "Koh-I-Noor" Polycolor Wax Crayon Pencil. "Made in 64 sunfast colors. Excellent for rendering and sketching and when used with a solvent produces pleasing wash effects. May also be used for coloring photographs." (Art Brown, *General Catalogue Artists' Materials Drafting Materials Screen Process Supplies* [New York, 1942], p. 107.)

No. 702 "Mona Lisa" L & C Hardtmuth CZECHOSLOVAKIA [yellow]
Manufactured by L & C Hardtmuth Austria, Czechoslovakia/Czech Republic/USA. L & C Hardtmuth offered a Mona Lisa line of oil chalk crayons in 1942; however, the wood-encased pencil version of this product has not been located in any art-supply catalogues.

VENUS-UNIQUE - THIN LEAD - CHROME YELLOW - 1229 / NEW PROCESS SUPER THIN COLORED LEAD MADE IN USA (fig. 29)
VENUS-UNIQUE - THIN LEAD - PURPLE - 1210
VENUS-UNIQUE - THIN LEAD - RED - 1207
Manufactured by American Pencil Company, Hoboken, New Jersey. "Venus-Unique Colored Pencils—Wax Crayons, Thin Leads. Venus-Unique Strong Thin Leads are encased in fine cedar wood enameled to resemble the actual color. These fine thin lead colored pencils are perhaps the best known and most widely used and therefore need no lengthy introduction." (Charles Bruning Company, *General Catalog 13th Edition* [New York, 1939], p. 248.) The color numbers in this catalogue description are the same as those on the pencils themselves.

MADE IN USA DIXON B . . . [green] (fig. 30)
Full imprint: MADE IN USA DIXON BEST GREEN — [color number]. Manufactured by Joseph Dixon Crucible Co., Jersey City, New Jersey. The back of a box of Dixon pencils with the label "Made in U.S.A. Joseph Dixon Crucible Company, Jersey City, New Jersey. Date Pkd 11/53." reads as follows: "Strong leads of smooth, even texture. Brilliant and permanent colors for drawing, sketching, drafting, map coloring, and bold checking. The finest type of colored pencil used extensively by Architects, Artists, Draftsmen, Engineers."

Conté à Paris Sanguine
Manufactured by Conté in France. A traditional wood-encased conté pencil.

. . . N CABINET .720 - No. 2
Manufacturer unknown.

MADE IN CZECHOSLOVAKIA EVERGREEN BLUE U.S. PENCIL CO. NEW YORK, USA COPYING NO. 503
Manufactured by U.S. Pencil Company, New York.

GENERAL'S SUPREME Purple Copying USA - 579
Manufactured by General Pencil Company, Jersey City, New Jersey. In addition to graphite and clay, copying or indelible pencils contain a water-soluble aniline dye. Developed in the late nineteenth century, copying pencils were used to make duplicates of office correspondence and receipts by placing the original document against a moistened tissue page of a letter-copying book. Placed into a copy press overnight, the moistened page of the letter-copying book absorbed the bright dye of the copying pencil, revealing a mirror-image copy, which could be easily read by holding it up to the light. Copying pencils were ubiquitous in offices and studios well into the twentieth century.

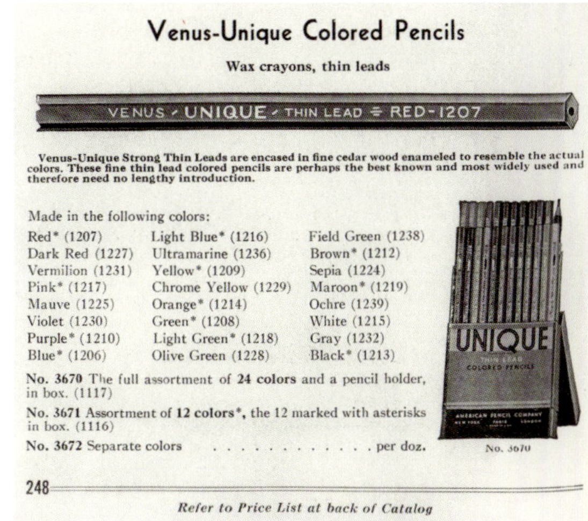

Venus-Unique Colored Pencils

Wax crayons, thin leads

VENUS - UNIQUE - THIN LEAD = RED-1207

Venus-Unique Strong Thin Leads are encased in fine cedar wood enameled to resemble the actual colors. These fine thin lead colored pencils are perhaps the best known and most widely used and therefore need no lengthy introduction.

Made in the following colors:

Red* (1207)	Light Blue* (1216)	Field Green (1238)
Dark Red (1227)	Ultramarine (1236)	Brown* (1212)
Vermilion (1231)	Yellow* (1209)	Sepia (1224)
Pink* (1217)	Chrome Yellow (1229)	Maroon* (1219)
Mauve (1225)	Orange* (1214)	Ochre (1239)
Violet (1230)	Green* (1208)	White (1215)
Purple* (1210)	Light Green* (1218)	Gray (1232)
Blue* (1206)	Olive Green (1228)	Black* (1213)

No. 3670 The full assortment of **24 colors** and a pencil holder, in box. (1117)

No. 3671 Assortment of **12 colors***, the 12 marked with asterisks in box. (1116)

No. 3672 Separate colors . . . . per doz.

UNIQUE

No. 3670

248

Refer to Price List at back of Catalog

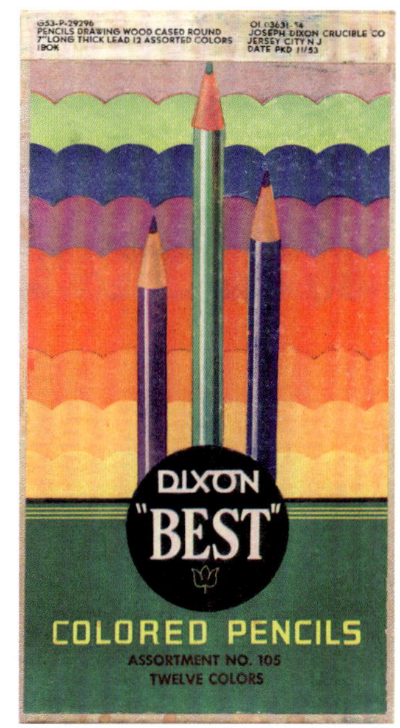

FIG. 29
Venus-Unique Colored Pencils, as they appear in Charles Bruning Company, *General Catalog 13th Edition* (New York, 1939), p. 248

FIG. 30
Packaging for Dixon "Best" Colored Pencils. Private collection

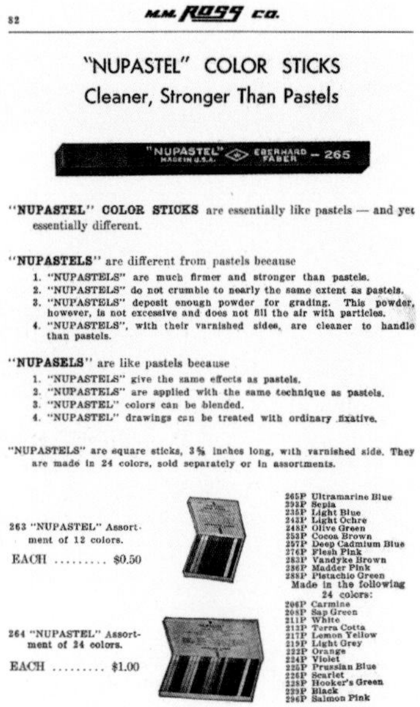

82 M.M. ROSS CO.

"NUPASTEL" COLOR STICKS
Cleaner, Stronger Than Pastels

"NUPASTEL" MADE IN U.S.A. EBERHARD FABER – 265

"NUPASTEL" COLOR STICKS are essentially like pastels — and yet essentially different.

"NUPASTELS" are different from pastels because

1. "NUPASTELS" are much firmer and stronger than pastels.
2. "NUPASTELS" do not crumble to nearly the same extent as pastels.
3. "NUPASTELS" deposit enough powder for grading. This powder, however, is not excessive and does not fill the air with particles.
4. "NUPASTELS", with their varnished sides, are cleaner to handle than pastels.

"NUPASELS" are like pastels because

1. "NUPASTELS" give the same effects as pastels.
2. "NUPASTELS" are applied with the same technique as pastels.
3. "NUPASTEL" colors can be blended.
4. "NUPASTEL" drawings can be treated with ordinary fixative.

"NUPASTELS" are square sticks, 3⅝ inches long, with varnished side. They are made in 24 colors, sold separately or in assortments.

263 "NUPASTEL" Assortment of 12 colors.
EACH $0.50

264 "NUPASTEL" Assortment of 24 colors.
EACH $1.00

Made in the following 24 colors:
265P Ultramarine Blue
293P Sepia
235P Light Blue
243P Light Ochre
248P Olive Green
253P Cocoa Brown
257P Deep Cadmium Blue
276P Flesh Pink
283P Vandyke Brown
286P Madder Pink
288P Pistachio Green
206P Carmine
208P Sap Green
211P White
212P Terra Cotta
217P Lemon Yellow
219P Light Grey
222P Orange
224P Violet
225P Prussian Blue
226P Scarlet
228P Hooker's Green
229P Black
296P Salmon Pink

FIG. 31
Eberhard Faber's Nupastel Color Sticks, as they appear in M.M. Ross Co., *Catalog Artists' Materials and School Supplies* (Boston, n.d.), p. 82

III. Pastels and Crayons

EBERHARD FABER NUPASTEL MADE IN USA 203 [Reddish Brown] (fig. 31)
EBERHARD FABER NUPASTEL MADE IN USA 224 [Violet]
EBERHARD FABER NUPASTEL MADE IN USA 228 [Hooker's Green]
EBERHARD FABER NUPASTEL MADE IN USA 246 [?]
EBERHARD FABER NUPASTEL MADE IN USA 253 [Cocoa Brown]
EBERHARD FABER NUPASTEL MADE IN USA 276 [Flesh Pink]
EBERHARD FABER NUPASTEL MADE IN USA 285 [Blue]
EBERHARD FABER NUPASTEL MADE IN USA 286 [Madder Pink]
EBERHARD FABER NUPASTEL MADE IN USA 296 [Salmon Pink]
Manufactured by Eberhard Faber, New York. "NUPASTELS are firmer and stronger than pastels and will not crumble, yet they will deposit enough powder for grading. They give the same effect with the same technique being applied and the drawing can be treated with ordinary fixatif. Nupastels are square sticks 3 5/8 inches long with varnished sides." (Bert L. Daily Inc., *Sign Writers Supplies and Artists Materials Catalog Number 26* [Dayton, Ohio, 1953], p. 84.)

A. W. FABER "CASTELL" Polychromos [No. 8?] Bark Chrome Bavaria Light-Proof
A. W. FABER "CASTELL" Polychromos No. 12 Mineral Green Bavaria Light-Proof
A. W. FABER "CASTELL" Polychromos [No. 20?] Prussian Green Bavaria Free From Poison
A. W. FABER "CASTELL" Polychromos No. 31 Pink Madder Lake Bavaria Free From Poison
A. W. FABER "CASTELL" Polychromos [No. 33?] Rose Pink Bavaria Light-Proof
A. W. FABER "CASTELL" Polychromos No. 48 Terra Cotta Bavaria Light-Proof
A. W. FABER "CASTELL" Polychromos [No. 49?] Indian Red Bavaria Free From Poison
A. W. FABER "CASTELL" Polychromos [No. ?] Light Green Bavaria Light-Proof
Manufactured by A. W. Faber, Newark, New Jersey, and Stein, Germany. A listing of these colored chalks has not been located in any art-supply catalogues.

IV. Inks

HIGGINS YELLOW Drawing Ink Waterproof Higgins American Drawing Ink No. 4025 – 3/4 oz. – Made in USA – When necessary to dilute add distilled water only (fig. 24)
HIGGINS NEUTRAL TINT Drawing Ink Waterproof Higgins American Drawing Ink No. 4255 – 3/4 oz. – Made in USA – When necessary to dilute add distilled water only
Identical bottle of red ink with dropper with black rubber bulb; label missing
Manufactured by Higgins Ink Co. Inc., Brooklyn, New York. "Higgins American Inks are the standard drawing inks of the world." (Bert L. Daily Inc., *Sign Writers Supplies and Artists Materials Catalog Number 26* [Dayton, Ohio, 1953], p. 72.)

Ozalid WATERPROOF DRAWING INK BLACK 1 oz. Made expressly for Ozalid Products Division General Aniline & Film Corporation Johnson City, N.Y. by F. Weber Co., Philadelphia, USA. Recommended FOR DRAWING ON MATTED ACETATE FOIL AND SHEETING
Manufactured by F. Weber Co., Philadelphia. Bottle capped with cork stopper. Very black, dense inks were required to make diazo reproductions of line drawings. Like copy pencils, these inks were found around art and commercial drafting studios.

V. Miscellaneous Materials and Tools

6 droppers with black rubber bulbs (fig. 24)
3 mouth atomizers (fig. 24)
Aluminum paint in rectangular-shaped bottle (approx. 3 oz.) with red metal screw-on cap; no label
Dri-Kwik Rubber Stamp Ink, with brush in cap
One soft, long-bristled dusting brush

NOTES

Friends and colleagues cited in the following notes are to be recognized for their unfailing generosity, as well as Jennifer Vorbach, Patty Tang, Reba Snyder, Martha Fitzpatrick, Rachel Mustalish, Elise Effmann, Kevin Martin, and Dan Biddle for their technical assistance and patience. I am grateful to William S. Lieberman, former Jacques and Natasha Gelman Chairman of the Department of Twentieth Century Art at the Metropolitan Museum of Art, New York, for launching my quest to better understand and interpret the "stuff" of Pollock.

1. Jackson Pollock, draft of statement for the review *Possibilities*, circa 1947, in Helen A. Harrison, ed., *Such Desperate Joy: Imagining Jackson Pollock* (New York: Thunder's Mouth Press, 2000), p. 23.

2. Jackson Pollock, interview with William Wright, late 1950, broadcast on radio station WERI, Westerly, Rhode Island, 1951, in Pepe Karmel, ed., *Jackson Pollock: Interviews, Articles, and Reviews* (New York: Museum of Modern Art, 1999), p. 23.

3. Harrison, op. cit., p. 23.

4. Pollock's thorough acquaintance with the working properties of his materials ultimately afforded him more freedom, as pointed out by James Coddington, Chief Conservator of the Museum of Modern Art, New York, in an interview with Anna Hammond:
http://www.moma.org/collection/conservation/pollock/interview1.html.

5. The parallel between the texture of Japanese paper and that of unprimed canvas was pointed out in Bernice Rose, *Jackson Pollock: Drawing into Painting* (New York: Museum of Modern Art, 1979), p. 25, note 17.

6. "Technic is the result of a need—new needs demand new technics." Jackson Pollock, handwritten statement, in Karmel, op. cit., p. 24. This was neither the first nor the last time this sentiment has been expressed. El Lissitzky, for example, in 1920, asserted that "the frayed point of the paintbrush is at variance with our concept of clarity." Sophie Lissitzky-Küppers, ed., *El Lissitzky: Life, Letters, Texts*, trans. Helene Aldwinckle and Mary Whittall (London: Thames and Hudson, 1968), p. 333. Axel Horn wrote of the participants of the Siqueiros Experimental Workshop led by the Mexican artist David Alfaro Siqueiros in 1936, including Pollock and himself: "We were going to put out to pasture the 'stick with hairs on its end' as Siqueiros called the brush." Horn, "Jackson Pollock: The Hollow and the Bump," *The Carleton Miscellany* 7, no. 3 (summer 1966), pp. 80–87; reprinted in Karmel, op. cit., p. 108.

7. Six droppers and three mouth atomizers were found in Pollock's studio after his death. They may have been used as early as 1944 to apply spattered ink (see pls. 21, 33, and 38). I am grateful to James Coddington for discussing with me Pollock's possible use of mouth atomizers to apply lightly pigmented varnishes in *Lavender Mist* (1950, JPCR 2:264). It would appear that ink droppers preceded the turkey basters introduced in 1951.

8. According to Lee Krasner, Pollock "indulged in materials very heavily. That is to say for drawings, he had the most fantastic collection of pens I had ever seen. He would go into Rosenthal's art supply store before we moved out to Springs and would pick out every new form of pen that would come out." Barbara Rose, "Jackson Pollock at Work: An Interview with Lee Krasner," *Partisan Review* 47, no. 1 (1980), pp. 82–92; reprinted in Karmel, op. cit., p. 43. William Rubin described Pollock's "continuous unbroken line" in his "Jackson Pollock and the Modern Tradition," *Artforum* (February–May 1967); reprinted in Karmel, op. cit., p. 129.

9. Henry Petroski, *The Pencil* (New York: Alfred A. Knopf, 1990), p. 291.

10. Petroski, op. cit., p. 296. The location of Joseph Dixon Crucible Co.'s interim graphite mine in Ticonderoga, site of an infamous Revolutionary War battle, gave rise to an advertising campaign celebrating the U.S. Marines "from Ticonderoga to Tokyo 1775–1944."
See www.the-pencil-place.freeserve.co.uk/pen_ads.htm.

11. Quoted in Christopher Busa, "'Being a Great Man Is a Thesis Invented by Others': Peter Busa on Jackson Pollock," in Harrison, op. cit., p. 199.

12. Art Brown [Arthur Brown and Bro.], *General Catalogue Artists' Materials Drafting Supplies* (New York, 1942), p. 2.

13. Manila paper was marketed as "extremely tough; will withstand abuse remarkably well" in Keuffel & Esser Co., *Catalogue* (Hoboken, N.J., 1944), p. 10. Office-document papers used by Pollock are variously watermarked and include Macadam Bond Rag Content and Basingwerk-Parchment, among others.

14. Horn, in Karmel, op. cit., p. 104. Grocers' pencils had thick leads of uneven quality that broke easily.

15. By using papers from sample books, Pollock was able to experience more expensive papers than he could otherwise afford. For example, paper-type information appearing on JPCR 3:456 indicates that it is a high-quality Vidalon Verge No. 832, a Canson paper from France. The source of another sheet, JPCR 3:782, having the imprint Agecroft Text, remains unknown. I thank Judith Walsh, Conservator, and Michelle Facini, Andrew W. Mellon Fellow, both in Paper Conservation at the National Gallery of Art, Washington, D.C., for their generous help in identifying these papers and others.

16. Francis V. O'Connor and Eugene V. Thaw, eds., *Jackson Pollock: A Catalogue Raisonné of Paintings, Drawings, and Other Works*, vol. 3 (New Haven, Conn.: Yale University Press, 1978), pp. 74–117.

17. My thanks to Elizabeth (Liz) Lunning, Chief Conservator of the Menil Collection, Houston, for this observation.

18. Lee Krasner makes reference to a Rosenthal in Rose, "Jackson Pollock at Work," in Karmel, op. cit., p. 43. It seems likely that the store called Robert Rosenthal was moved and renamed Philip Rosenthal sometime between 1939 and 1942. An undated order blank found in Art Brown's 1942 *General Catalogue Artists' Materials Drafting Supplies* refers to Philip Rosenthal at 47 East Ninth Street. Four checks made out to Philip Rosenthal, dated 1947, 1949, 1950, and 1954, are among Pollock's papers at the Pollock-Krasner House and Study Center, The Springs, New York. Two checks made out to the Cooper Union Supply Store, dated 1946 and 1947, are also among Pollock's papers. The address of Joseph Mayer is found on the stiff cardboard back of a pad measuring 14 x 11 inches that was used for JPCR 3:639. My thanks to Helen A. Harrison, Director of the Pollock-Krasner House and Study Center, for providing photographs of the canceled checks.

19. Art Brown, *General Catalogue Artists' Materials Drafting Supplies*, p. 11. Art Brown was located at 67 West Forty-fourth Street.

20. Ibid. Notebooks having spiral bindings appeared in 1924.

21. Strathmore Drawing Board or Bristol was quite flexible as opposed to Strathmore Illustration Board, which was rigid. Illustration Board was also available in different sizes.

22. I am grateful to Liz Lunning for this confirmation.

23. Kimberley Schenck, Director of Conservation/Paper Conservator of the Baltimore Museum of Art, generously examined their drawing (pl. 27) and confirmed that it is a partial sheet of Strathmore.

24. JPCR 3:670 and JPCR 3:693 are on partial sheets of Georgian manufactured by the Worthy Paper Company in North Agawam, Massachusetts. I am indebted to Ida Balboul, Research Associate of the Metropolitan Museum of Art, for confirming numerous details regarding the Pollock drawings in their collection.

25. These drawings are all in the 1982 gift from Lee Krasner to the Metropolitan Museum of Art.

26. My thanks are extended to Karl Buchberg, Senior Conservator of the Museum of Modern Art, for this watermark information.

27. *[Drawing for P.G.]* (ca. 1943; pl. 30) is on MBM Ingres d'Arches. I suspect that a close examination of JPCR 3:789, 3:790, 3:793, and 3:795 will reveal that their papers are MBM Ingres d'Arches also, in addition to the already documented drawings JPCR 3:724 (pl. 33), 3:791, 3:792 (pl. 64), and 3:794. My thanks to Harriet Stratis, Paper Conservator of the Art Institute of Chicago, for examining JPCR 3:724. In the Stevens-Nelson Paper Corporation's catalogue *Specimens* (New York, 1953), MBM Ingres d'Arches in all weights is available only in 18 3/4 x 24 3/4 inches. I thank Judith Walsh for directing me to this reference.

28. Pollock, interview with Wright, in Karmel, op. cit., p. 22.

29. I am grateful to Betty Fiske, Paper Conservator of the Winterthur Museum and Gardens, Winterthur, Delaware, and Hiromi Katayama of Hiromi Paper for this information.

30. S/j, S/k, S/l, and S/m in O'Connor and Thaw, op. cit., vol. 4, p. 164.

31. Rose, op. cit., p. 25, note 17.

32. Douglass Morse Howell, artist and papermaker, lived in Westbury, Long Island. He created unique handmade papers using flax, which he grew himself, as well as linen tablecloths, denim, and bits of lace and flowers. Pollock met Howell at the Betty Parsons Gallery exhibition of the collages of Anne Ryan in 1951.

33. Pollock's pastel lines are more cohesive and less fluffy than traditional pastels, indicating that the pastel sticks probably contained more binder and possibly some oil. Because they were less smudgeable, a fixative was not necessary, nor did Pollock appear to have used one. On the question of "madeness," see Clement Greenberg, "Jackson Pollock: 'Inspiration, Vision, Intuitive Decision,'" in Karmel, op. cit., p. 113.

34. Axel Horn remarked: "Jack's drawings . . . were painfully indicative of the continuous running battle between himself and his artist's tools." Horn, "Jackson Pollock: The Hollow and the Bump," in Karmel, op. cit., p. 106.

35. The job of transcribing labels and imprints fell to Helen A. Harrison, Director of the Pollock-Krasner House and Study Center, and Grace Jan, a graduate student at the Institute of Fine Arts, New York University. Rebecca Capua, also a graduate student at the Institute of Fine Arts, carried out further research. In addition, Helen Harrison answered numerous questions and generously provided photographs of all of these materials. I am enormously grateful to them all. It should be noted that some of the features and imprints of the chalks and pencils varied slightly during World War II, due to labor and material shortages. For example, the War Production Board restricted the addition of metal ferrules and rubber erasers. Curiously, only one of Pollock's pencils has an eraser.

36. Margaret Holben Ellis (with M. Brigitte Yeh), "The History, Use, and Characteristics of Wax-Based Drawing Media," *The Paper Conservator*, no. 22 (1998), pp. 48–55.

37. Margaret Holben Ellis, "The Fiber-Tipped Pen as a Drawing Tool," *Drawing* 16, no. 6 (March–April 1995), pp. 126–29, and Ellis, "The Porous Pointed Pen as Artistic Medium," *Institute of Paper Conservation Conference Papers Manchester* (Leigh: Institute of Paper Conservation, 1992), pp. 11–18. Federic Taubes, in his book *Pen-and-Ink Drawing* (New York: Watson-Guptill, 1956), extolled the virtues of the new pen as combining all the advantages of dry and wet mediums; ironically, in other publications Taubes virulently attacked the Abstract Expressionists, including a thinly veiled Pollock (p. 24).

38. From advertisements in *American Artist* 16, no. 9 (November 1952), p. 1, and *American Artist*; 13, no. 8 (October 1949), p. 15.

39. The pen probably wasn't available in 1938, the date Pollock gave to these drawings.

40. Phil Patton, "Delivery Systems for Wordsmiths," *The New York Times*, October 3, 2003, p. F12.

41. See Robert Storr, "A Piece of the Action," and Carol Mancusi-Ungaro, "Jackson Pollock: Response as Dialogue," in Kirk Varnedoe and Pepe Karmel, eds., *Jackson Pollock: New Approaches* (New York: Museum of Modern Art, 1999), pp. 59 and 149, respectively.

42. James Coddington discusses the composition of these paints in "No Chaos Damn It," in Varnedoe, op. cit., pp. 101–13.

43. No attempt has been made here to deconstruct the techniques used for drips, spatters, splatters, and pours. For this, see Francis V. O'Connor, "Pollock in Utopia: A Tour of the Exhibition," http://members.aol.com/FVOC/archive.html.

44. The floor of Pollock's studio was uncovered in 1987–88 by New York Conservation Associates in preparation for its opening to the public. Transcriptions of the paint cans were provided to me in 1995 by Harriet Irgang, Conservator, New York Conservation Associates, and Chris McNamara,

former Assistant to the Director, Pollock-Krasner House and Study Center. See Helen A. Harrison, "Jackson Pollock's Floor: Uncovering the Secrets," *IFAR Journal* 4–5, no. 1 (2001–02), pp. 34–40.

45. "Inherent vice" refers to the inevitable deterioration of an artwork resulting from the chemical or physical instability of its support and mediums or the unsound techniques used to create it.

46. Rodman, "Jackson Pollock" (interview), 1956, in Harrison, op. cit., p. 57.

47. While the decision to reinforce the skinned paper seems straightforward, whether to remove the distracting paper fuzz on the recto, evidence of the creative process, is not. The illustration of JPCR 3:786 in O'Connor and Thaw, op. cit., vol. 3, clearly shows paper remnants; these were subsequently removed following documentation.

48. Karen Colby, "A Suggested Exhibition/Exposure Policy for Works of Art on Paper," *Journal of the IIC: Canadian Group*, no. 17 (1992), pp. 3–11.

49. As calculated by the Light Damage Slide Rule devised by the Canadian Conservation Institute, *CCI Notes*, (December 1988), pp. 1–10.

50. Mrs. Helen S. Faye, speaking to Christine McNamara, Pollock-Krasner House and Study Center, August 1, 1993, quoted in O'Connor and Thaw, op. cit., vol. 4, p. 85.

EXHIBITION HISTORY OF WORKS ON PAPER

The exhibitions during Jackson Pollock's lifetime featuring the artist's works on paper are listed. Works are numbered according to the archival system as indicated in Francis V. O'Connor and Eugene V. Thaw, *Jackson Pollock: A Catalogue Raisonné of Paintings, Drawings, and Other Works,* 4 vols. New Haven and London: Yale University Press, 1978, and Francis V. O'Connor, Supplement One, 1995.

1935

Brooklyn Museum, New York, *Eighth Exhibition of Watercolors, Pastels, and Drawings by American and French Artists*, February 1–28. Works include *Threshers* (4:935).

1937

WPA Federal Art Gallery, New York, October. Pollock exhibits an unidentified watercolor in the inaugural show.

1943

Art of This Century, New York, *Exhibition of Collage*, April 16–May 15. Works include possibly 4:1041.

Art of This Century, *Jackson Pollock: First Exhibition–Paintings and Drawings*, November 9–27. Pollock exhibits fifteen paintings and an unspecified number of gouaches and drawings, all executed between 1941 and 1943. Gallery sales suggest that the following works were exhibited: 3:697; pl. 23; *Animals and Figures* (4:961); pl. 24; and an unidentified gouache and drawing. *[Drawing for P.G.]* (pl. 30), given to Peggy Guggenheim as a gift, was also included.

Art of This Century, *Natural, Insane, Surrealist Art*, December 1–31. Works include 3:694.

1945

The Arts Club of Chicago, *Jackson Pollock*, March 5–31. The exhibition, organized by Peggy Guggenheim, includes seventeen paintings and eight untitled drawings and is essentially a reprise of Pollock's first solo exhibition held at Art of This Century in November 1943. The exhibition travels to the San Francisco Art Museum (August 7–26).

Art of This Century, *Jackson Pollock*, the artist's second one-person exhibition, March 19–April 14. Pollock exhibits thirteen paintings and an unspecified number of gouaches and drawings. Gallery sales suggest that the following works were exhibited: 4:978; 4:1012; 4:1013; pl. 37; and two unidentified drawings and one unidentified gouache.

1946

The Society of the Four Arts, Palm Beach, Florida, *Abstract and Expressionist Paintings*, January 18–February 10. Princess Zalstem-Zalesky lends 4:978.

Art of This Century, *Jackson Pollock*, the third exhibition of the artist's work, April 2–20. Pollock exhibits eleven oils and eight works on paper. Gallery sales suggest that the following works were exhibited: pl. 41; pl. 43; 4:976; 3:766(?); one unidentified drawing; and four unidentified gouaches.

1948

The Whitney Museum of American Art, New York, *Annual Exhibition of Contemporary American Sculptures, Watercolors, and Drawings*, January 31–March 21. Works include one watercolor, *Dancing Forms* (not identified in JPCR).

Art Institute of Chicago, *59th Annual American Exhibition of Water Colors and Drawings*. Works include pl. 33.

Fine Arts Center, Indiana University, Bloomington, *First Indiana Print and Drawing Show*, May 1–31. Works include *War* (pl. 36), also included the following year in *Prints & Drawings*, The State University of Iowa, Iowa City.

XXIV Venice Biennale, Greek Pavilion, *La Collezione Peggy Guggenheim*, May 29–September 30. Pollock is represented by five paintings and one work on paper, *[Drawing for P.G.]* (pl. 30). An installation photograph indicates that 3:632 was also included, but not recorded in the exhibition catalogue. The exhibition travels to the Palazzo Strozzi, Florence (February 19–March 10, 1949) and the Palazzo Reale, Milan (June–July 1949).

1949

Betty Parsons Gallery, New York, *Jackson Pollock*, January 24–February 12. Pollock exhibits 26 paintings on canvas and paper, all executed in 1948. The small-scale paintings on paper include *Number 4: Gray and Red* (pl. 50); *Number 6 (Blue, Red, Yellow)* (2:209); *Number 12A: Yellow, Gray, Black* (2:200); *Number 14* (pl. 55); *Number 15: Red, Gray, White, Yellow* (pl. 54); *Number 19* (2:190); *Number 20* (2:191); *Number 21* (2:214); *Number 22A, 1948* (pl. 52); and *Number 23* (2:199).

The Museum of Modern Art, New York, *Sculpture by Painters*, August 3–October 5. Organized by the Department of Circulating Exhibitions, the presentation includes *Number 4, 1948: Gray and Red* (pl. 50). The exhibition travels to twelve American cities from November 1949 to May 1951.

Betty Parsons Gallery, *Jackson Pollock*, November 21–December 10. Pollock exhibits 34 paintings on canvas and paper, all executed in 1949, and three wire and plastic sculptures for a model of a museum for Pollock's work designed by Peter Blake. The small-scale paintings on paper include *Number 12* (2:233); *Number 13* (pl. 61); *Number 14* (2:256); *Number 15* (2:236); *Number 16* (2:244); *Number 17* (pl. 60); *Number 18* (2:226); *Number 19* (2:229); *Number 20* (pl. 57); *Number 21* (Supplement 5); *Number 30 (Birds of Paradise)* (2:237); *Number 31* (2:242); *Number 33* (pl. 56); and *Number 34* (pl. 59).

The Museum of Modern Art, New York, *Children's Holiday of Modern Art*, December 7, 1949–January 11, 1950, includes *Number 12, 1949* (2:233).

The Whitney Museum of American Art, *Annual Exhibition of Contemporary American Painting*, December 16, 1949–February 5, 1950, includes *Number 14, 1949* (2:256).

1950

Detroit Institute of Arts, *The Little Show of Work in Progress*, February 20–March 24. Works include *Number 4, 1948: Gray and Red* (pl. 50) and *Number 31, 1949* (2:242).

University of Illinois, Urbana, *Contemporary American Painting*, February 26–April 2, includes *Number 12A, 1948: Yellow, Gray, Black* (2:200).

Rutgers University, New Brunswick, New Jersey, February 28–March 23. Pollock exhibits *Number 21A, 1948* (2:214), *Number 13, 1949* (pl. 61), and *Number 20, 1949* (pl. 57).

Society of the Four Arts, Palm Beach, Florida, "From the Armory Show to the Present," March 9–31, includes *Number 22, 1949* (Supplement 6).

XXV Venice Biennale, American Pavilion, June 3–October 15. Pollock is represented by two works on canvas, 2:186 and 2:223, and two paintings on paper, *Number 12A, 1948: Yellow, Gray, Black* (2:200) and *Number 12, 1949* (2:233).

Ala Napoleonica, Museo Correr, Venice, *Jackson Pollock*, July 22–August 12/15. The exhibition represents the entire collection of works by the artist then owned by Peggy Guggenheim; 23 works in total, including two gouaches (pl. 44 and 4:1009) and one drawing, *[Drawing for P.G.]* (pl. 30) and one painting on paper, *Number 16, 1949* (2:244).

University of Michigan, Ann Arbor, *Post-War American Painting*, June 28–August 28, includes *Number 20, 1949* (pl. 57).

Forum Gallery, Provincetown, Massachusetts, summer, includes *Number 13, 1949* (pl. 61).

Calligraphic and Geometric: Two Recent Linear Tendencies in American Painting, organized by the Museum of Modern Art Traveling Exhibitions for 25 American venues, October 1953–May 1954. *Number 31, 1949* (2:242) is replaced in November 1953 with *Number 12, 1948* (2:200).

The Museum of Modern Art , *Children's Holiday Carnival of Modern Art*, December 1950–January 1951, includes *Number 13, 1949* (pl. 61).

Munson-Williams-Proctor Institute, Utica, New York, *Current Trends in British and American Painting*, December 3–31, includes *Number 20, 1948* (2:191) and *Number 34, 1949* (pl. 59).

1951

Stedelijk Museum, Amsterdam, *Surrealisme & Abstractie*, January 19–February 26. The exhibition presents the collection of Peggy Guggenheim and includes pl. 41, 4:1008, 4:1009, and *Number 16, 1949* (2:244). The exhibition travels to the Palais des Beaux-Arts, Brussels (March 3–28) and Kunsthaus Zurich (April 15–May 15) as *Moderne Kunst aus der Sammlung Peggy Guggenheim*.

Galerie Nina Dausset, Paris, *Véhémences Confrontées*, March 8–31, includes *Number 30, 1949 (Birds of Paradise)* (2:237).

The Whitney Museum of American Art, *Annual Exhibition of Contemporary American Sculpture, Watercolors, and Drawings*, March 17–May 6, includes *Watercolor Number 1, 1951* (not identified in JPCR).

Brooklyn Museum, *International Water Color Exhibition: Sixteenth Biennial*, May 9–June 24, includes *Number 3, 1951* (pl. 67).

University Gallery, Department of Art, University of Minnesota, Minneapolis, *40 American Painters, 1940–1950*, June 4–August 30, includes *Number 22A, 1948* (pl. 52).

Hilltop Theatre Art Room, Lutherville, Maryland, June 26–July 8, exhibits twelve Pollock paintings on paper including *Number 4, 1948: Gray and Red* (pl. 50); *Watercolor Number 1*, 1951 (not identified in JPCR); and *Watercolor Number 2*, which became *Number 18, 1951* (3:826).

1952

Blue Hill Pavilion, Blue Hill, Maine, exhibits 4:1021.

Studio Paul Facchetti, Paris, *Jackson Pollock, 1948–1951*, March 7–31, includes *Number 17, 1949* (pl. 60, 2:243).

The Whitney Museum of American Art, *Annual Exhibition of Contemporary American Sculpture, Watercolors, and Drawings*, March 13–May 4, includes *Number 7, 1951* (3:815).

Williams College Museum of Art, Williamstown, Massachusetts, *Williams Alumni Loan Exhibition*, May 5–June 16, includes 4:951.

Guild Hall, East Hampton, New York, *What Businessmen Collect*, July, includes *Number 23, 1948* (2:199).

Art Gallery of Toronto, *Canadian National Exhibition*, August 22–September 6, includes *Number 12, 1949* (2:233).

1953

Design Research, Cambridge, Massachusetts, exhibits 4:1021.

The Metropolitan Museum of Art, New York, *The Edward Root Collection*, February 12–April 12, includes *Number 20, 1948* (2:191) and *Number 34, 1949* (pl. 59).

States of Mind, organized by the Museum of Modern Art Traveling Exhibitions, October 21, 1953–May 20, 1956, includes *Number 21, 1949* (Supplement 5). The exhibition travels to sixteen American venues, mostly university art galleries.

1954

Phoenix Fine Arts Association, Arizona, *American Painting*, January 18–31, includes *Number 12, 1949* (2:233).

Vassar College, Poughkeepsie, New York, *Mid-Century Painting*, May 13–June 20, includes *Number 12, 1949* (2:233). The exhibition travels to the Institute of Contemporary Arts, Washington, D.C. (December 12, 1954–February 20, 1955).

1955

Kunsthalle Bern, Switzerland, *Tendances Actuelles 3*, January 29–March 6, includes *Number 16, 1949* (2:244).

The Whitney Museum of American Art, *The New Decade*, May 11 –August 7, includes *Number 2, 1951* (4:1039). The exhibition travels to San Francisco Museum of Art (October 6–November 6), Art Galleries of the University of California at Los Angeles (November 20, 1955–January 7, 1956), Colorado Springs Fine Arts Center (February 9–March 20, 1956), and City Art Museum of St. Louis (April 15–May 15, 1956).

1956

Marquette University, Milwaukee, Wisconsin, *Festival of the American Arts*, April 20–May 10, includes *Number 12, 1949* (2:233).

SELECTED BIBLIOGRAPHY

Most citations provide original-publication information only. Reprints or later versions are given if commonly referenced or significantly revised from the originals, or if original sources are difficult to access. Sources may appear in more than one section of the Selected Bibliography.

ARTIST'S STATEMENTS AND INTERVIEWS

"Jackson Pollock. A Questionnaire," *Arts & Architecture* (Los Angeles) 61, no. 2 (February 1944), p. 14. Reprinted in Karmel, pp. 15–16.

Statement, in Sidney Janis, *Abstract and Surrealist Art in America*. New York: Reynal and Hitchcock, 1944, p. 112.

"My Painting," *Possibilities* (New York) 1 (Winter 1947–1948), pp. 78–83. Reprinted in Karmel, pp. 17–18.

[Roueché, Berton]. "Unframed Space." *The New Yorker* 26, no. 24 (August 5, 1950), p. 16. Interview with Jackson Pollock and Lee Krasner. Reprinted in Karmel, pp. 18–19.

Interview with William Wright, The Springs, Long Island, New York, late 1950. Broadcast on radio station WERI, Westerly, Rhode Island, 1951. Reprinted in Karmel, pp. 20–23.

Interview with Selden Rodman, Spring 1956. In Rodman, *Conversations with Artists*. New York: The Devin-Adair Co., 1957, pp. 76–87.

INTERVIEWS WITH LEE KRASNER

Du Plessix, Francine, and Cleve Gray. "Who was Jackson Pollock?" *Art in America* (New York) 55, no. 3 (May–June 1967), pp. 48–51. Reprinted in Karmel, pp. 30–35.

Glaser, Bruce. "Jackson Pollock: An Interview with Lee Krasner." *Arts Magazine* (New York) 41, no. 6 (April 1967), pp. 36–39. Reprinted in Karmel, pp. 25–30.

Friedman, B. H. "An Interview with Lee Krasner Pollock." In *Jackson Pollock: Black and White*, exh. cat. New York: Marlborough-Gerson Gallery, Inc., 1969, pp. 7–10.

Rose, Barbara. "Jackson Pollock at Work: An Interview with Lee Krasner." *Partisan Review* (New York) 47, no. 1 (1980), pp. 82–92. Reprinted in Karmel, pp. 39–47.

MONOGRAPHS AND EXHIBITION CATALOGUES

Cernuschi, Claude. *Jackson Pollock: Meaning and Significance*. New York: Icon Editions, HarperCollins Publishers, 1992.

Frank, Elizabeth. *Jackson Pollock*. New York: Abbeville Press, 1983.

Friedman, B. H. *Jackson Pollock: Energy Made Visible*. New York: McGraw-Hill Book Co., 1970.

Harrison, Helen A., ed. *Such Desperate Joy: Imagining Jackson Pollock*. New York: Thunder's Mouth Press, 2000.

Jackson Pollock, exh. cat. New York: The Museum of Modern Art, 1967. Essay by Francis V. O'Connor.

Jackson Pollock, exh. cat. Paris: Musée national d'art moderne, Centre Georges Pompidou, 1982. Essays by Daniel Abadie, G. C. Argan, Dominique Bozo, E. A. Carmean Jr., Flavio Caroli, Françoise Choay, Hubert Damisch, Marcelin Pleynet, Georges Raillard, Pierre Restany, Barbara Rose, William Rubin, and Yoshiaki Tono.

Jackson Pollock, exh. cat. New York: The Museum of Modern Art, 1998. Essays by Pepe Karmel and Kirk Varnedoe.

Jackson Pollock: The Black Pourings, 1951–1953, exh. cat. Boston: The Institute of Contemporary Art, 1980. Essay by Francis V. O'Connor.

Jackson Pollock: Defining the Heroic, exh. cat. Houston: The Museum of Fine Arts, 1996. Essay by Barry Walker.

Jackson Pollock: Drip Paintings on Paper, 1948–1949, exh. cat. New York: C&M Arts, 1993. Essay by Carter Ratcliff.

Jackson Pollock: The Early Years, exh. cat. Santa Fe: The Gerald Peters Gallery, 1988. Essay by William S. Lieberman.

Jackson Pollock, New-Found Works, exh. cat. New Haven, Conn.: Yale University Art Gallery, 1978. Essays by David Bourdon, Andrea Spaulding Norris, Francis V. O'Connor, and Eugene V. Thaw.

Jackson Pollock: Paintings and Drawings, 1934–1952, exh cat. London: Anthony D'Offay Gallery, 1989.

Jackson Pollock. Pollock in the Mid-Forties: A Close-Up, exh. cat. New York: Jason McCoy Inc., 1992. Essay by Elizabeth Frank.

Jackson Pollock: "Psychoanalytic" Drawings, exh. cat. Durham, N.C.: Duke University Museum of Art, 1992. Essay by Claude Cernuschi.

The Jackson Pollock Sketchbooks in the Metropolitan Museum of Art, exh. cat. New York: The Metropolitan Museum of Art, 1997. Essays by Katharine Baetjer, Lisa Mintz Messinger, and Nan Rosenthal.

Jackson Pollock in Venice / The "Irascibles" and the New York School, exh. cat. Venice: Museo Correr, 2002. Essays by Ellen G. Landau, William S. Lieberman, Philip Rylands, and Kirk Varnedoe.

Karmel, Pepe, ed. *Jackson Pollock. Interviews, Articles, and Reviews*. New York: The Museum of Modern Art, 1999.

Landau, Ellen G. *Jackson Pollock*. New York: Harry N. Abrams, Inc., 1989.

Lewison, Jeremy. *Interpreting Pollock*. London: Tate Gallery Publishing Ltd, 1999.

Lieberman, William S. *Jackson Pollock: The Last Sketchbook*. New York: Johnson Reprint Corporation, Harcourt Brace Jovanovich, 1982.

Naifeh, Steven, and Gregory White Smith. *Jackson Pollock: An American Saga*. New York: Clarkson N. Potter, Inc., 1989.

Namuth, Hans. *Pollock Painting*. Edited by Barbara Rose. New York: Agrinde Publications Ltd., 1980.

O'Connor, Francis V., and Eugene V. Thaw. *Jackson Pollock: A Catalogue Raisonné of Paintings, Drawings, and Other Works*, 4 vols. New Haven, Conn. and London: Yale University Press, 1978.

O'Connor, Francis V. *Jackson Pollock: A Catalogue Raisonné of Paintings, Drawings, and Other Works. Supplement Number One*. New York: The Pollock-Krasner Foundation, Inc., 1995.

O'Hara, Frank. *Jackson Pollock*. New York: George Braziller, Inc., 1959.

Potter, Jeffrey. *To a Violent Grave: An Oral Biography of Jackson Pollock*. New York: G.P. Putnam's Sons, 1985.

Ratcliff, Carter. *The Fate of a Gesture: Jackson Pollock and Postwar American Art*. New York: Farrar, Straus & Giroux, 1996.

Robertson, Bryan. *Jackson Pollock*. New York: Harry N. Abrams, Inc., 1960.

Rohn, Matthew L. *Visual Dynamics in Jackson Pollock's Abstractions*. Ann Arbor: UMI Research Press, 1987.

Rose, Bernice. *Jackson Pollock: Drawing into Painting*. New York: The Museum of Modern Art, 1979.

Siqueiros/Pollock, Pollock/Siqueiros, exh. cat. Düsseldorf: Städtische Kunsthalle Düsseldorf, 1995. Essay by Jürgen Harten.

Varnedoe, Kirk, and Pepe Karmel, ed. *Jackson Pollock, New Approaches*. New York: The Museum of Modern Art, 1999.

Wysuph, C. L. *Jackson Pollock: Psychoanalytic Drawings*. New York: Horizon Press, 1970.

SELECTED ARTICLES

Alloway, Lawrence. "Notes on Pollock." *Art International* (Zurich) 5, no. 4 (May 1, 1961), pp. 38–41, 90.

Carmean, E. A., Jr. "Jackson Pollock: Classic Paintings of 1950." In *American Art at Mid-Century–The Subjects of the Artist*, exh. cat. Washington, D.C.: National Gallery of Art, 1978, pp. 127–53.

________. "The Church Project: Pollock's Passion Themes." *Art in America* (New York) 70, no. 6 (Summer 1982), pp. 110–22.

Chave, Anna C. "Pollock and Krasner: Script and postscript." *RES* 24 (Autumn 1993), pp. 95–111.

Clark, Timothy J. "Jackson Pollock's Abstraction." In Serge Guilbaut, ed. *Reconstructing Modernism: Art in New York, Paris, Montreal 1945–1964*. London and Cambridge, Mass.: MIT Press, 1990, pp. 172–243.

Fichner-Rathus, Lois. "Pollock at Atelier 17." *Print Collector's Newsletter* (New York) 13, no. 5 (November–December 1982), pp. 162–65.

Fried, Michael. "Jackson Pollock." *Artforum* (New York) 4, no. 1 (September 1965), pp. 14–17. Reprinted in Karmel, pp. 97–103.

Goodnough, Robert, with photographs by Hans Namuth. "Pollock Paints a Picture." *Art News* (New York) 50, no. 3 (May 1951), pp. 38–41, 60–61. Reprinted in Karmel, pp. 74–78.

Goosen, E.C. "The Big Canvas." *Art International* (Zurich) 2, no. 8 (November 1958), pp. 45–47. Reprinted in Gregory Battcock, *The New Art*. New York: E. P. Dutton, 1973, pp. 57–65.

Gordon, Donald E. "Pollock's 'Bird,' or How Jung Did Not Offer Much Help in Myth-Making." *Art in America* (New York) 68, no. 8 (October 1980), pp. 43–53.

Greenberg, Clement. "The Present Prospects of American Painting and Sculpture." *Horizon* (London) 16, no. 93–94 (October 1947), pp. 20–30. Reprinted in John O'Brian, ed., *Clement Greenberg: The Collected Essays and Criticism*, 4 vols. Chicago: University of Chicago Press, 1986–1993, vol. 2, pp. 160–70.

________. "The Crisis of the Easel Picture." *Partisan Review* (New York) 15(1), no. 4 (April 1948), pp. 481–84. Revised version published in Greenberg, *Art and Culture: Critical Essays*. Boston: Beacon Paperback, 1965, pp. 154–57.

________. "Jackson Pollock's New Style." *Harper's Bazaar* (New York) 85, no. 2883 (February 1952), p. 74. Reprinted in Karmel, p. 80.

________. "'American-Type' Painting." *Partisan Review* (New York) 22 (Spring 1955), pp. 179–96. Reprinted in O'Brian, ed., *Clement Greenberg: The Collected Essays and Criticism*, vol. 3, pp. 217–35.

________. "Jackson Pollock: 'Inspiration, Vision, Intuitive Decision.'" *Vogue* (New York) 149, no. 7 (April 1, 1967), pp. 160–61. Reprinted in Karmel, pp. 110–14.

Horn, Axel. "Jackson Pollock: The Hollow and the Bump." *The Carleton Miscellany* 7, no. 3 (Summer 1996), pp. 80–87. Reprinted in Karmel, pp. 104–09.

Kaprow, Allan. "The Legacy of Jackson Pollock." *Art News* (New York) 57, no. 6 (October 1958), pp. 24–26, 55–57. Reprinted in Karmel, pp. 84–89.

Krauss, Rosalind. "Jackson Pollock's Drawings." *Artforum* (New York) 9, no. 5 (January 1971), pp. 58–61. Reprinted in Karmel, pp. 176–79.

________. "Contra Carmean: The Abstract Pollock." *Art in America* (New York) 70, no. 6 (Summer 1982), pp. 123–31, 155.

________. In *The Optical Unconscious*. Cambridge, Mass.: MIT Press, 1993, pp. 243–93.

Langhorne, Elizabeth L. "Jackson Pollock's 'The Moon Woman Cuts the Circle.'" *Arts Magazine* (New York) 53, no. 7 (March 1979), pp. 128–37. Reprinted in Karmel, pp. 202–19.

________. "Jackson Pollock: Early Sketchbooks and Drawings" and "Focus: Pollock and Printmaking." *Art Journal* (New York) 58, no. 2 (Summer 1999), pp. 111–15.

Leja, Michael. "Pollock & Metaphor," in *Reframing Abstract Expressionism: Subjectivity and Painting in the 1940s*. New Haven, Conn. and London: Yale University Press, 1993, pp. 275–327, 365–69.

Morris, Robert. "Anti Form." *Artforum* (New York) 6, no. 8 (April 1968), pp. 33–35.

O'Connor, Francis V. "The Genesis of Jackson Pollock: 1912 to 1943." *Artforum* (New York) 5, no. 9 (May 1967), pp. 16–23.

Perchuk, Andrew, "Pollock and Postwar Masculinity." In Andrew Perchuk and Helaine Posner, eds. *The Masculine Masquerade: Masculinity and Representation*, Cambridge, Mass. and London: MIT Press, 1995, pp. 31–42.

Polcari, Stephen. "Jackson Pollock and Thomas Hart Benton." *Arts Magazine* (New York) 53, no. 7 (March 1979), pp. 120–24. Reprinted in Karmel, pp. 192–201.

Rose, Barbara. "Hans Namuth's Photographs and the Jackson Pollock Myth. Part One: Media Impact and the Failure of Criticism," and ". . . Part Two: *Number 19, 1950*." *Arts Magazine* (New York) 53, no. 7 (March 1979), pp. 112–16, 117–19.

Rosenberg, Harold. "The American Action Painters." *Art News* (New York) 51, no. 8 (December 1952), pp. 22–23, 48–50.

________. "The Search for Jackson Pollock." *Art News* (New York) 59, no. 10 (February 1961), pp. 35, 58–60. Reprinted in Karmel, pp. 90–96.

Rosenblum, Robert. "The Abstract Sublime." *Art News* (New York) 59, no. 10 (February 1961), pp. 39–41, 56–57.

Rubin, William. "Jackson Pollock and the Modern Tradition." Parts I–IV. *Artforum* (New York) 5, no. 6 (February 1967), pp. 14–22; 5, no. 7 (March 1967), pp. 28–37; 5, no. 8 (April 1967), pp. 18–31; 5, no. 9 (May 1967), pp. 28–33. Reprinted in Karmel, pp. 118–75.

________. "Pollock as Jungian Illustrator: The Limits of Psychological Criticism," parts I–II. *Art in America* (New York) 67, no. 7 (November 1979), pp. 104–23; 67, no. 8 (December 1979), pp. 72–91. Reprinted in Karmel, pp. 220–61.

[Seiberling, Dorothy]. "Jackson Pollock: Is he the greatest living painter in the United States?" *Life* (New York) 27, no. 6 (August 8, 1949), pp. 42–45. Reprinted in Karmel, pp. 63–64.

Siegel, Jeanne, "Materiality is the Message." *Art Journal* (New York) 58, no. 2 (Summer 1999), pp. 109–12.

Stuckey, Charles F. "Another Side of Jackson Pollock." *Art in America* (New York) 65, no. 6 (November–December 1977), pp. 80–91. Reprinted in Karmel, pp. 180–91.

Valliere, James T. "De Kooning on Pollock." *Partisan Review* (New York) 34 (Fall 1967), pp. 603–05.

________. "The El Greco Influence on Jackson Pollock's Early Works." *Art Journal* (New York) 24, no. 1 (Autumn 1964), pp. 6–9.

Wagner, Anne M. "Krasner's Presence, Pollock's Absence," in Whitney Chadwick and Isabelle De Courtivron, eds., *Significant Others*, London: Thames and Hudson, 1993, pp. 223–53.

Weinberg, Jonathan. "Pollock and Picasso: The Rivalry and the 'Escape.'" *Arts Magazine* (New York) 61, no. 10 (Summer 1987), pp. 42–48.

SOLOMON R. GUGGENHEIM FOUNDATION

PHOTOGRAPHY CREDITS

Unless noted below, photographic material has been supplied by the owner.

PLATES

Michael Tropea: 2
Robert Mckeever/Gagosian Gallery: 8
Robert E. Mates: 9
Damian Andrus: 10
David Heald: 11, 62
Hester + Hardaway: 12, 16, 18, 22
Rick Gardner: 13
Point Seven Studios: 15
Courtesy Gagosian Gallery: 23, 37
Janet Woodard: 24
Sheldan C. Collins: 25
Digital Image, The Museum of Modern Art/Licensed by SCALA /Art Resource, N.Y.: 26, 35, 41, 65, 72, 73, 78
Ricardo Blanc: 28
Antonia Reeve: 31, 69
John Seyfried: 32
John Lamka: 39
Lee Stallsworth: 40
Marcus J. Leith: 46
Ron Jennings: 54
Courtesy C&M Arts: 57
Jacqueline Hyde/CNAC/MNAM/Dist. Réunion des Musées Nationaux/Art Resource, N.Y.: 58
Courtesy Sotheby's: 60
Hickey-Robertson: 66
Rod del Pozo: 67
Rodney Todd-White & Son: 77

FIGURES

Arnold Newman/Getty Images: Frontispiece
Courtesy Art Resource, N.Y.: 1, 3, 11, 12, 21
Martha Holmes/Time Life Pictures/Getty Images: 4, 6
Express/Express/Getty Images: 5
Estate of Hans Namuth, courtesy Pollock-Krasner House and Study Center: 7, 8
B. Hatala, Réunion des Musées Nationaux/Art Resource, NY: 13
David Heald: 14
Andrew Bordwin: 16
Gjon Mili/Time Life Pictures/Getty Images: 18, 19
Maurice Berezov, courtesy Pollock-Krasner House and Study Center: 22, 23
Helen A. Harrison, courtesy Pollock-Krasner House and Study Center: 24, 25
Courtesy Margaret Holben Ellis: 26, 27, 28, 29, 30, 31